BACK TO BASICS
FOR THE
REPUBLICAN PARTY

MICHAEL ZAK

Back to Basics for the Republican Party
Copyright © 2000 by Michael Zak

ISBN 0-9700063-0-6

For further information or to order additional copies:

www.republicanbasics.com

Michael Zak
3023 N. Clark St.
PMB 733
Chicago, Illinois 60657

<u>Cover photographs</u>
Upper left: Abraham Lincoln (Chicago Historical Society)
Upper right: Thaddeus Stevens (Chicago Historical Society)
Lower left: Charles Sumner (Chicago Historical Society)
Lower right: Ronald Reagan (Reagan Presidential Library)

Printed by:

Thiessen Printing & Graphics Corp.
Chicago, Illinois

Contents

The best time to plant a tree was twenty years ago. The second best time is today.

Chinese Proverb

Chapter One

OVERVIEW

"The Republican Party is *the Party of Lincoln.*" Though Republican candidates may say this occasionally during campaign season, we forget just as soon as they do. What does "the Party of Lincoln" actually mean? And more importantly, what should it mean, for us Republicans and the country we love?

How many Americans know why our Republican Party began or what its original purpose was? Not many! How many Americans know, for example, that the 1964 Civil Rights Act and the 1965 Voting Rights Act were reforms that our Republican Party struggled for in vain during the Reconstruction era a hundred years earlier? Fewer still. The 13th amendment banning slavery, the 14th amendment extending the Bill of Rights to the states, and the 15th amendment according voting rights to blacks – all three were enacted by the much-maligned Radical Republicans in the face of fierce Democrat opposition. How many Americans know that? Again, very few.

Now whose fault is it that so much past glory of our Republican Party goes unnoticed today? Who should we blame? Ourselves, of course. How can we hope to convince voters to place their confidence in us when we lack confidence in our own heritage? And how can we Republicans battle Democrats effectively on economic, foreign policy, and other fronts when we act as if the world began the day we were born?

To retake the ideological high ground and fight off the socialism at the core of the Democratic Party we Republicans must embrace the

GOP's original reform agenda that is at once pro-free market and pro-constitutional rights. The founders of our Party understood that to win and to deserve to win, there should be no separating the two. To understand this original vision of our Republican Party we look to the site of the 2000 Republican National Convention. Philadelphia is not only where the Constitution was written but where in 1856 the first Republican National Convention met in order to save it, for their generation unto ours.

Throughout <u>Back to Basics for the Republican Party</u>, we will run through our fingers the links in the chain of events between then and now. Placing events in context means reaching back to the drafting of the Constitution to describe the point of view of patriots in the 1850s who were alarmed that the slave system was extending itself northward, threatening the free market society we still cherish today.

⸺⬥⸺

That first Republican National Convention took place just five years before the outbreak of the Civil War. Looking back so many years later we tend to think of the fighting as having waged between the North and the South, but that is not how those who "gave the last full measure of devotion" saw it. Devotion? Devotion to what? To the section of the country north of the Mason-Dixon line? No, Republicans and other patriots shared a devotion to "the last, best hope of earth" and the Constitution which made it possible. Their cause, as Abraham Lincoln said, was "a struggle for maintaining in the world, that form, and substance of government, whose leading object is to elevate the condition of men – to lift artificial weights from all shoulders – to clear the paths of laudable pursuit for all – to afford all an unfettered start and a fair chance, in the race of life." As echoed later in the Gettysburg Address, dedication to this "great task remaining before us" was the core ideology of the Republican Party then and should be now.

The common perception that Democrats are somehow less respectful of the Constitution, that they often delight in stretching and twisting it to suit their purposes, is valid. The misty origins of the Democratic Party lie, as we shall see, in the movement to oppose ratification of the Constitution, while most people who advocated ratification formed the Federalist Party, ancestor of our Republican Party. Democrats spent decades before and after the Civil War yammering about states rights, a doctrine they invented to preserve slavery, and used later to defend racial discrimination. In contrast, the theme of the first Republican administration was Lincoln's struggle to "preserve, protect, and defend the Constitution of the United States."

Republicans correctly viewed the Civil War as a battle for supremacy between the slave system and the free market society. Would the United States become all slave or all free? Those two visions still contend for dominance in the country today. The slave system, the very opposite of the free market society our Republican Party advocated, required a vast regulatory and enforcement infrastructure to keep people enchained for the benefit of others, just as the socialist policies of the Democratic Party do today. Trapped in the role once filled by slaves before the war and then afterward by poor blacks during the Jim Crow era, an underclass today maintains the political and economic power of the Democratic Party elite and those in their employ, if indirectly, in the government bureaucracy. No underclass would mean no immense bureaucracy to run the welfare state established by the Democrat Lyndon Johnson administration.

Why did our Party, born as a mass constitutional rights movement, lose the policy initiative to a party whose socialist policies have recreated a vile new version of the slave system? Rather than history repeating itself, what we have is a political version of the Law of Inertia; that is, forces continue until stopped by other forces. What stopped our Republican Party from completing Lincoln's "unfinished work," and why has the Democratic Party not been stopped from extending socialism?

The answers to these questions are to be found by recognizing that the history of the United States is the story of the Civil War, apart from which one cannot comprehend our Republican Party then or now. Everything that happened in our country before the Civil War was prologue, and we continue to live out the epilogue. This is what historians of the future will write, and this is what we would readily understand today had we the vantage point of outsiders looking in.

As far back as the Washington presidency, the overriding issues of the day were those which led inexorably to the Civil War. From the very first Cabinet meeting onward, Alexander Hamilton and Thomas Jefferson passionately articulated competing visions for the country which broke down generally North-South. As early as 1803, there was a secessionist movement – in the North. It took the Missouri Compromise to squelch rumbles of civil war felt as early as 1818. Jefferson described that furor over slavery in Missouri as "a fire bell in the night," and John Quincy Adams wrote: "The present question is a mere preamble – a title-page to a great, tragic volume." After around 1830, the two sides hardened in their determination to have their way, and only adroit but shaky compromises kept the country together another thirty years, by which time economic development had advanced enough in the North to enable Union forces to overcome the rebellion.

The United States emerged from the Civil War a vastly different country. Supremacy of the federal government stood unchallenged. No longer could Democrats hinder economic progress so as to protect the slave system. Once most Democrats in Congress had gone with the Confederacy, Republicans met little opposition in enacting their progressive economic agenda: a national banking system and a national currency, free land for farmers in the Plains states, land-grant colleges, the transcontinental railroad, and other structural reforms that brought forth the industrialization that soon made the United States the wealthiest country in the world.

But what about the South? Was our Republican Party able to carry out its agenda there – to free the slaves and guarantee their constitutional rights? You already know: yes to freeing the slaves but no to guaranteeing their constitutional rights. Why was that? The force that stopped our Republican Party from implementing its constitutional rights agenda was the murder of the Great Emancipator.

The man who would take over the presidency for the next four years of Reconstruction, Andrew Johnson, was a southern Democrat racist, who did all in his power to prevent blacks from experiencing Lincoln's "new birth of freedom." The southern Democrat state governments set up by that first President Johnson quickly reduced blacks to near slavery with "black codes" shockingly similar to their previous "slave codes." This was a man who while President offered to contribute $20,000 toward defeating ratification of the 14th amendment. The Republicans had to override his veto – the first time that had ever happened incidentally – of the 1866 Civil Rights Act, which Johnson then refused to enforce.

Knowing that 64 of 80 Democrats in the House of Representatives had voted against passage of the 13th amendment in January 1865, congressional Republicans feared that once the southern states were back in the Union a new Democrat majority along with a Democrat such as Johnson in the White House might undo all they had accomplished for blacks. What if they rescinded the Emancipation Proclamation, as many Democrats had demanded, or repealed the Republicans' Civil Rights Act? To keep the precepts of that law safe from any future Democrat Congress, the Radical Republicans drafted and enacted the 14th amendment, every Republican in Congress voting for it and every Democrat voting against. Republicans today must bear in mind that the reason the Republican constitutional rights agenda was not carried out in the postwar South was that until they managed to override another Johnson veto to pass the Reconstruction Act of 1867, President Johnson and the former Confederate leadership were completely in charge of the South.

That's right, two years elapsed after the war ended before our Republican Party's Reconstruction policies even began. To illustrate, how would Germany look today if after World War II, Nazi regimes had remained in power at the provincial level well into 1947? What if General MacArthur had not instituted land reform, restructured the

Japanese economy, or extended the suffrage to women? No way the Allies would have been able to root out every vestige of the Third Reich or Imperial Japan if they had been compelled first to wait two years. Think of how immensely difficult and painful the postwar decades would have been for Germany and Japan. Think of the frustrating and daunting challenge for the Allies of 1947 to have had to intercede on behalf of slave laborers in Germany, say, or conscripted Korean workers in Japan.

Fortunately, this tragedy did not occur overseas in the 1940s; in reality, the Allies swept away the conquered regimes immediately and "reconstructed" them as modern, free market democracies. Unfortunately, this tragedy did occur in the southern United States in the 1860s. The subject people were never fully liberated and Lincoln's "unfinished work" never completed. Just as sadly, our Republican Party was forced off its original course. Now you may appreciate that most social problems today are due to the lamentably inadequate resolution of the central conflict in our history. Similarly, we are burdened by ignorance of our past with the mistaken impression that now and in the future we have but a limited set of policy options to deal with these problems. As knowledge is power, we must understand how trends from the past entrap us today, for "You shall know the truth and the truth shall set you free."

We are all familiar with the general outline of the Civil War – from Fort Sumter to Appomattox, Lincoln and his armies endured two years of defeats before Gettysburg and Vicksburg turned the tide toward victory – but with Lee's surrender our perspective tends to shift. Perhaps we read something about how a defenseless South endured "harsh" Reconstruction policies imposed by the Radical Republicans. Why is it that Americans today tend to view the Civil War itself from the patriots' point of view but the postwar era from the rebels' point of view? Now you know why. History is indeed written by the winners, and as Samuel Eliot Morrison observed: "The North may have won the war, but the white South won the peace."

To this day, we Republicans owe our Party's muddled message and inability to battle the Democrats effectively to our own ignorance about the Reconstruction era. What you think you know, aside from the slanted histories, is very much the product of two huge best-selling books and the blockbuster movies made from them. These were no mere books and movies, they were culture-shaping sensations.

After the Civil War, the Ku Klux Klan operated as the terrorist wing of the Democratic Party, massacring hundreds of white and black Republicans in the South, until it was crushed by the federal government once the presidency was back in the hands of the GOP. You would not know that, however, from the 1905 novel <u>The Clansman: A Historical Romance of the Ku Klux Klan</u>, the basis for the 1915 movie <u>The Birth of a Nation</u>. That racist epic portrayed the KKK as virtuous men riding around in white sheets to protect the southern way of life from evil ex-slaves and their graspy white pals. Woodrow Wilson screened the movie in the White House and said famously it was "terribly true...like writing history with lightning." The movie had such an impact on the popular consciousness that it spawned the modern-day Klan, which adopted cross-burning and other rituals as described in the book.

Did a movie that glorified the Ku Klux Klan also give us a mistaken view of the Radical Republicans? You bet! The other phenomenon to warp our understanding of the Reconstruction era was of course <u>Gone with the Wind</u>. Though still distorted, the movie considerably toned down the racist, pro-secessionist slant of the book, from which millions of readers came away lamenting that by defeating the rebellion and freeing the slaves those horrid Republicans had ruined everything for Scarlett O'Hara and her friends. Already weakened by President Wilson's favorite movie, our Republican Party's appreciation for its postwar crusade faded completely soon after <u>Gone with the Wind</u> hit the theaters in 1939.

Just who were these Radical Republicans, and what about their "harsh" Reconstruction policies? From the very beginning of our Party there was a difference of opinion on how to oppose slavery. The most conservative Republicans merely wanted slavery contained, hoping that one day the institution would die out on its own. Other Republicans went further, calling for some moderate anti-slavery measures while being careful not to upset the Democrats too much. Those with the most radical position were the abolitionists; they were the Radical Republicans. If you had been alive then, would you have taken a conservative stance against slavery? Would you have been only moderately against slavery? Or would you have been radically against slavery? Would you not have wanted the slaves set free immediately? And after the war would you not have wanted to end forever the power of the former masters over their former slaves?

You would have been a Radical Republican.

Prior to Fort Sumter there was plenty of reason for Republicans not to be too radical in their opposition to slavery, lest the South try to secede. Early on in the war, there remained good reason for Republicans not to push for emancipation too hard. The Union had only a tenuous hold on Kentucky and other loyal slaveholding areas, and many northern Democrats vowed not to support the war effort if its aim became to free the slaves. But as the war drew to a close, most Republicans – and some northern Democrats too – adopted the Radical position. They realized that the time had come to rid the country of the institution that had caused so much misery for so long.

During the war, President Lincoln also shifted his position on slavery somewhat toward the Radical view, but with a war to run he dared not move too far too fast. While the Radicals were more eager than he to seize the moment and uproot the entire slave system, there was nowhere near the discord between Lincoln and the Radicals that most historians would like us Republicans to believe. Lincoln, after all, was a highly partisan President whose chief opponents were the Confederacy and the Democratic Party. He counted many congressional Radicals, including Massachusetts Senator Charles Sumner, among his closest friends. Salmon Chase, another prominent Radical Republican, he named Secretary of the Treasury and then Chief Justice of the Supreme Court.

Throughout the Civil War, our Republican Party was strongly united. There were no significant differences on economic or foreign policy. All Republicans agreed that they must fight on until victory was theirs. While most Democrats voted against it, support for the 13th amendment among congressional Republicans was unanimous. Only on the issue of how vigorously to move against slavery could Republicans be counted as Radicals or moderates or conservatives. As public opinion in the North turned more radically against slavery, it was Abraham Lincoln, as we shall see, who was out of the mainstream of our Republican Party. This shift within our Party accelerated once peace was restored.

The House of Representatives elected in the first postwar elections, in November 1866, was three-quarters Republican, most of them being radically committed to doing for the South what the Allies did for Germany and Japan after World War II. Not until March 1867 then was our Republican Party able to disregard the Democrat President, Andrew Johnson, and radically sweep away the quasi-slavery regimes set up by the Democratic Party. During this time, the former Confederacy had been doing its damnedest to reestablish as much of the slave system as possible. A leading Radical, Thaddeus Stevens, warned: "The whole fabric of the South must be changed and never can it be done if this opportunity is lost." Another predicted "a century of serfdom" for blacks if they were denied their rights. The two years of Democrat rule since the war ended proved to be too long a delay before proper Republican Reconstruction of the South could begin. This opportunity was indeed lost, and a century of serfdom is just what blacks got.

What all Republicans wanted, Radicals especially, was "a new birth of freedom" for the South. They saw the Civil War as a chance to fulfill for the region the promise of the American Revolution. Republicans did not want to keep the South down; rather, they wanted to unite the country by extending to the South the free market system they had helped make so successful in the North. But just as sacrificing all else to maintaining the slave system had impoverished the South before the war, white Democrats in control of the postwar South would again deny economic development for the region by making subjugation of blacks their top priority.

Those Republicans radically opposed to slavery were highly resolved to ensuring that the hundreds of thousands of men who had given their lives for freedom "shall not have died in vain." The Radical Republicans did not want a century to pass before the slave system was completely abolished. They wanted freedom now. Was this "harsh"? Harsh treatment of the defeated traitors would have been to hang their leaders by the hundreds – the usual practice after an insurrection was put down – or to parade prisoners through northern cities. Instead, General Grant, President during most of the Radical Republican attempt to reconstruct the South, simply let the Confederate soldiers go home. This was "malice toward none." Harsh would have been to pillage the South. Instead, Republican teachers, administrators, businessmen, missionaries, and philanthropists tried to bring to the South the blessings of constitutional rights and the free market system. This was "charity for all," white and black.

Once in charge, Radical Republicans smashed the neo-Confederate regimes that had emerged in the South after Appomattox. Alarmed that President Johnson had permitted the southern states to revive their state militias, often led by former rebel officers wearing Confederate uniforms, Republicans disbanded them. Ominously, the 1868 Democratic Party platform demanded that the South regain control over their state militias. Rebellion may very well have broken out again in the South if there had been no Republican Reconstruction.

Though tragic for the region as a whole, the failure to reconstruct the South proved especially devastating for blacks, who though legally free, found themselves once again ruled by the same class of white southern Democrats who had been their slave masters just a few years before. With no land of their own, former slaves became sharecroppers, totally at the mercy of the landowners. As soon as they were back in power in the southern states, Democrats closed down most of the public school system that Republican administrations had established for blacks as well as poor whites. For decades thereafter, the Democratic

Party kept southern blacks poor and badly educated, and the conse-quences of this calamity are with us still.

During the second decade of this century, blacks began to move north in large numbers, attracted by plentiful industrial jobs for unskilled workers that paid well enough to support families. For a time they prospered, and their children received decent educations. By the 1960s, however, the world economy had advanced such that those well-paying industrial jobs which their parents had held were beginning to move overseas.

It was at this point that the second President Johnson declared his War on Poverty, which tended to hinder private sector job creation in the cities. While the quality of public school education declined markedly, what jobs were created were mostly in the government bureaucracy being expanded by the Democrat administration, effectively returning blacks to the Democratic Party control they had tried to escape half a century before.

To be sure, Lyndon Johnson was not a racist. He genuinely cared for the welfare of blacks (Hispanics too), but he wanted to put them in their place, which in his view was firmly back under the control of the Democratic Party. Being placed again under the control of whites, however well-intentioned, proved ruinous to blacks. Some blacks would succeed in breaking free, but many others would become a per-manent underclass, just as the slaves were. And as before, the Democratic Party thrives off the chief product of those trapped in the underclass – before it was cotton, now it is misery.

During the Civil War and Reconstruction, to be black was to be a Republican, as our Party was committed to their freedom. With the Democrats back in charge of the South, blacks could no longer vote and whites who had become Republicans generally were shut out of politics. Efforts to create a Republican Party coalition of blacks and poor whites had come to nothing, because white southerners across the political spectrum had united within the Democratic Party. Allied with northern Democrats, this Solid South would threaten nation-wide Republican policies as well.

Deploying thousands of soldiers had failed to guarantee the constitutional rights of blacks in the postwar South, so Republicans began to wonder what more could be done. Many asked themselves whether it would be better to concede victory to the southern Democrats. Since blacks in the South could not vote anyway, these Republicans considered, what was to be gained by antagonizing the whites who might agree with our Party on other issues?

This debate shaped our Republican Party during the Populist and Progressive eras of the late 19th and early 20th centuries. Radical Republicans such as Frederick Douglass, the black abolitionist and friend of Abraham Lincoln, argued strenuously that no matter what the political price, the Grand Old Party should remain true to its founding principles. Other Republicans disagreed. It was time to move on, they said, to new issues reflecting industrialization, advanced agriculture, and the country's growing prominence in world affairs. Henry Cabot Lodge, grandfather of Richard Nixon's 1960 running mate, led the Republicans' final charge of their postwar battle to protect constitutional rights. In 1890, his Federal Elections Bill passed the House of Representatives but was blocked in the southern Democrat-dominated Senate.

Not just blacks, but our entire Republican Party would suffer because of its inability to eradicate the slave system after the Civil War. Douglass turned out to be right, and political expediency was wrong. Even though there was no longer much our Republican Party could do for them in the South, blacks resented having been written off. As a consequence, when blacks began to move North in appreciable numbers after 1914, they took with them no great allegiance to our Republican Party. President Wilson was the worst racist to occupy the White House since Andrew Johnson, so at first the Democrats were no more attractive. Eventually, however, the Democratic Party's traditional focus on urban ethnic politics would show results.

Northern machine Democrats cared little about the southern Democrats' desire to keep blacks out of politics. For them, blacks moving into northern cities were just another immigrant group to be integrated into their party. Being on the bottom rung of the economic ladder, blacks in northern cities tended to suffer even more than whites during the Great Depression, so they responded enthusiastically to the New Deal combination of federal government assistance to the poor and traditional urban Democrat paternalism. Franklin Roosevelt's own empathy for blacks, as well as that of his wife Eleanor, further attracted blacks to the Democratic Party.

Nonetheless, our Republican Party held on to considerable support by blacks for several more decades. Blacks could not easily forget that the party of the New Deal was also the party of brutal repression in the South. Republicans were more progressive on racial issues than were Democrats, but having only a small number of seats in Congress at the time our Party had little influence over national policy.

The Republican presidential candidate in 1944 and 1948, New York Governor Thomas Dewey, could boast of a more progressive constitutional rights record than either of his Democrat opponents. In 1952 and again in 1956, more blacks supported Dwight Eisenhower than the Democratic Party nominee. In 1960, Richard Nixon was much more progressive on constitutional rights protection for blacks than was John Kennedy, but he lost that close election in part because of his unwise decision to downplay this stance in order to appeal to southern whites.

It was in 1964 that Republicans acquired their present reputation as being hostile to the interests of blacks and other minorities. That was the year our Republican Party paid dearly for having forgotten its Radical heritage. Republicans fought among themselves so viciously because each of the two main presidential contenders, Goldwater and Rockefeller, seized on only half the original Republican pro-free market and pro-constitutional rights agenda.

While denouncing New Deal socialism Goldwater figuratively wrapped himself in the Confederate flag so despised by his forebears. Rockefeller had his heart in the right place on constitutional rights, but his enthusiasm for socialist economic policies was alien to Republican tradition. The founders of our Party had understood that unchecked government power, whether exercised blatantly by a slave state or more subtly by a socialist bureaucracy, is the worst threat to constitutional rights; they knew that protecting constitutional rights is the foremost free market policy. As Radical Republicans would have foreseen, no good would come from tearing their legacy in half.

By muddling together two distinct concepts – promoting the free market society and tolerating unconstitutional racial discrimination – Goldwater enabled the Democrats to do some muddling of their own. Three distinct concepts made up the Democratic Party's agenda in the mid-1960s; Lyndon Johnson's "Great Society" label was all they had in common. Cutting taxes was a tremendous success, though Democrats have since managed to hand that issue to the Republicans. Another concept was enforcing the Constitution, through the 1964 Civil Rights Act and the 1965 Voting Rights Act. Using a War on Poverty to advance socialism was a third.

To this day, the Great Society legacy misleads most people into thinking that to oppose a socialist welfare state is to oppose the Constitution. Most Republicans today, never having thought through just what a "right" is, find themselves unable to counter Democrat charges that our Party is against the right to this or that or just about any noble-sounding sentiment. Armed with a thorough understanding of the Constitution, Radical Republicans were impervious to such clever manipulations.

A much higher percentage of Republicans than Democrats in Congress voted for the 1964 Civil Rights Act. Few of the Republicans who voted for it though recognized that the legislation was little more than Charles Sumner's Civil Rights Act of 1875 rewritten to get around an 1883 Supreme Court decision that stuck it down. If only the achievements of the Radical Republicans had not been long forgotten, our Party could have reclaimed much of its constitutional rights heritage that year. Instead, the Republican standard-bearer shamed our Party by bitterly denouncing this attempt to enforce the Constitution in the South, claiming it violated states rights.

Ever since the New Deal, the dominant ideology in this country has been the notion that most problems can be solved by enabling government employees to exercise more power over other people. In some instances, Republicans fall prey to this mentality. For the most part, however, it is Democrats who advocate imposing a regulation on this person or taxing more money from that one in order to achieve some goal. Arguing with them about specific policies and programs, Republicans find themselves outmaneuvered endlessly, because few understand that for most Democrats this accumulation of power by government over individuals is not a means to some end, but the end in itself.

At the core of the socialist outlook on life is what Friedrich Hayek described as "the fatal conceit." Far from any conscious or conspiratorial intent, a socialist's fatal conceit stems from his egotistical assumption that any problem would disappear if he were able to impose his will on it. Government employees, whom he projects would somehow act on his behalf, serve as the proxy for imposing his will on society. A faceless bureaucracy is too impersonal, however, for some socialists, who prefer a proxy with a face. These people prefer to focus their aspirations on some charismatic leader, whose cult of personality attracts people across the political spectrum who might otherwise not agree on anything else. What does matter to these socialists is that they can all dream about how the great leader would impose their own will on society if only he were in charge of everything!

Relieved of the burden of having to think for themselves, these fascists – yes, that's what they are – can easily find their political passions unrestrained by reason. In a political system too weak to limit its effects, this fascist mentality can produce the brutish zealotry of a Napoleon or Mussolini or Peron regime. In the United States, our constitutional system has had to contend with Huey Long in the 1930s and, more recently, several other embodiments of fascist aspirations.

For both mainstream socialism and the fascist variant, reality is an enemy. Attempting to stay one step ahead of reality is the mechanism by which the expansion of socialist policies knows no bounds. As a second problem arises to complicate a naive solution devised for the first, the recourse for the socialist is to try and impose his will, via the government, on that second problem; and so on. This sorry scramble, not some wicked lust for power, is why for Democrats the failure of one social program means it is time for two or three more. This is also why for Democrats the solution to every problem is ultimately to be found in the federal government. A socialist is like the proverbial farmer who does not want to own all the land in the world, just the land next to his.

Socialism does not require government ownership of anything. In times past, outright possession of the means of production was the only effective way for those in charge to exercise control, but no longer. Now, just about any government regulation or directive can serve that purpose, regardless of who owns what. Socialists do require enemies, the more the better. There are groups to be demonized domestically and countries to be vilified internationally.

The days of the monolithic organization are over. American society owes its dynamism to individual initiative. Decentralization and bottom-up decision-making have made our economy the envy of the world. Concentration of power at the top leads to oppression and stagnation. We Republicans hold these truths to be self-evident for the government too. We know that to the greatest extent possible consistent with the Constitution, government power should be exercised away from Washington, at the state and local levels, where individuals can more readily shape the policies which affect them. We know that having misspent six trillion dollars on the War on Poverty the federal government is far less capable than states and cities of dealing with social problems. We know that most of the enormous expansion of the federal government has had nothing to do with protecting constitutional rights. We know the Democratic Party to be the great trampler of constitutional rights.

And yet, the best our Party can manage is to slow down the spread of socialism, however fitfully and ineffectually. Why? Because after more than three decades, our Republican Party remains crippled by Goldwater's use of the old Democrat states rights argument to oppose socialism. The Radical Republicans vigorously enforced constitutional rights and promoted the free market society just as vigorously. A century later, having forgotten our Radical roots, modern Republicans can be thrown on the defensive on nearly any issue with charges that our motives are racist.

Worse, frustrated by not knowing how to fight the battle for the free market society, Republicans too easily dissipate their energies into symbolic distractions, such as campaigns to criminalize flag-burning. Moralists in our Party, who may not see the true cause of their discontent, are especially prone to being diverted away from making real progress. As the Radicals could appreciate, any Republican's ire at specific grievances would be better focused on sweeping away the entire socialist apparatus.

During their first decade of existence as a Party, Republicans accomplished their policy objectives – saving the Union, ending slavery, and laying the foundation for the modern American economy – because they seized and held the policy initiative. Stevens, Sumner, Lincoln, and other Republican leaders were acutely aware that to preserve the free market society, the drift toward a nationwide slave society had to be stopped. To get the job done, they charged right at the Democratic Party in a battle of ideas, their best weapon a clear vision of the free market society they were fighting for.

Ronald Reagan, the Radical Republican of our time, shared with the earlier Radicals the dream of the free market society for all Americans. He understood, as did Thaddeus Stevens and Charles Sumner, the futility of tinkering with a system of institutionalized government oppression. His vision stirs us still: "You and I are told we must choose between a left or right, but I suggest there is no such thing as a left or right. There is only an up or down. Up to man's age-old dream – the maximum of individual freedom consistent with order or down to the ant heap of totalitarianism." Though his bold policies did invigorate the economy and help defeat Soviet communism, he could not eradicate socialism in the United States. More to blame than the Democrat-controlled House of Representatives were Reagan's views about the Constitution that contradicted Radical Republican principles.

Today's Republican Party places itself at an immense disadvantage. Rather than express clearly what we should be for – the free market society we Republicans won the Civil War to preserve – on too many issues, too often our Party's policy is merely that we are against whatever Democrats are for, or perhaps we want less of it than they do. Our Party is an athlete who has lost his balance – we are in good shape, with plenty of drive, but until we regain our footing we are going nowhere.

Chapter Two

(1848-1861)

A GRAND NEW PARTY

Three decades of truce between North and South came to an end with the Mexican-American War of 1846-48. The Missouri Compromise of 1820 had been devised to deal with territory acquired by the Louisiana Purchase, but annexation of the Republic of Texas and swift conquests to the west brought to everyone's mind the question of what to do with all that new land. Would slavery be allowed in Arizona or California? In August 1846, even before the fighting stopped, Pennsylvania Representative David Wilmot introduced into Congress a bill to prohibit slavery in any territory which might be won from Mexico.

This "Wilmot Proviso" bill passed the House but failed in the Senate. Though it did not become law, the "Wilmot Proviso" had a tremendous impact. No longer could the American people put off deciding whether slavery would remain a regional exception or a national norm. So consumed by this issue was the country that the election campaigns of 1848 were fought over little else.

Though the Whigs had not been as eager as the Democrats to acquire more southern territory, in 1848 the party nominated for the presidency war hero General Zachary Taylor. A southerner whose military experience had given him a more nationalist outlook, Taylor promised to let congressional Whigs take the policy initiative. Notably, Representative Abraham Lincoln had urged his fellow Whigs to go with Taylor instead of his hero, Henry Clay, preferring victory of some of his policies over the defeat of all of them. The Democratic

Party countered with a northern presidential candidate of southern sympathies, Michigan Senator Lewis Cass. Taylor ran without a platform because the northern and southern wings of the Whig Party could not agree on one.

In a narrow victory the Whigs won New York, and so the presidency, because of a third party challenge in that state; where the Free Soil Party, a recent fusion of anti-slavery Whigs and Democrats, and the Liberty Party, had split the Democrat vote by nominating former President Van Buren.

The new House of Representatives would be 112 Democrats and 109 Whigs, with 12 from the Free Soil Party holding the balance of power. The Democrats and the Whigs, each having members on both sides of the slavery issue, dared not take official stands on whether to permit slavery in the territories. Party identities broke down, resulting in a Congress elected that year that was so divided that it took sixty-three ballots just to elect a Speaker of the House. One ominous theme throughout these rancorous preliminaries was discussion of a convention of southern states to form a voting bloc in Congress and perhaps form an independent country later on. Even if the North were inclined to let seceding states go, which side would control the rich new territories meant war would be inevitable. Everyone knew it.

So bitter were disputes over the disposition of the new territories that President Taylor had to repeat Andrew Jackson's threat to use military force against any secessionist movement and hang any secessionists he could find. Taylor became fatally ill at the July 4, 1850 groundbreaking ceremony for the Washington Monument and was succeeded by his thoroughly Whig Vice President, Millard Fillmore of New York.

Three great figures dominated debate over what would become of the territories, and by implication, the country. Whig Senator Daniel Webster, a former Federalist, spoke for most northerners. John Calhoun, former Vice President and current Democrat Senator from South Carolina, advocated the predominant southern position. Holding the middle ground was Kentucky Senator Henry Clay, after whom fellow-Whig and fellow-Kentuckian Abraham Lincoln modeled his own political agenda.

Under the Compromise of 1850, California would be admitted as a free state (meaning no slavery allowed) to balance Texas which had already been admitted as a slave state. In territories south of the Missouri-Arkansas border, residents would vote on whether to allow slavery; territories above that line would be free. This compromise, worked out by Henry Clay, did avert civil war for another ten years, but all remained unresolved. Just before he died in March 1850, Calhoun declared: "The cords that bind the States together are snapping one by one."

Another part of the Compromise did bind the states together more tightly. A new Fugitive Slave Act, replacing the lax version from 1793, extended into the North much of the southern slave system that had previously been something of an abstract, faraway horror. Under the new federal law, government agents could arrest any black* person, authorized by a mere affidavit, and with no trial send him south into slavery. Escaped slaves and free blacks alike were to be hunted down as remorselessly in, say Columbus, Ohio as in Columbia, South Carolina. Alarmed that this particular "southern way of life" was taking root in the North, many state governments there refused to permit their law enforcement officers to assist federal authorities with the manhunts.

In 1852, the Whigs nominated another southern war hero with nationalist political sympathies, General Winfield Scott. With a war veteran of their own, former New Hampshire Senator Franklin Pierce, the Democrats recaptured the presidency with 51% of the popular vote, to 43% for the Whigs and 6% for the Free Soil Party. During the Pierce administration, as the Democrats adopted much of the Whig economic agenda, slavery became the only issue anyone really cared about. The Democratic Party, since the Tyler administration, was dominated by slave interests, but the Whigs were unable to take a stand. Pro-slavery Whigs, North and South, drifted to the Democratic Party, while anti-slavery Whigs in the North were unsure of their political future.

---

* Reflecting the dynamic between racial groups, this term is used throughout the book instead of the worthy "African-American."

One of those northern Whigs was Abraham Lincoln, who had begun his political career in the Illinois legislature at the age of 25. While in the legislature he married Mary Todd, whose father was a close friend of Henry Clay. Strongly supporting Clay's American System, Lincoln pressed for state infrastructure projects and a charter to replace the Bank of the United States at the state level. At 27, his Whig colleagues elected him party leader. After eight years in state government, Lincoln returned to his legal practice full time, though he did travel to Indiana in 1844 to campaign for Whig candidates there. In 1846, he was elected to the House of Representatives but did not seek reelection. While in Congress, the devoted Whig traveled to New England in 1848 to campaign for Zachary Taylor.

Our Republican Party was born as a protest movement against a very specific outrage perpetrated by the Democrats. The elections of 1852 had given the Democratic Party a two-thirds majority in the House of Representatives and nearly so in the Senate. Virtually the first order of business of the new Congress was to repeal the Missouri Compromise of 1820, specifically, the prohibition of slavery in territories north of Arkansas. The Kansas-Nebraska Act, drafted by Stephen Douglas, the Democrat Senator from Illinois and owner of a slave plantation in the South, provided that voters in each territory could decide whether or not to allow slavery. Nearly all Democrats in Congress voted for the Act, and Democrat President Franklin Pierce signed it into law in May 1854. Even more so than the Wilmot Proviso, the Kansas-Nebraska Act forced all Americans to choose sides. One was either for the Act or against it, for the slave society or for the free market society – there was no middle ground.

The Nebraska Territory included the Dakotas and Montana too, so the slave system could now spread to most of the United States. Implicitly, once a territory voted for slavery, it would be federal law that enforced it. And if the federal government could legislate in favor of slavery in the territories, why not in the free states as well? Everyone could feel which way the wind was blowing. After straddling the slavery issue for decades, the majority Democratic Party had chosen to side with slavery. Already fading, the minority Whig

Party feared that firm opposition to slavery would cost the party its remaining support in the South. What could be done to oppose the extension of slavery?

The Whigs could have survived, perhaps to this day, had they come down hard against slavery, but instead their caution cost them everything. The party fell apart that year as most southern Whigs joined the Democratic Party, resulting in the Solid South that was to last more than a century. In the North, the Whig Party tried for a while to stay true to the middle-of-the-road policies of Henry Clay, the Great Compromiser, but the days of compromise were over. What was once regarded as statesmanship most northern Whigs now saw as appeasement. Millions of Whigs left the party, but unlike the southern Whigs they had no ready place to go. The only other national party, the adamantly anti-slavery Free Soil Party, they believed, was too-abolitionist, too-northeastern, and too-Democrat in its economic policies.

Shocked by the Kansas-Nebraska Act, most northerners were outraged at slavery, the South, and the Democratic Party. They realized that soon territories as far north as Minnesota could enter the Union as slave states, transforming the nation's dominant economic and social system from free market to slavery. Amid the intense reaction, so-called "anti-Nebraska" groups sprang up all across the North in early 1854 to oppose the extension of slavery into the northern territories. In hundreds of town meetings and demonstrations, Whigs, Free Soil members, and dissident Democrats united with a single purpose: "Enough concessions to the 'Slavocrats'! We draw the line right here. NO SLAVERY IN THE TERRITORIES." Over the next few months these groups would coalesce into our Republican Party.

Though the Democratic Party is still with us, it lost most of its anti-slavery members at the time over the Kansas-Nebraska Act. In January 1854, two Free Soil Party Senators, Charles Sumner and Salmon Chase, along with several other prominent politicians, wrote the "Appeal of the Independent Democrats," calling on anti-slavery Democrats to resist the Kansas-Nebraska bill and their party's proslavery stance overall. Published widely, the "Appeal" led many anti-slavery Democrats to abandon their party.

Several sites share the credit as the birthplace of our Party. At one "anti-Nebraska" town meeting in a Ripon, Wisconsin schoolhouse on February 28, 1854, the leader, Alvan Bovay, called for another meeting the following month to organize a new political party, to be called the "Republican Party." Though only fifty-three people were present at that second small town meeting on March 20, 1854, this was the first time the name "Republican" was used for the new political party. The first state Republican Party convention, attended by 10,000 people, took place in Jackson, Michigan on July 6, 1854. Dozens of members of Congress pledged themselves to our new Party. The Republican Association, forerunner of the Republican National Committee, met for the first time in June 1855. The first national organizational meeting of newly-minted Republicans was in Pittsburgh in February 1856, followed four months later by the first Republican National Convention, chaired by party icon David Wilmot.

Horace Greeley, editor of the <u>New York Tribune</u>, was an early booster of both the new party and the term "Republican," a name with a past as well as a future. Opponents of slavery had chosen the term "Republican" to contrast themselves with the aristocrats who lorded it over slaves and poor whites down South. Thomas Jefferson and his followers had also been known as "Republicans." Then there were James Madison, James Monroe and other "Democratic-Republicans." Before settling on the "Whig Party," opponents of Andrew Jackson had called themselves the "National-Republicans."

Several factors explain why our Republican Party was so phenomenally successful from the very start, growing in just two years into one of the country's two major parties. Careful to avoid the overly narrow focus of the Free Soil Party, the Republicans achieved a synthesis of the best of Jefferson and Hamilton, combining that first Republican's defense of "life, liberty, and the pursuit of happiness" with the Whigs' Hamiltonian agenda for economic growth. Whigs looking for a new home and Democrats unwilling to join their Whig or Free Soil rivals had no problem uniting in a new party. Our

Republican Party grew rapidly as northerners who saw the futility of placating the South recognized the potential of not having to straddle the slavery issue as the Whigs had done, or actually abetting the spread of slavery like the Democrats.

Since the Kansas-Nebraska Act had violated the Compromise of 1850, northerners opposed to slavery no longer saw any reason to enforce the Fugitive Slave Act, which had been a concession to the South. Their attitude tended to shift from noncompliance to active opposition. Five years later, northern state governments would ignore a Supreme Court decision ordering them to comply with the Fugitive Slave Act. The day after the Kansas-Nebraska Act became law, it took hundreds of soldiers to battle a crowd of angry Bostonians to arrest and ship back one escaped slave. A policeman was killed in the riot.

The Kansas-Nebraska Act cost hundreds more lives in the months leading up to the vote on whether Kansas would have a free or slave territorial government. Rival free and slave administrations were set up, and northern "Jayhawkers" and southern "bushwhackers" fought it out. This mini-Civil War became known as "Bleeding Kansas."

Just as the Fugitive Slave Act thrust the slave system into the northern states, "Bleeding Kansas" brought the slave master's brutality to the floor of the U.S. Capitol. Elected by a Whig-Free Soil coalition to replace Daniel Webster as Senator from Massachusetts, Charles Sumner was an outspoken critic of slavery, blaming the "peculiar institution" for the degeneracy of the masters as well as the evils inflicted on their slaves. During Senate debates, Sumner strongly denounced the proposed Kansas-Nebraska Act. Over the course of two days in May 1854, Sumner delivered a blistering assault on slavery in the South and its Democrat collaborators in the North. Entitled "The Crime Against Kansas," his speech mocked the slave-holders for presuming to be civilized and gentile, and said the penetration of slavery into Kansas was "the rape of a virgin territory." So infuriated was one Democrat that two days later as Sumner was working at his desk on the Senate floor this South Carolina Representative bashed his head with a heavy cane.

Senator Sumner spent the next three years in a wheelchair, and never fully recovered from the severe skull and spinal injuries. While slavery zealots in the South sent the assailant replacement canes, Charles Sumner became a hero in the North, particularly among Republicans. He joined our Republican Party in 1856 and came in third place for our Party's vice presidential nomination that year. In 1857, Sumner was reelected to the Senate by the state legislature nearly unanimously.

The other principal co-author of the "Appeal of the Independent Democrats" was also to become a pillar of the early Republican Party. Salmon Chase rose to prominence for serving, however futilely in most cases, as pro bono attorney for dozens of runaways, earning the sobriquet "Attorney General for Escaped Slaves." In 1848, Chase helped organize the Free Soil Party and was elected to the Senate from Ohio the following year by a coalition of his party and anti-slavery Democrats. Senator Chase thundered against the Fugitive Slave Law and other concessions to slave interests. Failing to win reelection, because his Free Soil Party had faded away by 1855, he then joined our Republican Party and was twice elected Governor of Ohio. Chase was a strong contender for the first Republican presidential nomination, in 1856.

Second only to Abraham Lincoln as champion of Republican ideals during the Civil War era was Pennsylvania Representative Thaddeus Stevens. Though little known today, as the most powerful member of Congress during the war, Stevens oversaw the financing of the war effort and masterminded the tremendously successful Republican economic agenda. Born in 1792 during the Washington presidency, with a severely deformed foot, Stevens began his career of public service long before our Republican Party made its debut. During his twenty-six years living in Gettysburg he was instrumental in establishing Pennsylvania's public school system in the 1830s. He opposed a new state constitution because it prohibited blacks from voting. Having entered politics as a Federalist just before that party disappeared, Stevens become a Whig in 1844. Due to Stevens' renown as an effective advocate for Whig policies, freshman Whig Representative Abraham Lincoln wrote to ask him for his views. In 1848, Stevens was elected to the House of Representatives from Lancaster by a Whig-Free Soil coalition.

Even more than for his firm grasp of economic policy, Thaddeus

Stevens was revered for his tireless work on behalf of the slaves. After losing his seat in the Democrat landslide of 1852, Stevens joined our Republican Party at the Lancaster County founding convention in 1855. As a Republican, Stevens won his old House seat back in 1858, and became so popular that in 1860 he was reelected with 96% of the vote. The firm backing of his constituents is all the more remarkable considering that he was as married to a black woman as a white man could be in those days. In 1848, when he was 56, a widowed free black woman, Lydia Smith, along with her two young sons, moved in with the never-married Stevens to serve as his housekeeper. As demonstrated by their devotion to each other until his death, their relationship evolved into husband and wife. Mindful of the prejudices of the age, Stevens was always careful to refer to her as "Mrs. Smith," but Lancaster neighbors knew to call her "Mrs. Stevens."

Henry Wilson, who would later be elected Vice President, was another influential Republican during the formation of our Party. He began his career as a Whig, then helped establish the Free Soil Party. After a brief stint as a moderate in the American (or Know-Nothing) Party, Wilson joined our Republican Party and was elected to the Senate by the Massachusetts legislature. One of the most zealously anti-slavery members of Congress was Illinois Representative Owen Lovejoy, brother of slain abolitionist Elijah Lovejoy.

Sumner, Chase, Stevens, Wilson, Lovejoy. These men were all leaders of the Radical Republicans, that is, Republicans who were radically against slavery. The most prominent conservative Republican early on was New York Senator William Seward. Though he opposed the Kansas-Nebraska Act and the Fugitive Slave Law, Seward was more willing than the Radicals to tolerate slavery where it already existed. As a Whig, Seward had first been elected Governor of New York in 1838. Joining our Party in 1855, as a Senator from New York Seward was perhaps the most powerful Republican in the pre-war years. The conservative Republican leadership also included William Dayton of New Jersey, Montgomery Blair of Maryland, and Simon Cameron of Pennsylvania.

After his one term as a Whig member of the House of

Representatives (1847-49), Abraham Lincoln had been in private legal practice for five years when the Kansas-Nebraska Act jolted him back into politics. A devoted follower of Whig founder Henry Clay, Lincoln was more reluctant than most other prominent Whigs to abandon the party, even after it disintegrated in 1854. To avoid having to choose between the Whigs and the Republicans, Lincoln left Springfield the morning of an October 1854 meeting called by Owen Lovejoy and others to establish an Illinois Republican Party, and had his name taken off the first state party committee roster.

At first, Lincoln considered our Republican Party too strongly abolitionist to have much of a future in national politics. He also had to be sure the Republicans would adopt the Whigs' economic growth agenda. Still calling himself a Whig, Lincoln nearly won election to the U.S. Senate in 1855, coming six votes short in the Illinois legislature before throwing his support to the eventual winner, anti-slavery Democrat and future Republican, Lyman Trumbull.

In May 1856, Lincoln, realizing the Republicans had indeed replaced the Whigs as a major political party, agreed to be a delegate to the Illinois state convention at Bloomington. His reputation as a moderate on the slavery question intact, he helped organize the event and gave the keynote address. His extemporaneous remarks so grabbed the audience that no one took down the words or even took notes. Lincoln's "Lost Speech" made him the leader of our Republican Party in Illinois.

Though our Party was only months old, the Republicans had made tremendous gains in the 1854 fall elections, winning some 40% of the House of Representatives. Another 20% were members of another opposition group which had emerged to fill the void left by the Whigs. The American Party, more commonly known as the "Know-Nothings," claimed not to know anything about violence used against its opponents. Just as the Whigs did, the American Party split over slavery and faded away soon after this initial success.

In 1855, Lincoln wrote this famous passage denouncing the Know-Nothings: "As a nation, we began by declaring that 'all men are created equal.' We now practically read it 'all men are created equal, except negroes.' When the Know-Nothings get control it will read 'all men are created equal, except negroes, and foreigners, and catholics.' When it comes to this, I shall prefer emigrating to some country where they make no pretense of loving liberty – to Russia, for instance, where despotism can be taken pure, and without the base alloy of hypocrisy."

As dissident Democrats and other opponents of the Kansas-Nebraska Act shifted over to the Republicans, our Party – less than three years old – won control of the House of Representatives with the election of Massachusetts Representative Nathaniel Banks* as Speaker of the House in February 1856.

Heading into the 1856 general elections, Republicans, who until recently had been divided among the Whig, Democratic, and Free Soil parties, were united in their determination to save the country. They came out squarely against slavery and the South's economic system, based on slave labor. Consequently, our Republican Party began with no strength at all in the South. Free from having to mollify slave-holding interests, Republicans easily found agreement on progressive economic policies for growth, taken straight from the Whig agenda. The future of slavery, however, was the only real issue in the campaign, and the electoral contest was generally between North and South.

In June 1856, that first Republican National Convention convened in Philadelphia, where the Constitution had been written three score and nine years before. The delegates settled on an excellent choice for their presidential nominee. Famous for having helped conquer California and explore the West, former Democrat Senator John Fremont** was a southern-born abolitionist married to the daughter

---

* Banks would become better known as one of the Unions generals defeated by Stonewall Jackson in the Shenandoah Valley.
** During the Civil War, Fremont was the second of three generals defeated by Stonewall Jackson in the Valley. The third, James Shields, had decades before met Abraham Lincoln to duel with swords before the fight was called off at the last minute.

of a powerful Senator from a border state. To the Free Soil slogan "Free labor, free speech, free Kansas" Republicans could now append "and Fremont!" Lincoln came in second in the balloting for the vice presidential nomination; the nominee, former Whig Senator William Dayton, would later be Lincoln's ambassador to France.

By 1856, as nearly every American opposed to slavery had joined our Republican Party, the Democratic Party had become firmly pro-slavery. The Democrat platform touted the Kansas-Nebraska Act as a glorious achievement. The presidential nominee, James Buchanan, a Lancaster neighbor of Thaddeus Stevens, had been serving as ambassador to Britain during most of the previous four years, and so was unencumbered by any public record on the slave issue. The vice presidential nominee would five years later become a Confederate general. What remained of the Whig Party and the American Party together nominated former Whig President Millard Fillmore for another term.

Many southerners warned that their states would secede if Fremont won. Fear of war plus Buchanan's inclination to appease the South to keep it in the Union cost Fremont the support of many voters in the North who would otherwise have voted for him. Fremont did win most northern states (114 electoral votes) and Fillmore won Maryland (8); while the Solid South, Pennsylvania, Indiana, and Illinois went for Buchanan (174). Results in the House of Representatives were 54% for the Democrats and 39% for the Republicans.

In his inauguration address, President Buchanan hinted that the Supreme Court would soon render a decision that he believed would settle the question of slavery in the territories. Two days later, on March 6, 1857, the Supreme Court did indeed announce its infamous Dred Scott decision. The slave Dred Scott, having traveled to Illinois and Wisconsin, where he was free, was suing for his freedom after he returned to Virginia. The Justices had been wrestling with how a person could be a slave, then free, then a slave again depending where he was.

The solution for the seven Democrats on the Supreme Court (the two Republicans dissented) was that blacks could not be citizens anywhere, North or South, so they had no standing to sue in court for anything. Despite the fact that free blacks had fought in the

Revolution and the War of 1812, voted for five of the state conventions that ratified the Constitution, and could vote in several northern states, the Court declared that a black man had no rights a white man was bound to respect.

Atrocious as that was, the really explosive part of the Dred Scott decision was the striking down of a law for the first time since Marbury v. Madison in 1803. The majority opinion written by Chief Justice Roger Taney, Andrew Jackson's former Secretary of the Treasury, declared unconstitutional the Missouri Compromise of 1820, which banned slavery in the territories north of Arkansas. Congress, he wrote, did not have the authority to ban slavery anywhere because to do so would violate the Bill of Rights, specifically the 5th amendment's safeguard against being deprived of one's property without due process.

Every Republican could see that the Democrat Justices were violating the Constitution in order to impose their pro-slavery agenda. If the weak Congress under the Articles of Confederation could ban slavery in the territories and the first session of Congress after ratification of the Constitution could ban slavery in the territories, then surely such a measure was constitutional. Still worse, the Supreme Court went far beyond the Constitution in asserting that slaves were property, hence not fully human; though the Constitution mentioned "Person held to Service or Labour" it nowhere said that masters actually owned their slaves as property.

Republicans believed that Buchanan and the Democrat Justices were in league to destroy their principal opposition party by declaring unconstitutional its central tenet: NO SLAVERY IN THE TERRITORIES. By the Democrats' logic, if a congressional ban on slavery violated the 5th amendment, then northerners had reason to fear that the Supreme Court was just one step away from declaring slavery legal in every state from Maine to California. A vote by no more than five Justices transforming the entire country into a slave society could come at any time. And, if the Supreme Court could revoke the citizenship of free blacks, why not naturalized citizens, or any citizen at all? For the infuriated Republicans, the stretching and twisting of the Constitution by the Democrats to suit their purposes had gone too far.

As Lincoln pointed out throughout his career, the Framers of the Constitution had been ashamed of slavery and had expected that the institution, confined to a region, would eventually die out. By the 1850s, however, many white southerners touted slavery (not for themselves, of course) as a blessing they would be glad to see conferred on the North. Slaves, they alleged, were much better off than free white workers. "Free Society!", declared a prominent Georgia newspaper, "We sicken at the name."

Though slavery may have been economically ruinous for the South, it was not all on the verge of death. Just as the cotton gin increased demand for slaves in the 1790s, industrialization could easily have done so again. Many southern politicians were already calling for the South to industrialize itself through the use of slave labor in mining and manufacturing. Some were even calling for the enslavement of poor whites too. Soviet labor camps and Nazi slave factories prove how readily this system could have been implemented. Just before the Civil War, there was even wild talk throughout the South of conquering the whole Western Hemisphere in order to set up a vast slave empire. If the South were allowed to secede, northerners wondered, how long before the breakaway nation attempted to add parts of the North to its slave empire?

In 1858, Democrat Senator Stephen Douglas came up for reelection. At the June 1858 Republican state convention that nominated him for the Senate, Lincoln delivered his famous "House Divided" speech, which was then widely printed throughout the North: "I believe this government cannot endure, permanently half slave and half free... It will become all one thing, or all the other." Since Douglas had written the law which sparked the creation of our Republican Party, everyone expected the two candidates to debate whether the nation would become all slave or all free. In their first debate, Lincoln summed up our Party's position: "The Republican Party think it [slavery] is wrong – we think it is a moral, a social, and a political wrong... [A] sentiment which holds that slavery is not wrong...is the Democratic policy."

The second debate, held in the northwestern Illinois town of

Freeport, in August 1858, was the most important one. This was the final undoing of attempts to reconcile two contradictory Democrat positions – states rights and the right to enslave others. It also cost Douglas the presidency two years later. Lincoln asked him: "Can the people of a United States Territory, in any lawful way, against the wish of any citizen of the United States, exclude slavery from its limits prior to the formation of a state constitution?" Saying yes argued against the Dred Scott decision, while saying no would contradict the Kansas-Nebraska Act. Douglas' reply was to say that a territory could, despite Dred Scott, keep out slavery by simply not enacting slavery laws. This admission by Douglas that a territory could legally exclude slavery enraged southern whites. One could almost hear snapping the last strand holding the two halves of the country together.

With slavery the sole issue during the campaign, Republican candidates for the Illinois legislature outpolled the Democrats. Nevertheless, since northern Illinois was underrepresented in the legislature, Democrats took a majority of the seats and reelected Douglas. Lincoln did come away from his loss a national figure, thanks to the printing and distribution of transcripts of the debates, as they occurred, by Greeley's <u>New York Tribune</u>.

Nationwide, Republicans did very well, winning control of most northern state governments and a plurality in the House of Representatives, which would have 113 Republicans to 101 Democrats, and some two dozen Know-Nothings. Amid Democrat denunciations of their principal opposition as "a bunch of radicals," the new House wrangled for weeks over electing a Speaker. John Sherman, whose older brother would become the famous general, ultimately had to give way to a more moderate Republican. To ensure slavery for all territories whether the people there wanted it or not, southern Democrats demanded a federal slave code. Douglas, to his credit, was firmly opposed. North and South, no longer on speaking terms politically after the elections, faced the specter of war after John Brown's unsuccessful attempt to spark a slave insurrection in October 1859 whipped many southern whites into a wild-eyed frenzy.

For the 1860 presidential election, the remnants of the Whigs and the Know-Nothings renamed themselves the "Constitutional Union Party." Few voters were attracted by the policy of its presidential nominee, Tennessee's John Bell, to ignore the slavery issue. Just as the Whigs had been unable to straddle the growing chasm between North and South, in 1860 it was the turn of Democrats to split up over the slavery issue. At the Democratic National Convention that year in Charleston, South Carolina, delegates could not agree on a standard-bearer. Southern Democrats, who began calling themselves Constitutional Democrats, walked out, nominating Vice President Breckinridge in Richmond two months later. In Baltimore, Stephen Douglas received the presidential nomination of northern, or National Democrats.

Contention for the Republican presidential nomination already underway, Lincoln traveled to New York City in February 1860 to deliver a major address at the Cooper Union. Calmly, logically, and convincingly, he demolished the Democrat position on slavery by outlining the history of the crisis from the very origins of the country. Even more than his debates with Douglas, this widely-reprinted speech left northeastern Republicans mightily impressed with the midwestern lawyer. As he had done in 1858 and in 1859, Lincoln then went on a speaking tour, helping forge national Republican policy with speeches in Connecticut, Rhode Island, and New Hampshire. He returned to Illinois a serious contender for the nomination.

Propitiously for Lincoln, the 1860 Republican National Convention, again chaired by David Wilmot, was held in Chicago. Delegates convened in the "Wigwam," a specially built wooden structure which stood downtown at what is now the corner of Lake Street and Wacker Drive. Republicans did not care that very few southern delegates were present. With the Democrats divided, all our Party had to do was carry the North. Lincoln was the ideal candidate to win over moderates in the northern and border states. Seward, the Republican heavyweight, had little support west of Pennsylvania. Drawbacks for Chase, Banks, Dayton, and others included long public records to defend.

Lincoln, sufficiently well known nationally but no longer in public office, had on the record only his relatively moderate speeches. He was no abolitionist, but given the "House Divided" speech, Radicals could be sure his containment policy would eventually eliminate slavery. He beat out Seward on the third ballot to win, after which his nomination was made unanimous. To balance the moderate midwestern former Whig Representative at the top of the ticket, the convention nominated Radical northeastern former Democrat Senator Hannibal Hamlin for Vice President.

Following the tradition at the time, Lincoln stayed home in Springfield, but Republicans across the spectrum, from Seward and other conservatives to Radicals such as Stevens, Sumner, and Chase, did campaign for him vigorously. Since an 1857 speech, Lincoln's opinion on the difference between our Party and the Democrats was no secret: "The Republicans inculcate, with whatever of ability they can, that the negro is a man; that his bondage is cruelly wrong, and that the field of his oppression ought not to be enlarged. The Democrats deny his manhood; deny, or dwarf to insignificance, the wrong of his bondage; so far as possible, crush all sympathy for him; and cultivate and excite hatred and disgust against him; compliment themselves as Union-savers for doing so; and call the indefinite out-spreading of his bondage 'a sacred right of self-government.'" The strong prospect of victory over slave-holding interests raised in the North popular enthusiasm for the Republican ticket to heights incomprehensible to modern voters.

Lincoln embodied our Party's dedication to achieving Thomas Jefferson's ideals through Alexander Hamilton's free market system. Like Hamilton, Lincoln was a self-made man who had raised himself up from poverty. The popular image of Lincoln the Railsplitter signaled to northern workers that, in contrast to Democrat disdain for "mudsills and greasy mechanics," Republicans revered the free market system. Unlike the Democrats, Lincoln was genuinely devoted to Jefferson's humanitarianism; "All honor to Jefferson," he would say. Unnerved that the Republicans had taken to heart Thomas Jefferson, the man they claimed as their founder, Democrats accused them of being "Black Republicans," as if mentioning our Party's regard for the rights of blacks was some sort of insult.

Many years before, the Virginian George Mason had foreseen the ill effects of slavery: "Slavery discourages arts and manufactures. The poor despise labor when performed by slaves... They produce the most pernicious effect on manners. Every master of slaves is born a petty tyrant. They bring the judgment of Heaven on a country." The Republican campaign was also on behalf of the millions of poor southern whites exploited by the slave system, who could be kept down by the white elite with the solace that at least they were not as bad off as the slaves.

Far from being engaged in a contest between regions, Republicans sought to extend to the South the economic growth and social progress underway in the North. They understood that slavery and the free market were mutually exclusive, since it was the heavy hand of government's regulatory and enforcement infrastructure that permitted some people to enslave others. "The free labor system opens the way for all – gives hope to all, and energy, and progress, and improvement of condition to all," wrote Lincoln.

For decades, so intimidated by southern secessionist threats were northerners in Congress that none dared speak publicly about the actual suffering of the slaves, restricting themselves instead to generalities and abstract rhetoric. That all changed when Charles Sumner returned from Europe after three years recuperating from his injuries. His first speech back in the Senate in June 1860, "The Barbarism of Slavery," had a tremendous impact across the country. Slavery, he observed, had warped the southern culture and economy, producing a class of semi-literate, violence-prone, slave-holding white barbarians. He cited blood-curling examples of how "the chivalry of the South" enforced their slave codes – by whipping, cutting off noses and ears, burning people alive.

That was not all. If slaves, as it was alleged, were property like cattle, slave masters, Sumner noted, were still plenty willing to have sex with their female livestock. The Senator's language was roundabout, but his implication was stunningly straightforward: slave-holders were either perverts or criminals. Seeing their reflection in Sumner's mirror, southern Democrats howled. Throughout the North,

Republicans cheered their hero – at last, someone with the courage to tell the truth. No longer would the political debate be about what might happen in the future; the 1860 campaign would be fought over the stark alternatives of the present.

Free from having to appease a southern wing, the Republican Party of 1860 was more united than the Whigs had ever been. Since Lincoln would not even appear on the ballot in ten southern states, the 1860 Republican platform aimed to appeal exclusively to northern industrial workers, farmers, and merchants. In the days when conventions actually chose the nominees, party platforms were very important. Lincoln, for example, regarded himself bound by it, as a solemn obligation to those who voted for him. First, though the anti-slavery rhetoric was toned down from the 1856 platform in the hope of attracting some Democrat voters, our Party would not yield an inch on the slavery issue.

On economic policy, Republicans adopted the full Whig agenda. Planks called for agricultural and mechanical colleges, and land grants to farmers (a measure long opposed by the Democrats, who wanted the Plains states reserved for slave plantations). Other planks were for a transcontinental railroad and higher tariffs. Another plank criticized the anti-immigration stance of the Know-Nothings.

The November 1860 elections were a tremendous success for the Republicans. Our Party won majorities in both the Senate and the House of Representatives. Moreover, every state in the North would have a Republican Governor. Among the notable winners was John Andrew of Massachusetts, the Radical Republican Governor who would later form the famed 54th Massachusetts regiment of black soldiers portrayed in the movie <u>Glory</u>.

In the four-candidate presidential race, Lincoln's 40% of the vote (up from Fremont's 33%) was enough to win. Douglas came in second in the popular vote with 29%, followed by Breckinridge with 18% and Bell with 12%. In the Electoral College, Lincoln received 180 votes, to 72 for Breckinridge, 39 for Bell, and only 12 for Douglas. Mere vote totals, however, do not reflect the fact that basically there were two separate elections. Lincoln and Douglas split the northern vote, while the South and the border states chose between Breckinridge and Bell.

For the secessionists, it was now or never. While the South stagnated, the North was growing ever stronger and more populous. As soon as Lincoln's victory was confirmed in the Electoral College, South Carolina declared its secession from the Union. Only moderately anti-slavery at the time, the President-elect declared that as President he would have no authority to abolish slavery where it already existed. Nevertheless, six states soon followed South Carolina in proclaiming their independence.* In his inaugural address, in a desperate attempt to keep the rebellion from spreading, Lincoln went so far as to endorse a constitutional amendment guaranteeing slavery in the South forever.

At first, President Lincoln followed his predecessor's do-nothing approach until the rebels could be maneuvered into firing the first shot. Once Fort Sumter was fired upon, the President called for volunteers to crush the rebellion. Four more southern state governments then announced their secession, and the Civil War began.

The majority of Democrats being southerners, most party members joined the rebellion. The reaction of Democrats in the North varied widely, from patriotism to collaboration. Stephen Douglas, who signaled his loyalty by holding Lincoln's hat as he was sworn in, announced: "Before God it is the duty of every American citizen to rally around the flag of his country." In the middle, many Democrats found neutrality appealing. At the other end of the spectrum, New York Mayor Fernando Wood actually tried to get the city to join the rebellion.

Rebels spoiling for a fight might be understandable enough. Wealthy southerners had everything vested in the slave system, while poor whites would fight to stave off social equality with blacks. But what about the hundreds of thousands of northerners, many who had just recently immigrated from Europe, rushing off to fight the rebels?

---

* One notable holdout was Sam Houston, hero of Texas independence and Governor of the state in 1861. Houston was removed from office for refusing to swear allegiance to the Confederacy.

Enthusiasm for the war among Republicans and other northern patriots is difficult to comprehend under the impression that the fighting was a "War Between the States," or a war between North and South. Why not just let the South go in peace?

People living then understood much better than most do today that a clean break was just not possible; the regions were too intertwined. Clearly, even if there were an armistice, fighting would surely break out again over any number of disputes. Given the pro-Confederate sentiment in southern Illinois, for example, or the Unionist sentiment in eastern Tennessee, where exactly would the border be drawn? Which side would get the border states? What about Arizona and California? Would the Midwest retain access to the lower Mississippi? And then there were the slaves. How could an independent South keep its slaves from escaping north across the border?

As one Virginia Senator explained at the time, the Civil War was really "a war of sentiment and opinion by one form of society against another form of society." Our country would ultimately become all slave or all free, and the war would decide the issue. Believing they had been pushed around long enough by the "Slavocrats," patriots were eager for a showdown. In their view, the United States Constitution had made our country the best in the world, and they would fight to keep it that way. They fervently believed what Daniel Webster had proclaimed thirty years before: "Liberty and Union, now and forever, one and inseparable!"

THE RULES
BY WHICH WE LIVE

In his inaugural address, speaking for our entire Party, Lincoln said: "The Union is perpetual...[and] is much older than the Constitution. It was formed, in fact, by the Articles of Association in 1774. It was matured and continued by the Declaration of Independence in 1776." Several months later, pointing out that it was the national government that created the states, Lincoln declared: "Our States have neither more, nor less power, than that reserved to them, in the Union, by the Constitution." For the new administration, not only could a state not secede, any proclamation to the effect was as meaningless as, say, green-eyed or left-handed people proclaiming their secession from the Union.

Millions would fight, hundreds of thousands would die to settle the question of whether our country was a pact among states (the predominant Democrat view) or a perpetual union created by "We, the People of the United States" (the Republican position). Lincoln understood that differences of opinion about the origin and meaning of the Constitution lie at the core of every political issue that our country would ever face – before, during, or since the Civil War.

The events which led to the creation of the United States are no less relevant to us today than they were to the people listening to Lincoln's words as the nation teetered on the brink of civil war. Just as patriots later fought to prevent rebels from destroying their "Liberty and Union," American patriots in the 1770s went to war to protect from British tyranny what they regarded as the freest society in the world. In September 1774, delegates from the colonies met to formulate a national policy toward the British. It was this First Continental Congress that Lincoln argued was the founding of the country, nearly two years before the Declaration of Independence of July 1776. The Second Continental Congress that convened in Philadelphia in May 1775 took upon itself governing authority over the entire country.

That month, Congress called upon the colonies to set up state governments independent of the British Crown, and selected George Washington to command the rebel army which had gathered around Boston. Not only was Washington an experienced British army veteran, being from Virginia he would help rally the South, where dedication to the patriot cause was weaker than in the North. Though hampered by its lack of taxation power, Congress handled military and foreign affairs as well as could be expected, and by 1780 had established departments for finance and foreign affairs. The most important achievement of this rudimentary form of national government was the subordination of military power to civilian authority.

The same month Jefferson's Declaration of Independence was approved, Pennsylvania's John Dickinson delivered to Congress his draft of the first American constitution, the Articles of Confederation. Congress adopted the Articles the next year, though they did not go into effect until ratified by the last of the states in March 1781. The country's second national government consisted of Congress and five departments. There was no Chief Executive to carry out or "execute" the laws, though the Congressman elected annually to preside over debates was known as the "President." To promote national unity, Article 4 required each state to accord to residents of other states all the "privileges and immunities" accorded to its own residents.

Not much could be accomplished since each state had one vote in Congress, as cast by its legislature, and major decisions had to be unanimous. Congress again could not levy taxes and had only limited powers aside from military and foreign affairs. The national government was so ineffective that it could not even pay army officers their years of unpaid salaries after the war. Only Washington's dramatic intervention headed off an attempt by the military to march on Philadelphia and perhaps seize power for itself. Despite its weaknesses, as Lincoln would note, the Confederation was to be a "Perpetual Union" of the states. The most important achievement of our nation's second form of national government was the Northwest Ordinance of July 1787, which prohibited slavery in the territory later to become Illinois, Indiana, Ohio, Michigan, and Wisconsin.

In 1786, a revolt broke out in western Massachusetts among impoverished farmers. After Congress proved incapable of quelling "Shays' Rebellion," it fell to the state militia to restore order, forcing most Americans to realize that if the nation was to survive, a stronger form of national government was needed. Alexander Hamilton warned: "Who can determine what might have been the issue of [the] late convulsions, if the malcontents had been headed by a Caesar or a Cromwell? Who can predict what effect a despotism, established in Massachusetts would have upon the liberties of New Hampshire or Rhode Island, of Connecticut or New York?" To the dismay of most of his countrymen, Thomas Jefferson approved of the unrest, writing: "A little rebellion now and then is a good thing; the tree of liberty must be refreshed from time to time with the blood of patriots and tyrants."

In September 1786, delegates from five states from the Chesapeake Bay area met in Annapolis, Maryland to discuss interstate trade squabbles. They also suggested a subsequent convention of all the states to revise the Articles of Confederation. Congress endorsed this idea and called for another convention in Philadelphia in May 1787. Though Congress did not expressly authorize discussion of a new constitution, many Congressman had long advocated it, so the result of the Constitutional Convention did not come as an unwelcome surprise. In fact, Congress promptly submitted the proposed Constitution to the states for ratification, arranged the elections of the new Congress, and set the early March presidential inauguration date that was to endure until the 1930s.

The Constitutional Convention deliberated from May to September 1787, during which time Thomas Jefferson was in Paris serving as ambassador. The new national government was to have far greater powers than its predecessor, though not enough to suit New York's foremost delegate, Alexander Hamilton. Congress would be able to levy taxes and tariffs, to regulate interstate commerce, and to make all laws "necessary and proper" to exercise its powers. The "privileges and immunities" clause would be retained, to prevent out-of-state residents from being treated as foreigners. Most significantly, the Constitution and federal laws were to be the supreme law of the land. Delegates assumed that the first President would be George Washington, who presided over the Convention, and the position was designed with him in mind.

The Convention explicitly rejected a British-style parliamentary system, in which the leader of the largest group of legislators typically would serve as Prime Minister to a nominal head of state. Instead, the writings of English philosopher John Locke and French philosopher Charles Montesquieu would be the basis for dividing power among legislative, executive, and judicial branches of government. This system of checks and balances reflected a profound understanding of human nature. "If men were angels, no government would be necessary," James Madison observed. Recognizing that vices and lust for power lurk in the heart of everyone, he advocated "the subordinate distributions of power, where the constant aim is to divide and arrange the several offices in such a manner as that each may be a check on the other that the private interest of every individual may be a sentinel over the public rights."

Even though swift action by the federal government was designed to be nearly impossible, in our time Democrats in particular heap criticism on a "do-nothing" Congress that is too slow to enact whatever policy it is they want. They go on, for example, about a health care "crisis" or a child care "crisis" or an environmental "crisis." "It's an emergency," they say. "No time to think it over. The government must take action now, now, now!"

To illustrate just how much freedom we owe to James Madison's foresight, consider the fate of our republic if in 1993 there had been a parliamentary system. In the initial enthusiasm for his health care plan, a Prime Minister Clinton would have succeeded in nationalizing one-seventh of the economy. Happily, the scheme failed, because members of Congress, even those of the President's party, are separate from the administration. Republicans especially were not to be bullied into passing the measure before analyzing it thoroughly. Once exposed to the glare of public scrutiny, Hillary's horror receded into the shadows. Thanks to the Constitution, any impulse for hasty action is further restricted by a Congress divided into a Senate and a House of Representatives.

The mission of all Republicans to "preserve, protect, and defend the Constitution of the United States" is as vital now as in Lincoln's day. Democrats have devised a new and staggeringly ambitious assault on the separation of powers doctrine. Gigantic liability suits against particular industries could soon enable an administration to fund itself to a great extent without having to rely on Congress' power of the purse. Like cunning tyrants have done throughout the centuries, Democrat politicians chose their first victims with care: the unpopular cigarette and gun manufacturers. Aside from the fact that the wealth extracted from these industries actually comes at the expense of millions of shareholders, the settlements are a form of taxation, transferring billions of dollars from the private sector to government coffers.

Far from being innovative, this means of generating revenue has been around for thousands of years. Called "proscription," it was employed by Caligula and other Roman emperors, who would often fund their regimes by condemning opponents to forfeit assets to the government. If not stopped, "confiscation without representation" will soon be extended to other industries, and then to individuals.

The Constitution implied that apart from certain designated federal powers, state governments could do whatever they wanted. This is certainly true, since decentralization is as much a principle of our form of government as separation of powers. What states rights advocates would later overlook, however, is the fact that one of those designated federal powers that states must acknowledge is the authority to decide, with considerable latitude, the delineation between state and federal authority. This is not to imply that the federal government must exercise authority over any matter it can, just that the states cannot assert a certain power if the Constitution and federal law, as interpreted by the Supreme Court, determine otherwise.

Though political parties are not mentioned in the Constitution, they were from the start an integral part of the political process. During colonial times, parties had operated at the state level (as they mostly do today), and so this natural tendency of candidates and their supporters to link themselves together was very familiar to the drafters of the Constitution. Indeed, the two-party system we have today predates the Constitution, having arisen as those in favor and those opposed to its ratification confronted one other.

Integration of innumerable viewpoints into coherent policy options is among the chief benefits of political parties, which must strive to assemble a majority. That zealots seek to incorporate themselves into the major parties is a healthy sign; much worse would be a situation in which they saw no point in participating, spinning off instead into hardened mini-factions on what Theodore Roosevelt called "the lunatic fringe."

The manner in which a President is elected has evolved into a mainstay of the two-party system. Back in the 1780s when drafting the Constitution, delegates realized that a national election was logistically impossible. In such a vast land, before even the telegraph, how would voters even know who the candidates were? Having Congress elect the President would be too much like the parliamentary system. Having state legislatures do it would be too much like the Articles of Confederation. To solve this 18th century problem, the convention came up with the Electoral College, a single-purpose deliberative body.

So that the College could not become a rival of Congress, presidential Electors would cast their votes from the state capitals. Prior to the 1820s, each legislature selected the Electors for their state. Since then,* slates of

---

* South Carolina retained this method as late as 1860.

Electors in each state have been selected by popular vote, almost always on a winner-take-all basis. Because coming in second in a state is worthless, presidential candidates are forced to seek the broadest possible support. The United States has thereby avoided the plight of other countries where the national leader is often selected after the election through power-brokering that often affords small factions influence far out of proportion to their actual size.

Before the new Constitution could take effect, state conventions selected apart from the legislatures would have to approve it. Both Washington and Benjamin Franklin, the only other figure of national prominence, lent their prestige to the campaign in favor of ratification. Proponents could also count on the support of most Revolutionary War veterans, whose experiences had given them a sense of national identity. Many states ratified quickly, but several of the larger ones held back.

Already, a geographic pattern of party allegiance was taking shape. New England and Pennsylvania, Federalist, Whig, and then early Republican strongholds, were firmly in favor of the new Constitution. Opponents were strongest in New York and the South, areas which would become bastions of the Democratic Party. To win over crucial New York State, Hamilton, Washington's former military aide and later the first Secretary of the Treasury; future President James Madison; and John Jay, who would become the first Chief Justice, published a series of insightful articles now known as the "Federalist Papers."

Ever since the Constitution was ratified, our society has conducted itself according to this set of rules determined over two hundred years ago. To a greater extent than any other in the world, the Constitution of the United States stands apart from the normal political process. The procedure for amending it is an arduous one requiring approval of not only two-thirds of each house of Congress but of three-quarters the states as well.

Just as with any set of rules, there are those who find it to their advantage to violate them. "The Constitution is a living document," they say. "It must change with the times." Who is to determine how the rules "live" and "change with the times?" How, apart from amendment, are such decisions to be reached? What about those who prefer to play by the rules rather than see them changed as they go along? Advocates of the "living document" approach should consider how they would react to a bank deciding that their mortgage agreements are living documents that change with the times. Properly understood, while circumstances change with the times, the Constitution remains the same.

The famous "interstate commerce" clause serves to illustrate this vital distinction. The federal government was given authority to regulate commerce among the states. At first, most economic activity took place entirely within a state, so federal regulation was mostly limited to preventing interstate barriers to trade. As technology advanced, however, and virtually all economic activity took on an interstate character, the scope for federal regulation over the economy expanded. Thus, the Constitution did not change (or evolve or grow or adapt) at all – it was the nature of "interstate commerce" that changed. Similarly, economic globalization has expanded the definition of the "Commerce with foreign Nations" that the federal government is authorized to regulate.

As Jefferson wrote in the Declaration of Independence, governments derive "their just Powers from the Consent of the Governed." At Gettysburg, Lincoln said ours is a "government of the people, by the people, for the people." However, simple majority rule – Congress or the President decreeing whatever they want on behalf of the people who elected them – is not what they had in mind. Though in a sense we consent to the Constitution every instant it is in force, the set of rules for our political process is not an expression of the will of the majority of Americans today, but of the country two centuries ago.

Every provision in the Constitution limits the ability of the majority of the people, as expressed through their elected officials, to make decisions for themselves. In our system of government, five or more Justices on the Supreme Court can determine that a particular issue cannot be decided by popular vote because it was decided permanently two centuries ago. Judicial review is the Court's inherently anti-democratic duty to ensure that the actions our representatives and President take now conform to the document (as amended) that was drafted by the Constitutional Convention in 1787.

Underlying the concept of majority rule is the principle that in cases when people cannot be absolutely certain of the correct policy alternative it would be best to enact the policy that most people want at the time. "Should the government spend $10 million or $20 million dollars on this problem?" Put it to a vote! "Should that tax rate be 10% or 20%?" Let the people decide! "Should Smith or Jones be the next President?" It's up to the electorate.

"Should terms of Senators be six years or only five?" In this case, what most people want is irrelevant because the issue is not subject to majority will. How about if the people's representatives vote to abolish jury trials? Again no, such a measure would be impermissible because it is against the rules, even if they were written by men long since dead. On whether to abolish jury trials, for example, it is irrelevant what the majority may want, or what any particular person wants. In our democracy, voices and votes expressed on issues subject to majority rule are crucial, but opinions contrary to the Constitution mean nothing at all.

Civil rights. Inalienable rights. Human rights. Animal rights. Individual rights. Group rights. God-given rights. Sacred rights. Natural rights. Positive rights. Negative rights. Children's rights. Parent's rights. Patient's rights. Property rights. Personal rights. Basic rights. Fundamental rights. Just what is a right? Can some rights be more basic or fundamental than others? Which is more important, a basic right or a fundamental right? Do the rights of the many outweigh the rights of the few? Are rights absolute? One could assert whole new kinds of rights and then argue about where they fit in among all the other rights. How about essential rights, or core rights, or perhaps preeminent rights?

Definitions of the nature and origin of rights vary widely – from a gift from God, to one of Jefferson or Madison's tenets, all the way down to "a good thing" – but these disputes can be left to theologians and historians and scatterbrains. Let constitutional scholars debate the fine points of original intent or understanding (of each delegate? or the drafter of a particular clause? or the Convention as a whole? or Congress? or the ratifying state conventions?). All that matters with regard to rights is how they function within our constitutional system.

A person saying he has the right to XYZ, for instance, is saying that regardless of what other people want, he must have XYZ and society must give it to him. To admit there is such a right is not only to accept that the opinion of the majority on his having XYZ is meaningless, but that your opinion on the issue too counts for as little as your opinion on whether there should be jury trials. As anti-democratic limitations on the scope of majority rule, rights are like provisions of the Constitution. Indeed, they are one and the same, because in a practical sense – the only sense that matters – a right is a government policy that must be so regardless of majority will.

Any constitutional provision can be seen as a right. For example, Article I, Section 9, Clause 5 – "No Tax or Duty shall be laid on Articles exported from any State." – can just as easily be: "Every person has the right to export Articles from any State without a federal Tax or Duty being laid on it." The first part of Article II, Section 2 is the equivalent of "The President has the right to be Commander in Chief of the Army and Navy." One could say he has the right to veto laws and grant pardons. A Supreme Court Justice has the right to serve for life, and the Supreme Court has the right to original jurisdiction over cases involving foreign ambassadors. The residents of every state have the right to representation by two Senators. People have the right to have their federal laws enacted by a Congress consisting of a Senate and a House of Representatives. There are many more such variations on the theme, but the point is that the Constitution is nothing but a long list of rights; that is, government policies that must be so regardless of majority will.

In addition to provisions limiting the ability of Congress or the President to change the general structure of the government apart from the amendment process, the Constitution contains many specific limitations on government action that are more readily recognizable as rights. The narrow definition of treason means a person has the right not to be convicted of treason for a crime that does not fit the definition. The privileges and immunities provision is a right, as is the jury trial guarantee. The Constitution protects creditors by prohibiting states from voiding contracts (as they had done under the Articles of Confederation) or making anything but gold or silver legal tender. Congress may not pass a bill of attainder (a legislative pronouncement of guilt) or an ex post facto law (making an act illegal after it was committed). The habeas corpus protection against arbitrary arrest is one of the most important rights protected by the Constitution.

As Hamilton pointed out in Federalist 84, the Constitution contains these rights and more even without the amendments known as the Bill of Rights. Can the Bill of Rights protection against unreasonable searches somehow supersede the right to a jury trial spelled out in Article III? Does freedom of the press outrank freedom of speech? Is the 3rd amendment ban on quartering soldiers in private homes more important than the 13th, which banned slavery? Does the order in which they are listed matter, so that freedom of religion is more important than freedom of speech? No, to all these questions. Since the entire Constitution – every rule in the rule book – must be so regardless of majority will, every provision of the original text (where unamended), of the Bill of Rights, and of the later amendments is no more or less important than any other.

Most Americans are unaware that there are actually eleven amendments in the Bill of Rights, not ten. During the ratification process, many people were concerned that though each state constitution had one, the proposed Constitution did not have a list of restrictions on majority rule labeled as a Bill of Rights. Delegates had not included one because they assumed the federal government would have so little authority over individuals that it would be superfluous. To mollify these critics, Congress appointed James Madison to head a four-person committee, which drafted twelve proposed amendments for the Bill of Rights. After some debate and modifications, Congress approved all twelve and sent them to the states for ratification in September 1791. Ten of them were ratified by the end of the year. An eleventh, fixing the number of seats in the House of Representatives, never was approved. A twelfth, preventing congressional pay raises from taking effect until after the next election, lie unratified and forgotten until it achieved enough state ratifications in 1992 to become the 27th amendment.

Since the entire Constitution – from "We, the People" to "shall have intervened" – is one long right and rights can only be exercised within our constitutional framework, constitutional rights are the only kind with any meaning. As determined, ultimately, by the Supreme Court, an issue is either a political question – meaning it is to be decided by majority vote – or it is a constitutional right – meaning the correct decision, as determined by the Constitution, must be imposed on the country whether people want it or not. In the latter case, figuring out just what it was that the Constitutional Convention decided for us on a particular issue may be difficult for the courts to determine, but the task does not involve balancing one provision of the document against another.

Some rules in our society's rule book cannot outweigh other rules; they are all equally valid. Once understanding that any part of the Constitution, whether expressed as a provision or a right, is a policy that must be so, a person can see the absurdity of trying to balance one right against another. Gone are tussles between rights and responsibilities, positive rights and negative rights, the rights of the many and the rights of the few, personal rights and property rights, human rights and economic rights, group rights and individual rights, fundamental rights and not-so-fundamental rights. One person's rights do not end where another's begin. No constitutional right can be outweighed by some other consideration, because all constitutional rights are absolute. Either something is mandated by the Constitution or it isn't.

Every expansion, creation, or recognition of a right removes from the political arena an issue to be decided through the electoral process.

However justified in certain cases, restricting majority rule is to say: "No matter what most people might want, XYZ must be so." Here we arrive at the real reason people are not as engaged in the political process as they once were.

People vote less and less because, as more and more so-called rights are created, their opinions matter less and less. Democrats especially are fond of lawsuits to oppose expressions of majority will by elected officials. They want, for example, a Supreme Court that will transfer as many issues as possible from the political arena to the judicial arena, where, unlike politicians opting for what most people want, lawyers and judges seek the correct solution to be imposed on all concerned. To illustrate, while adequate health care is indeed vital for every American, establishing a right to health care means that most or perhaps the entire health care issue is to be decided in a manner regardless of what the majority wants. Your opinion on what this new right to health care entails would then be as meaningless as your opinion on any other provision of the Constitution.

Whether or not some policy is important has no bearing on whether it is a right. Proper health care for every American is of course at least as important as the ban against granting any "Title of Nobility." But under our system of government, decisions on health care policy are to be taken from time to time by the people's representatives, while the issue of granting a "Title of Nobility" was decided for us in 1787.

The pronounced inclination of Democrats to assert new rights to this or that is born of the urge to control. Whatever policy they want the government to adopt they can seek to make permanent, off-limits to future changes of voter sentiment, by claiming to discover more rights; that is, provisions of the Constitution which had somehow been overlooked all these years. A dictatorship, to be sure, is nothing but an all-encompassing set of government policies (or rights) that must be so regardless of majority rule. How easy it is for Republicans to be outmaneuvered with talk of the more rights the better. Confronted with, for example – "Aren't you for the right to safety, or the right to get enough sleep? Don't you want everyone to have more rights?" – Republicans are in a bind, because arguing with Democrats using their terms is pointless.

Once Republicans understand the role of the Constitution as well as did the founders of our Party, Democrats will have lost the most fearsome weapon in their rhetorical arsenal. A better term for an important government policy created by the voters of today (hence changeable by the voters of tomorrow) is an entitlement. We Republicans have sound reasons to be in favor of plenty of these.

Many of the worst government policies in our history have come about by being asserted as rights. The basis for the Dred Scott decision, after all, was the supposed right of a slave-holder to due process before being deprived of his property (another human being). For decades, attempts to improve working conditions or curb monopolistic business practices were fended off with claims that such regulations would violate some rights. And then of course there is the states rights argument used by southern Democrats to justify subjugating blacks. According to the supremacy clause of Article VI, there can be no geographic limitations on the federal government's responsibility for upholding the Constitution. Bearing in mind the distinction between a right and an entitlement, one knows that the federal government is not obligated, however, to impose on state residents policies that are not mandated by the Constitution.

The only sense in which the term "state right" has any meaning is as a provision of a state constitution. Just as the federal Constitution limits the scope for majority rule at the federal level, state constitutions, within the bounds set by the federal government, limit what state governments can do. For example, Article X, Section 1 of the Illinois State Constitution states: "Education in public schools through the secondary level shall be free." In other words, state residents must have recourse to a free primary and secondary education regardless of whatever the Illinois legislature may decide in the future. Other state constitutions provide for many such rights. Nothing in a state constitution, however, can supersede the federal Constitution or federal law.

Chapter Four

(1789-1848)

HOLDING A
WOLF BY THE EARS

Once the Constitution was in force, even the most vociferous "Anti-Federalists" were forced to admit its excellence. The administration of President Washington consisted of three departments. Henry Knox, Secretary of War under the Articles of Confederation, stayed in office. Alexander Hamilton became the first Secretary of the Treasury. The third Cabinet post, Secretary of State, went to Thomas Jefferson, back from serving as ambassador to France. Jefferson would not be "Secretary of Foreign Affairs" though, because early on the Department of State was a catch-all office for executive branch functions not military or financial. In later years, the creation of other Cabinet departments would leave the State Department focused almost entirely on foreign affairs. Originally, the Attorney General was just a part-time legal advisor to the President. Disliking Vice President Adams, Washington set a precedent that the Vice President would have no role in government other than presiding over the Senate. Not until Richard Nixon in the 1950s would a Vice President assume an active role in the administration.

The two political heavyweights could not have been more different, ideologically or personally. Born into the Virginia plantation aristocracy, Jefferson had no problem with the reality of slavery even while advocating freedom in the abstract. Having opposed ratification of the Constitution because he believed it made the federal government too strong, he wrote: "The government that governs least governs best."

Hamilton, in contrast to his antagonist's privileged upbringing, had to overcome being born poor and illegitimate, on a small Caribbean island. No friend of state autonomy, he feared that the federal government would in fact be too weak. Though scorning Jefferson's homage to the common man, the ardently anti-slavery Hamilton favored a free market society without barriers to social mobility.

From the very first Cabinet meeting, the overriding theme of the Washington presidency was the rancorous debate between Jefferson and Hamilton over the future of the United States. Into the second half of the next century, this ideological shouting match grew ever noisier. Would our country remain a loose arrangement of states, or become one nation? Would Jefferson's vision of an agrarian society win out over Hamilton's ambition for a commercial economy? Would we as a nation look backward or forward? Which system would prevail, the South's forced labor economy or the North's free market society? As Lincoln would later remark, would the United States become all slave or all free?

Proponents of Hamilton's vision for the country soon began to refer to themselves as the Federalist Party. This was largely an urban phenomenon, strongest among the merchants of New England. While opposed to the slave system, Federalists tended to favor the wealthy and educated, and discouraged popular participation in government. President Washington, though a slave-holding Virginia planter like Jefferson, was inclined toward Hamilton's point of view. Lengthy service leading a national army (mostly in the North), respect for his old friend's financial acumen, and recognition of the need for a government strong enough to control the frontier made Washington a Federalist in all but name. In retirement, he became very pro-Federalist, even to the extent of freeing his slaves, effective upon his wife's death.

A few months into the new administration, Treasury Secretary Hamilton delivered to Congress his plan for strengthening the nation's finances. No one had a problem with his proposal that the federal government assume the Confederation's foreign debt. Where he ran into considerable opposition was in urging Congress to assume not only the Confederation's domestic debt but the pre-Constitution debts of all the states as well. By then, the Confederation debt had depreciated and was mostly in the hands of northern speculators.

No matter, wrote Hamilton, paying less than par would dishonor the original loan commitments. Virginia and other states which had already paid their debts complained about federal taxpayer money going to pay other states' debts. For Hamilton, however unfair, this assertion of federal government primacy over the states was crucial. For this reason, Jefferson opposed the assumption of state debts, though he and other southern politicians eventually did agree to the whole package in return for moving the national capital from New York City to the banks of the Potomac River.

Hamilton's proposal for managing this enormous financial burden was a work of genius that solved two problems at once. During the Confederation, so little gold and silver coinage circulated that interstate commerce was hardly possible. Paper money issued within one state had little value in another. For the federal government just to print some of its own, with no gold or silver reserves to back it, would bring on a ruinous inflation in no time. Following his suggestion, Congress redeemed all the assumed debts with long-term interest-bearing federal government securities which could then circulate as money. They would maintain their value because they would pay 6% annually and be supported by a sinking fund to repurchase some should their price fall. A permanent federal government debt, Hamilton noted, would not only create a national bond market but provide a powerful incentive for holders of the securities to see that the federal government survived.

There were at the time no banks in a true sense. To "promote the general Welfare," Hamilton proposed a Bank of the United States, patterned after the Bank of England but with branches throughout the country. In this way, capital could be mobilized, notes issued by the Bank could serve as a common currency, and people and the government could transfer funds around. Generally, the mercantile North favored the Bank, while the agrarian South was rather less enthusiastic.

With firm Federalist support, Congress passed the Bank bill and Washington signed it into law in 1791 over Jefferson and Madison's objections that setting such a precedent for the "implied powers" clause could justify almost any federal government measure. For the Treasury Secretary, Congress' power to "make all Laws which may be necessary and proper for carrying into Execution the foregoing Powers" was authority enough.

The economy took off, and the United States soon had the best credit in the world. Almost single-handedly, Alexander Hamilton had laid the foundation for the financial system of the United States. He also wanted federal spending to improve transportation links and high tariffs to protect emerging industries, but this President Washington thought was beyond the federal government's role.

In 1794, farmers in western Pennsylvania rebelled against federal excise taxes on whiskey distillation, about their only source of cash. At the head of an enormous army, Washington and Hamilton crushed the insurrection, though Hamilton was soon afterward forced out of office. As had happened in Shays' Rebellion, the rebels were rounded up, then pardoned, setting the precedent for Appomattox.

In the 1796 election to succeed Washington, his Federalist Vice President, John Adams, defeated Jefferson, who had resigned from the Cabinet three years before to go into opposition. Under the electoral procedure then in force, Jefferson the runner-up became Vice President. During the Adams administration, the Federalist majority in Congress provoked tremendous popular resentment with their anti-immigration, authoritarian Alien and Sedition Acts of 1798.

The uproar against these laws not only crippled the Federalist Party but spawned the states rights argument that would bring on no end of trouble. In reaction to the Alien and Sedition Acts, Jefferson drafted one resolution for the Kentucky legislature declaring that the federal government could not go beyond the powers specifically delegated by the Constitution, and another that a state could nullify any federal law. Madison too wrote similar resolutions for the Virginia legislature. These future Presidents were implying that the Constitution had established a league of states, from which any state could secede, despite the fact, as Federalists observed, that it says "We, the People," not "We, the States," right at the top.

Until very recently, the Democratic Party was an alliance between two very different groups – southern white agrarian interests and northern ethnicity-based political machines. Among northern states, New York felt a special kinship with the Solid South. How did this partnership ever get started? In the summer of 1791, Jefferson and Madison traveled to New York to seek common cause with the chief opponents there of Hamilton's policies – Governor George Clinton, a principal foe of ratification several years earlier, and his protégé, Aaron Burr, who had converted a fraternal organization, "The Society of Saint Tammany," into our nation's first political machine.

Implying that the Federalists were actually monarchists, Jefferson, Madison, Clinton, Burr, and their followers called themselves "Republicans." Federalists retaliated by calling the Republicans "Democrats," a word which in those days conjured up specters of mob rule. The Republicans held their first congressional caucus in 1792, and each side set up a newspaper to blast away at the other. In 1800, the Federalists nominated John Adams again, and another New Englander for Vice President. The savvier Republicans cemented the South-New York alliance by nominating Jefferson for President and Burr for Vice President.

The Republicans won big majorities in both houses of Congress and the presidency, though just who the President would be – Jefferson or Burr – was unclear. Until the electoral process was amended in 1804, Electors cast two votes without specifying which for President and which for Vice President. The unfortunate result, a tie between the two Republicans, went to the House of Representatives to be decided. After a lengthy deadlock, Hamilton persuaded the Federalists to vote for his adversary Jefferson over the devious Burr, who had refused to take the second spot as pre-arranged. Four years later, the miffed Vice President killed Hamilton in a duel, and went on to lead a failed scheme to carve himself an independent empire out of U.S. territory west of the

Appalachians. Hamilton's other New York nemesis, George Clinton, replaced Burr in Jefferson's second term.

Just as the Anti-Federalists quickly accepted the Constitution, once in office the Republicans embraced most of the Federalist economic policies they had campaigned against. The new President did not undo any Hamiltonian measures. "We are all Republicans. We are all Federalists," Jefferson said in his first inaugural address. To secure the Louisiana Purchase of 1803, he was forced to accept the implied powers doctrine. His Treasury Secretary, Albert Gallatin (whose statue is in front of the Treasury Building, Hamilton getting his portrait on the ten dollar bill) proposed building national roads and other infrastructure projects. In 1808, Jefferson even signed legislation renewing the charter of the Bank of the United States.

Where Jeffersonian Republicans and Hamiltonian Federalists still disagreed completely was on the role of the federal courts. To the extent they had thought about it, most drafters of the Constitution assumed that the presidential veto would be sufficient protection against unconstitutional legislation. However, once the new government was in place, it became apparent to the Federalist majority in the first session of Congress that the court system would have to fulfill this role.

According to their Judicial Act of 1789, which established the federal court system, the Supreme Court would have the last word on any conflicts between laws. Article VI having established that the Constitution is "the supreme Law of the Land," judicial review was Federalist policy from the start, and as Hamilton had clearly anticipated, the Supreme Court would be the arbiter of constitutionality. Jeffersonian Republicans, however, would have none of it, so concerned were they that state governments be able to judge for themselves whether a federal law was constitutional.

In 1791, well before Marbury v. Madison, a federal court overturned a state law that violated a treaty. The following year, the Supreme Court refused to comply with a federal law that assigned to the courts the job of deciding military pension claims. Just before Jefferson took office, President Adams appointed as Chief Justice his Secretary of State, John Marshall. Knowing the incoming President's states rights views, he and the other Federalist Justices seized upon the Marbury case to fend off infringement on the Constitution by states rights advocates.

The landmark Marbury v. Madison decision of 1803, which stated "It is emphatically the province and duty of the judicial department to say what the law is," rather than a usurpation of power, was a firm defense of the Supreme Court's constitutional authority against Jefferson's meddling. In response, Jefferson tried to get rid of the Supreme Court Justices through impeachment. The acquittal in the Senate trial of the first Justice in 1805 proved to be as important as the Marbury v. Madison decision.

Further defending the Constitution, the Marshall Court firmly established federal supremacy over the states in the 1819 McCulloch v. Maryland decision. In 1824, the Gibbons v. Ogden case declared that federal authority over interstate commerce could extend to activities wholly within one state. In 1833, however, the Marshall Court explicitly refused to apply the Bill of Rights to the states, a mission later accomplished by the Radical Republicans' 14th amendment. It was when rung at a ceremony to mark the death of John Marshall in 1835 that the Liberty Bell cracked.

Though the Federalist Party had done a magnificent job in the early years of our country, the party outlived its usefulness. Once Presidents Jefferson and Madison adopted most of their policies, including the protective tariff of 1816, Federalists were left with little but their elitist tinge. Opposition to the War of 1812 nearly finished them off. In 1820, President James Monroe, the third consecutive Jeffersonian Republican from Virginia with a Vice President from New York, was reelected unopposed, and in another four years the Federalist Party had practically disappeared.

⁕

Our nation's experience with a one-party system did not last long before new political parties emerged. Though all four presidential candidates in 1824 called themselves Republicans, each headed a sharply distinct faction. Demonstrating the decline of the Republican establishment, Virginia-born William Crawford, Treasury Secretary under both Madison and Monroe, saw his bid for southern support eclipsed by the Tennessee war hero and Senator, Andrew Jackson. Speaker of the House Henry Clay was also from west of the Appalachians, but unlike Jackson, Clay favored policies more conducive to a commercial economy.

Jackson was the most popular candidate, but his lack of a majority in the Electoral College meant the election would be decided by the House of Representatives, where Clay threw his support decisively to the northern candidate, Secretary of State John Quincy Adams, son of the former President. This alliance between Clay, favorite son of the Midwest, and Adams, a Federalist Senator from Massachusetts before joining the Republicans, reflected the integration of states to the north of Clay's native Kentucky into the free market system.

Considering himself cheated out of the presidency, Jackson resigned from the Senate and immediately began campaigning for a rematch. He and his supporters took to calling themselves Democratic-Republicans, for contrast with the alleged aristocratic-Republican in the White House. Jackson's party held its first national convention in 1832, by which time the term "Democrat" had largely replaced "Democratic-Republican." A formal name change to the "Democratic Party" came in 1840. For a party symbol, the Democrats would eventually adopt a caricature of Jackson as a "jackass," or donkey, popularized in a cartoon decades later.

In the 1828 presidential election, the first in which nearly all Electors were selected by popular vote, the two-party system was reborn. Jackson crushed Adams 56% to 44%, and 178 to 83 in the Electoral College. Democrats swept to victory in most congressional and state contests as well. For the first time for any political party anywhere, the Democrats realized the importance of promoting their cause continuously, not just before elections. This meant grass-roots organizing among the poor, many of whom were able to vote for the first time as property qualifications were eliminated. By providing vital social services, Democrat political machines grabbed hold of most immigrants arriving in northern ports.

Andrew Jackson was the first President to attempt to lead the country, rather than just carry out the will of Congress, and the first to veto laws he admitted were constitutional but simply did not like. Under Jackson, the Democrats invented that party-building exercise known as the spoils system – handing out federal government jobs to party loyalists. He opposed most federal infrastructure spending, withholding his veto only from projects of a national character that a state government would not undertake. In a departure from Jefferson, though he disliked unwarranted federal government interference in state government affairs, President Jackson came down squarely on the side of federal supremacy, so adamantly in fact that on his deathbed he expressed regret he had not hanged the leader of the states rights movement, John Calhoun, who had been Vice President in his first term before resigning to become a Senator from South Carolina.

In 1816, Congress replaced a low tariff intended as a source of revenue for the federal government with a higher tariff that indirectly subsidized certain industries by protecting them from lower-priced foreign competition. Even higher tariffs were enacted in 1828, which were generally to the advantage of northern industries and the detriment of southern plantations. Taking the Kentucky and Virginia Resolutions to heart, an 1832 South Carolina state convention responded by declaring the tariffs null and void within the state and warned that South Carolina would secede from the Union if the federal government tried to collect them within its borders.

Though sympathetic to their complaints about the tariff, President Jackson did not take any guff from secessionists, warning: "If one drop of blood be shed in defiance of the laws of the United States, I will hang the first man of them I can get my hands on to the first tree I can find." No one who knew Jackson doubted that he would not have stopped until he ran out of rebels or ran out of trees. Congress did lower the tariff somewhat, but all this concession did was show slave-interest politicians that constant threats to secede would get them just about whatever they wanted, constantly. After using this tactic for three decades, South Carolina, followed by ten other states, would make good their threat to secede when voters for our Republican Party decided "Enough concessions to the Slavocrats!" and elected Abraham Lincoln President.

⋘

In the summer of 1832, during his reelection campaign, Jackson vetoed a bill to renew the charter of the Bank of the United States, which he had opposed long before becoming President. The Bank was unconstitutional, he said, despite the Supreme Court's 1819 McCulloch v. Maryland decision upholding it. Southern plantation magnates resented the Bank for having vastly improved business conditions for northern merchants. Not waiting for the charter to expire in four years, Jackson then killed "The Monster" by withdrawing all federal funds. Jackson's denunciation of the Bank for having concentrated economic power in the hands of wealthy northern and foreign shareholders left his critics unimpressed, especially after he deposited the bulk of the federal government funds in state banks controlled by his supporters. In addition to concentrating economic power in the hands of the Democratic Party, the demise of the Philadelphia-based Bank of the United States shifted the country's financial capital from that city to New York.

This bitter contention over the fate of the Bank of the United States – and all it implied for the country's future – was a continuation of the Hamilton v. Jefferson debate, as well as of the constitutional ratification struggle before that. People again divided themselves into two camps: those opposed to the Bank became Democrats while those in favor looked to the leadership of Henry Clay, whom Abraham Lincoln would later describe as "the man for whom I fought all my humble life." A generation later, the country would fight once more over the same issues, but with bullets instead of words.

Until the Jackson presidency, presidential candidates were nominated by legislative caucuses, but in 1831, John Quincy Adam's National-Republican Party held a convention in Baltimore and nominated Henry Clay for President. In May of the following year,

Democrats renominated Jackson at their first national convention. Taking no chances, the Democratic Party made sure of its traditional South-New York axis by nominating for the vice presidency, New York's Democrat kingpin, the former Senator and Governor, Martin Van Buren. Jackson easily defeated Clay, and his party won majorities in both houses of Congress.

Two years after their loss, the National-Republicans and other followers of the Hamiltonian Federalist tradition reorganized themselves as the Whig Party. Their early leadership consisted of former President John Quincy Adams, returned to the House of Representatives; Senator Henry Clay; and Massachusetts Senator Daniel Webster. Unlike the Federalists, the Whigs, who recognized no regional allegiances, had considerable support in the South, well into the 1850s. Craftsmen, merchants, and small farmers were at the core of the party.

The progressive Whigs stood for the "American System" of free market economic development, a national banking system, infrastructure projects such as roads and canals to bind the nation together, and a protective tariff to subsidize the emerging manufacturing sector. While there may have been half an argument back then for such subsidies, today's tariff support for declining industries bears no resemblance to the Whig position. Whigs rejected the Democrats' class warfare approach to politics, advocating instead advancement opportunities for all. They tended to push for universal education and scientific advancements, as well as moral causes such as prohibition. Nearly everyone opposed to slavery, including of course every free black, was a Whig.

For a name, the party had considered going with "Republican," to claim Jefferson's mantle, before deciding on "Whig," what Americans patriots often called themselves during the Revolutionary War. The term which had come into use in England during the 1680s to describe opponents of the king would now be used by opponents of "King" Andrew Jackson. Whigs resented Jackson's aspirations to be leader of the nation. It is the President's job, they countered, to carry out public policy as determined by Congress. Many of our

Republican Presidents – including Grant, Hayes, Arthur, Taft, Harding, and Coolidge – held this Whig view of the role of the presidency. Among the more activist Republicans in the White House were Theodore Roosevelt and Richard Nixon.

Mainly because the Whigs could not agree on a single presidential candidate in 1836, Vice President Van Buren was elected, narrowly edging out the principal Whig contender, war hero and Indiana Senator William Harrison. Soon after Van Buren took office, the folly of Jackson's war against the Bank of the United States became apparent to all. Filling the void left by the Bank, loosely regulated state banks sprang up across the country. Unrestrained by competition from the solid and cautious Bank, these "wildcat" banks printed money with abandon and made speculative loans with deposits, especially those federal funds Jackson had placed in Democrat-controlled institutions.

Jackson tried to slow down money supply expansion by ordering that only gold or silver could be accepted in payment of federal taxes, but all this drastic contraction did was cause the Panic of 1837. The ensuing depression lasted the duration of the Van Buren presidency. To compensate for the dearly departed Bank of the United States, the Democrats came up with a system of federal government strongboxes into which federal funds would be deposited. The money could not be lent out, however, so the money supply kept on contracting until the scheme was abolished a year later.

The dismal economy gave Whigs reason for confidence, but the party was careful to nominate the bland and more electable Harrison instead of their brilliant leader, Henry Clay, who had already lost twice. William Harrison, a midwesterner popular in the Northeast, narrowly defeated Van Buren in the 1840 rematch. Tragically for the Whig cause, Harrison died a month after taking office and was succeeded by his Vice President, John Tyler of Virginia. The new

President, barely a Whig to begin with, soon revealed such a pro-Democrat, pro-slavery bent that his appalled Cabinet resigned. Unfazed, Tyler filled their places with Calhoun and other southern Democrats. He vetoed most of the Whig legislative agenda, including a new charter for the Bank of the United States. Not satisfied with betraying just the Whigs, Tyler ended his career as a member of the Confederate Congress.

For the 1844 presidential election, the Whigs turned once again to their standard-bearer, Henry Clay. He narrowly lost crucial New York, and so the election, to former Tennessee Governor James Polk because Whigs in that state split the anti-Democrat vote with the nation's first anti-slavery party, the Liberty Party. For nine years, the United States had held back from annexing the Republic of Texas, knowing that it would mean war with Mexico. The new Polk administration promptly went ahead and admitted Texas into the Union. Showing surprising improvement from its performance in the War of 1812, the U.S. Army easily conquered vast new lands, for which territorial governments had to be established.

Early in our country's history, economic and cultural differences between North and South were much less sharp than in the decades leading up to the Civil War, as the northern free market and the southern slave system had yet to develop fully. Southern politicians tended to regard the "peculiar institution" as "holding a wolf by the ears. You don't like it, but you don't dare let it go." Many even considered gradually emancipating the slaves. By the 1830s, however, several developments had driven the North and the South in different directions. The cotton gin had made cotton farming immensely profitable, extending to Texas and beyond the plantation system, in which slaves lived in chain-gang misery. Alarmed by the 1831 and 1832 Nat Turner and Denmark Vesey revolts and the growing abolitionist movement in the North, southern whites cracked down hard, imposing further legal restrictions known as the slave codes.

Rather than productive investments, buying more slaves and more land in fertile areas to the west were about the only road to wealth in the South. The economy of proud Virginia declined to the point that its chief industry was breeding slaves for sale to other states. The South made itself completely dependent on northern factories and shipping. New Orleans was the only large city in the South. Meanwhile, the industrial revolution – of technology and factories, corporations and unions – was transforming the North, destination for nearly all the immigrants.

The slave system was the means by which the southern Democrat elite kept themselves in power. By keeping blacks down at the lowest level of a rigid class structure, upper class whites knew that poor whites would themselves put up with being exploited so long as they had other people to look down on and could hope to one day own slaves themselves. Grow cotton, borrow to plant more cotton, grow more cotton – these were the directives of "King Cotton" that made the South in effect a planned economy, organized for the benefit of some 15,000 families of the slave-holding gentry.

So dependent had they become to living off the labor of others, Democrats of the southern elite took to sneering at whites who worked for a living. In the bustling North, people tended to look forward – to a future made better through scientific, economic, and cultural achievement. Most southerners, on the other hand, looked back – to an imaginary past of chivalry and romantic adventures. Slaveholders often thought of themselves as feudal lords of the kind written about in the Sir Walter Scott historical romances they found so enthralling, an obsession Mark Twain later went so far as to blame for the Civil War.

In their idleness, the southern elite took to dueling and otherwise obsessing about their honor, rather than making a better world for their children. Literacy in the North neared 100%, but amid the "intellectual barrenness of the South," at least one in five whites could not read or write – not to mention one-third of the population, the slaves, who were forbidden to do so. Even some southerners admitted that the slave system was to blame for their economic and cultural backwardness.

Attitudes toward blacks varied too. In the South there was actually little racial prejudice, because the lowliest white had no reason to fear any black person, whom he could have crushed with a snap of his fingers. Most white northerners, in contrast, disliked blacks. Illinois and Indiana, to name two, actually had laws prohibiting blacks from entering the states. Not until the 1852 publication of <u>Uncle Tom's Cabin</u> did northern whites give much thought to the actual suffering of the slaves. Perhaps the biggest best-seller in U.S. history, the book opened millions of eyes in the North to the slave system, to which most southern whites reacted by rallying to its defense. A decade later, President Lincoln would call the author, Harriet Beecher Stowe, "the little lady who made this big war."

Chapter Five

(1861-1865)

REPUBLICANS TO THE RESCUE

Just as many northerners sympathized with the rebels, the onset of the Civil War found many southern patriots trapped behind enemy lines. Unionist sentiment was particularly strong among the mountain folk of Appalachia, a region never integrated into the slave system. During this war fought between Johnny Reb and Billy Yank, these Appalachian Yankees, or "Hill Billies," sided with the Union. When Union troops marched into eastern Tennessee, for example, cheering residents greeted them with American flags they had hidden from the Confederates. Southwest Texas, northwest Arkansas, Jones County in southern Mississippi, Winston County in northwest Alabama, and parts of Louisiana were other Unionist strongholds. For decades after the Civil War, these areas of the South would remain Republican islands in a Democrat sea.

As many as 100,000 southern whites – 30,000 from Tennessee – fought for the Union, and there were several dozen Union army units with southern designations, including the 1st Alabama (U.S. Volunteers), the 1st Mississippi Mounted Rifles (U.S.A.), the 2nd Florida Cavalry (U.S.A.), and the 10th Tennessee Infantry (U.S.A.). Among the southern officers who remained loyal to the United States Government were Virginia's General Winfield Scott and General George Thomas, Tennessee's Admiral David Farragut, and Georgia's Montgomery Meigs, Quartermaster General of the Union army.

Southern Unionists suffered a reign of terror by Confederate authorities far, far worse than even the most extreme accusations that the defeated rebels later hurled at the federal government during the Reconstruction era. Hundreds were hanged in eastern Tennessee, for example, for loyalty to the United States Government, and more than a hundred in Texas. Confederate General George Pickett hanged 22 prisoners from the 1st North Carolina (U.S. Volunteers). The tens of thousands of ex-slaves in the Union army also had reason to fear capture. In an incident that foreshadowed countless acts of savagery by white Democrats during Reconstruction, dozens of black prisoners of war were executed by General Nathan Bedford Forrest, who later became the first Grand Wizard of the Ku Klux Klan.

After the shooting started, Republicans stopped listening to Democrats defend states rights. "Whence this magical omnipotence of 'States Rights'?" wrote Lincoln in his July 1861 message to Congress. General Thomas spoke for all Republicans when after one battle he was asked if the dead should be buried by state: "No. Mix them up. I am tired of states rights." Complaints about the loss of rebel property also fell on deaf ears. In the summer of 1861, Congress passed the first Confiscation Act, authorizing seizure of rebel property used for the war effort. Property, as the rebels defined it, included slaves, so the implications of this law were enormous.

A year later, in July 1862, Congress passed with near-unanimous Republican support a second Confiscation Act that said rebel property could be seized whether or not it was used in the rebellion. Under the law, any slaves still held by rebels after 60 days were to be declared free, as well as all those who fled to Union lines. At Lincoln's insistence, language specifically authorizing confiscation of rebel-held land was taken out. The law also authorized the enlistment of black soldiers, for Radical Republicans knew that once in the army blacks could never be re-enslaved. Senator Sumner, among others, pointed out that since blacks were fighting in the military they could hardly be denied the right to vote, an argument echoed in the Vietnam War-era drive to lower the voting age to 18, accomplished by the 26th amendment in 1971.

In August 1862, Horace Greeley denounced Lincoln for not using his new legal authority to emancipate the slaves immediately, writing that "attempts to put down the Rebellion and at the same time uphold its...cause" were "preposterous and futile." Though he had already drafted the Emancipation Proclamation, Lincoln responded publicly in this way: "My paramount object in this struggle is to save the Union, and is not either to save or to destroy slavery. If I could save the Union without freeing any slave, I would do it; and if I could save it by freeing all the slaves, I would do it; and if I could save it by freeing some slaves and leaving others alone; I would also do that."

Here Lincoln was carefully presenting emancipation as a war measure, so as not to anger northern Democrats, especially those in the Union army, more than could be avoided. Nonetheless, most Democrat politicians and newspaper editors in the North were incensed by the Emancipation Proclamation, saying that they were for saving the Union but not freeing the slaves. Very few soldiers deserted, though thousands would have had Lincoln not timed the Proclamation so well. Another concern, that the Proclamation would spark a bloody slave uprising, proved groundless.

There is a common misperception today, abetted by Democrat-leaning historians who wish to distance Abraham Lincoln from our Republican Party heritage, that with the Emancipation Proclamation Lincoln just waved a presidential wand and freed the slaves. In fact, he was acting on authority granted to him by the Republican Congress in the second Confiscation Act, a copy of which Lincoln appended to the Proclamation. After complaining for months that Stevens, Sumner, and Wilson had been "haunting" him to proclaim the slaves free even ahead of specific congressional authorization, Lincoln discussed a preliminary Proclamation with his Cabinet five days after Congress passed the second Confiscation Act. At Seward's suggestion, he waited to make it public until Union forces won a victory, which came two months later at the Battle of Antietam. Since the authorizing legislation pertained to rebel property, the Emancipation Proclamation could not free slaves in Union-held territory, but three-quarters of all slaves in the country were legally emancipated immediately. And so many blacks from loyal border states were in the Union army that slavery in that area was effectively dead even though not officially abolished there until 1865.

Sixty days having passed since the second Confiscation Act became law, Lincoln could have proclaimed the slaves free at once. Instead, the Emancipation Proclamation, contrary to the will of Congress, actually delayed their freedom until January 1, 1863. The purpose of this delay was to entice rebels to lay down their arms by the end of the year; presumably, those rebels doing so could have kept their slaves. Lincoln had this eventuality in mind in December 1862 when, to the Radical Republicans' dismay, he proposed a compensated emancipation plan to be implemented gradually through the year 1900.

Abraham Lincoln showed exceptional skill in balancing our Republican Party's conservative and Radical wings. To his first Cabinet he named the foremost conservative, William Seward, as Secretary of State and the eminent Radical, Salmon Chase, as Secretary of the Treasury. Lincoln worked closely with both. Seward, for example, polished the first inaugural address (particularly the classic "mystic chords of memory" passage), and Chase, as well as Senator Sumner, did the same with the Emancipation Proclamation. Between these three men stood Edwin Stanton, the anti-slavery Attorney General in the final months of the Buchanan presidency, who headed the War Department from January 1862 onward. Lincoln's private secretary, John Hay, would later serve as Secretary of State during the McKinley and Roosevelt administrations.*

When President Lincoln was sworn in, the federal government had only $3 million on hand, and the new President immediately asked Congress for borrowing authority. This measure was tremendously important because Congress would after only a few days not be back in Washington until July. In those days, the House Ways and Means Committee handled both appropriations (Ways) and taxation

---

* A close friend of Theodore Roosevelt's father, Hay introduced him to Lincoln.

(Means), making its chairman, Thaddeus Stevens, the most powerful member of Congress. Stevens bulldozed right over parliamentary obstacles thrown up by obstructionist Democrats, having the Speaker of the House, Galusha Grow, whom he had hand-picked, call the House of Representatives into session as a committee of the whole, so that the rules could be suspended. Stevens saw to it that Lincoln got the borrowing authority, and for more money than he had requested. Treasury Secretary Chase then arranged for the loans.

Once Congress was back in session in July 1861, Stevens and Chase met to discuss long-term financing of the war effort. Under Stevens' direction, Vermont Republican Justin Morrill became the architect of a new taxation system while New York Republican Elbridge Spaulding devised a new national currency.

An array of excise taxes would be insufficient, so the first federal income tax was enacted in August 1861. It was simple and progressive: 3% on annual incomes over $300 (nearly an average worker's salary), later raised to $600, and 5% on incomes over $10,000. To generate more revenue and also to subsidize northern industries, tariffs were hiked considerably.

A paper currency was critical, since gold and silver were being hoarded, but financing deficit spending by merely printing money was out of the question. At Chase's insistence, the federal government would borrow instead, and some bonds would be sold directly to the public, the first time this had been done anywhere. Based on Alexander Hamilton's policies and also research Stevens had done on how Britain had financed its wars against Napoleon, Spaulding's plan called for the government to issue $100 million in legal tender notes exchangeable for 20-year, 6% Treasury bonds. Critics joked that the notes were backed, not by gold, but merely their green ink; the real backing of the "greenbacks," however, was the administration's solid creditworthiness due to its effective taxation policy.

A second Legal Tender Act, of July 1862, authorized the federal government to print another $150 million in greenbacks and to issue $500 million in 6% bonds, redeemable in gold and silver twenty years later. The promise to pay off the principal with precious metals was a compromise between Chase, who pressed for the interest to be paid in gold, and the more realistic Stevens, who wanted to do away altogether with a need for gold reserves. First appearing during the Civil War, the motto "In God We Trust" was something of a pun, replacing the implicit "In Gold We Trust" guarantee of previous paper money.

A third Legal Tender Act, in February 1863, authorized printing $150 million more in greenbacks and borrowing another $900 million. Seven years later, as Chief Justice, Salmon Chase wrote the decision striking down these greenback laws for going beyond constitutional authority to "coin money." Congress averted financial chaos by increasing the number of Supreme Court Justices from 7 to 9,* enabling President Grant to name two more Justices, who then voted to reverse "Hepburn v. Griswold." The greenback issue would remain bitterly contested for the rest of the 19th century.

Once most Democrats in Congress left to go with the Confederacy, Republicans enjoyed a three-fifths majority in both houses, and could count on the votes of some independents from border states too. Our Party was at last able to enact the economic agenda of Alexander Hamilton and Henry Clay. No economic expert, President Lincoln followed Whig tradition in allowing the tremendously productive Congress of 1861-62 to set the nation on course for unprecedented prosperity.

The banking system in place until creation of the Federal Reserve System was the brainchild of Salmon Chase and Thaddeus Stevens, two strong advocates for federal regulation of the banks. The National Banking Act of 1863 set up federally-chartered banks, which were generally sounder than state banks. Doing away with the assortment of bank notes printed by a multitude of state banks, federal bank notes were uniform and accepted throughout the country, like those once issued by the Bank of the United States. The Act required national banks to hold a portion of their capital in the form of U.S. Government bonds, thus vastly expanding the bond market.

A high priority of Speaker of the House Galusha Grow, the

---

* The number of Justices on the Court had been reduced to prevent Andrew Johnson from appointing any.

Homestead Act of May 1862 allotted free of charge 160 acres each to tens of thousands of small farmers, the land donated having been acquired by the federal government in the Louisiana Purchase. This measure, followed up by an 1870 law giving preference to Union army veterans, helped make America's heartland solidly Republican to this day. We owe many of the great state universities of the Midwest, such as the University of Illinois, to Justin Morrill's Land Grant College Act of July 1862, which gave federal land to state governments for the promotion of agriculture, engineering, and other technical subjects. Thaddeus Stevens pushed hard for the Pacific Railroad Act of July 1862, which chartered the transcontinental railroad from Omaha to San Francisco, a northerly route long opposed by Democrats intent on extending the slave system using instead a route through Texas. The U.S. Department of Agriculture was also established that year.

The Radical Republicans, also referred to as "Ultra Republicans" by pro-slavery Democrats, viewed the war as a moral crusade, not only to free the slaves, but to completely eradicate the slave system. As the fighting dragged on, our Party's Radical wing grew at the expense of the conservatives, who merely wanted slavery contained where it already existed. In the middle stood the moderate Lincoln, carefully calibrating his public stance against slavery to be no tougher than public opinion would tolerate. In early 1862, he hurriedly countermanded orders by two generals that proclaimed emancipation in areas under their control. Similarly, enlisting black soldiers too early might have cost him critical support from loyalist slave-holders in the border states, but he did go along with the Radical Republicans' demand that the army not return runaway slaves to their former masters.

Though he did not share the Radicals' zeal to liberate their black countrymen, Lincoln's cautious approach was rarely more than a few months behind the Radicals in implementing their policies. Unfortunately for the collective memory of our Party, deification of the martyred Lincoln has taken him out of this context, to the disparagement of the Radicals, who actually had better foresight than the more tactically-minded Lincoln.

Radical Republicans were quick to eliminate any traces of the slave system in the North. Kansas was admitted as a free state. At the urging of the Radicals, President Lincoln recognized the black-led governments of Haiti and Liberia. In 1862, Congress abolished slavery in the District of Columbia and in the federal territories, despite the Dred Scott decision. In their impatience for victory over the rebels, the Radicals sometimes did try to interfere with the President's conduct of the war. They were especially wary of General George McClellan, a Democrat whom they suspected did not want to defeat Confederate armies, just fight them off until an armistice could be arranged under which the South could keep its slave system. Certainly, any grief that the Radicals' Joint Committee on the Conduct of the War gave Lincoln was nothing compared to the many northern Democrats' outright opposition to fighting the rebels.

Thaddeus Stevens truly cared about the suffering of the slaves, and, in view of his domestic circumstances, unlike Lincoln he had no problem envisioning an integrated postwar society. From the start, he called for enlisting blacks into the Union army, and paying them equally with whites. Stevens also argued against allowing draftees to buy their way out by paying a $300 fee or finding a substitute. His bill to enable black residents of the District of Columbia to vote passed the House of Representatives but failed in the Senate. Way ahead of his time, Stevens was also an impassioned advocate for Native Americans and for Chinese immigrants in California. In 1863, he saw to it that Grow's successor as Speaker was another Radical, Schuyler Colfax, who would later be Vice President during Grant's first term. In 1868, Stevens would help convince a reluctant House of Representatives to appropriate the money to pay for the purchase of Alaska.

Not just an idealist, Thaddeus Stevens was a very witty guy. Once, when Stevens warned Lincoln that his first Secretary of War would steal anything except a red-hot stove, the offended party demanded a retraction, to which Stevens replied: "Mr. President, I now take that back. He would steal a red-hot stove." Another time, when Stevens heard that two Democrat Representatives intended to fight a duel, he suggested they do so with dung forks.

In addition to Stevens, Sumner, and Chase, most prominent Republicans in Congress were Radicals, including nearly all congressional committee chairmen as well as the Speaker of the House and President pro tempore of the Senate. New Hampshire Senator John Hale and Indiana Representative George Julian had been the 1852 Free Soil Party candidates for President and Vice President. Michigan Senator Zachariah Chandler had been one of the founders of our Republican Party in 1854. Massachusetts Senator Henry Wilson, responsible for repealing the District of Columbia law that enslaved any free black who married a white person, later became Grant's second Vice President. Vermont Senator Justin Morrill, Ohio Senator Ben Wade, Maryland Representative Henry Davis, and Illinois Representative Owen Lovejoy were also radically opposed to slavery. Perhaps the most famous Radical Republican outside of government was former slave Frederick Douglass, the great orator and abolitionist. The famous movie portrayal of Col. Robert Gould Shaw, who led his regiment of black soldiers to death and glory, depicts the quasi-religious fervor common among Radical Republicans serving in the Union army.

War-weariness and backlash against the Emancipation Proclamation proved costly to the Republicans in the fall 1862 elections. In the House, our Party lost only three seats, but its majority slipped to 103-80 due to the shift of most border state voters from independent to Democrat. Legislative advances were in no danger of being reversed, however, because control of most state legislatures actually gained the Republicans eight Senate seats.

In private, Lincoln always treated blacks as equals. In October 1864, he met with black abolitionist Sojourner Truth, who expressed amazement at being received so respectfully. Lincoln had many long conversations with Frederick Douglass, though during the war the President took care to meet with him away from the White House. At his second inauguration, the war virtually over, Lincoln was confident enough to go public about his friendship with a black man. Hearing that Douglass was being denied entry into the inaugural reception because he was black, the President had him shown in, greeting him with "Here comes my friend Douglass" and shaking his hand. Such a gesture was unprecedented, and could have scarcely been thought possible just a few years before.

—⊷⊶⊷—

The term "Reconstruction" came into use well before the end of the war, by both Lincoln and the Radicals. The President did not refer to rebuilding destroyed property, rather to how the Union of states was to be reconstructed. Radical Republicans wanted to go beyond that, to reconstructing southern society, for they thought of blacks as citizens whose constitutional rights were just as important as those of any white person. What was the point, they asked, of abolishing slavery if the blacks were to remain at the mercy of plantation lords? Leaving the old power structure in place, wrote abolitionist Wendell Phillips, "makes the negro's freedom a mere sham."

Radical Republicans in no way wanted personal vengeance against the rebels. Thaddeus Stevens set the tone; while he did want plantation lords displaced from their lands in favor of the blacks who actually worked it, he adamantly opposed any treason trials. What he and other Radicals wanted for the South was to uproot the slave system and replace it with the North's free market society – just the transformation Lincoln would later call "a new birth of freedom." They wanted to integrate the slaves and also poor southern whites into a nationwide economy of free enterprise and social mobility. In a March 1864 speech to the New York Workingman's Association, President Lincoln expressed this free market vision: "Property is the fruit of labor – property is desirable – is a positive good in the world. That some should be rich shows that others may become rich, and hence is just encouragement to industry and enterprise."

In December 1863, President Lincoln published his Proclamation of Amnesty and Reconstruction. According to the plan, any rebellious state where 10% of the voting populace swore allegiance to the United States could set up a loyalist government, and hold elections under a new state constitution. Full pardons could be had by all but high-ranking rebels. Lincoln's purpose was to restore the Union as quickly as possible, with little regard for the kind of social transformation the Radicals had in mind. The President's expectation was that these administrations would in time draw southerners away from the Confederate state governments.

This short-sighted policy failed to shorten the war by a day, but it did generate immense complications. Lincoln held that as President his power to pardon was all that was required to restore the Union. Aside from its complete breach with the Whig presidential tradition, this Proclamation did not make much sense constitutionally. Congress, not the President, would have to agree to seat any new Representatives and Senators from the seceded states.

Most congressional Republicans, whether they backed Lincoln or not, believed Congress, not the President, possessed the constitutional authority to be in charge of Reconstruction and that federal laws as enacted by Congress, not the President's power to pardon, were the proper means. Lincoln was indeed Commander-in-Chief of the military, but, they said reasonably enough, his assertion of authority over civil matters such as forming new southern state governments was an infringement on congressional prerogatives. Who could argue otherwise? To be sure, whatever their disagreements over timing and methods of dealing with the rebellion, differences between President Lincoln and the Radicals were still inconsequential compared to the policy chasm separating them from their common enemies, the Confederacy and the Democratic Party.

When Lincoln announced his reconstruction plan, he had already set up wartime civilian governments for Arkansas and Louisiana, states largely in Union hands. Popular support for these administrations was weak. In Louisiana, fewer than eight thousand people voted in elections to send two Representatives to Washington. Both men were unquestionably loyal to the United States, but they were seated despite the strenuous objections of Thaddeus Stevens that their elections had been illegitimate.

Though the new state constitutions were major improvements over the Confederate versions, most of the laws were copied from the rebel governments. Worse, the President said that as long as these new southern state governments acknowledged legal freedom for blacks and were committed to their education, they could make for the ex-slaves "any provision which may be adopted by such State…as a temporary arrangement." The southern state governments would seize this loophole to enact "black codes" little different from the slave codes, reestablishing slavery in all but name. Fearing competition for jobs, poor whites had the most to gain by keeping blacks down.

Slavery was gone from the statute books but blacks were to be serfs, that is, technically free but in reality legally bound to their masters by regulations or annual labor contracts. For plantation lords, abolishing slavery turned out to be a terrific deal; they could still exploit them economically without having to invest in their purchase or being encumbered by any obligation to provide them with food and shelter in sickness and old age. Typically, blacks were forbidden to operate their own businesses, assemble without white supervision, own guns, be on the street after sunset, or travel without permission from their white employers.

In the eyes of the Radicals, this was an astoundingly callous betrayal of not only the blacks but of all Union soldiers who had died for their country. President Lincoln did say he was open to other reconstruction plans, but those Republicans radically opposed to slavery were angry that he had infringed on the authority of Congress to make "all Laws which shall be necessary and proper." Reports of outrages against blacks perpetrated by Lincoln's southern state administrations caused Congress to expel the two Louisiana Representatives and refuse to seat anyone else from a "10%" state government.

Thaddeus Stevens, Charles Sumner, and other Radical Republicans determined that the only way to eliminate slavery forever in every state was to amend the Constitution. The amendment was needed, they believed, because the Emancipation Proclamation amounted to a wartime seizure of rebel property with meager constitutional underpinning. The proposed 13th amendment passed the Senate in 1863, but Democrat opposition kept the measure from achieving the necessary two-thirds majority in the House of Representatives.

Radical Republicans were alarmed. If Democrats regained control of the federal government, would they reimpose slavery nationwide as they had effectively done in Lincoln's "10%" state governments in the South? In June 1864, having passed the Senate again, the 13th amendment fell just a few votes short in the House. Reacting to this calamity, the first week of July Congress passed its own reconstruction plan, the Wade-Davis bill, named after its sponsors, Senator Ben Wade and Representative Henry Davis. Nearly every Republican voted for Wade-Davis — not just the Radicals — showing that on Reconstruction it was President Lincoln, not the Radicals, who was out of the mainstream of our Republican Party. The bill contained a nationwide ban on slavery, so that slavery could not reemerge while Congress was out of session.

Under Wade-Davis, a seceded state could be readmitted to the Union (by Congress, not the President), only after 50%, not 10%, of the voters swore loyalty to the United States. What is more, they would have to swear that they had never voluntarily supported the rebellion. Of course, since no state of the Confederacy could meet this standard, the purpose of Wade-Davis was to postpone Reconstruction altogether until Congress returned to Washington in December 1864, at the earliest.

Clearly, Radicals rejected the Lincoln approach of establishing loyal southern governments as a means of winning the war; no way did they want white-supremacist Democrats back in power even before the war was over. The mainstream Republican position was that the slave system had to be completely and permanently eradicated from a seceded state before it could be readmitted to the Union. Contrary to descriptions in pro-Democrat history books of Wade-Davis as harsh or punitive, Republicans intended for the postwar South nothing more than an interim period of federal government control much like the postwar administrations that reshaped Germany and Japan after World War II.

Two days after passing Wade-Davis, Congress presented the bill to President Lincoln for his signature, one hour before adjournment. Lincoln did not sign or veto the bill, but his not signing it by the time Congress adjourned had the effect of a veto. On July 8, 1864, Lincoln issued a second proclamation on Reconstruction, denying that Congress had the constitutional authority to abolish slavery aside from the wartime seizure and emancipation of rebel slave property. Another reason for the President's startling message was that, worried about his reelection prospects, he feared Wade-Davis could cost him the Electoral College votes of his "10%" southern state governments.

Wade and Davis published a critique on Lincoln's policy in August 1864: "[President Lincoln] must confine himself to his Executive duties – to obey and execute, not to make the laws – to suppress by arms armed rebellion, and leave political reorganization to Congress." Who could disagree? Representative Davis' ardently antislavery views cost him so much support from Maryland voters that he was defeated for reelection by a Democrat that November.

Far from being some kind of fiendish plot or coup attempt, opposition by many Republicans to renominating Lincoln for the presidency was normal politicking. After all, a second term was against even Lincoln's previously stated principles, and every President since Van Buren had been denied another nomination. Radicals tended to favor Chase, who as a tremendously successful Treasury Secretary would actually have been a very good postwar Chief Executive.

The ambitious Chase was all for it, going so far as to place his own portrait on the $1 bill. Upset that he was not going to get the nomination, Chase resigned from the Cabinet in June 1864. That October, Lincoln appointed him Chief Justice to replace the recently deceased Roger Taney, with the understanding that Chase campaign for Lincoln's reelection. Thaddeus Stevens, Charles Sumner, Henry Wilson, future President James Garfield, and other former Chase supporters also campaigned vigorously for President Lincoln. Among Chief Justice Chase's first official acts would be to swear in a black lawyer to argue before the Supreme Court.

The Republican platform called for passage of the 13th amendment and continuation of the war until total victory, plus planks for more immigration and further Whig economic policies. The Democratic Party came under attack for the pro-rebel sentiments of many of its members. To appeal to border states which the Republicans had lost in 1860, President Lincoln had his outspokenly anti-slavery Vice President, Hannibal Hamlin, dropped from the ticket. At Lincoln's insistence, the 1864 convention replaced him with Andrew Johnson, the loyal Democrat and former Senator from Tennessee whom he had appointed military governor of that state in 1862. Thanks to John Wilkes Booth, picking Andrew Johnson proved to be the biggest mistake of Abraham Lincoln's life.

To be a Republican meant, virtually by definition, to be in favor of fighting the rebels. Not so with the Democrats, who in the North were divided into War Democrats, such as General McClellan, and Peace Democrats, whom Republicans called Copperheads, after the venomous snake. In 1862, the Democrat majority in the Illinois legislature voted to demand that Lincoln rescind the Emancipation Proclamation. They even tried to withdraw the state militia from service in the Union army. To prevent this threat to the war effort, Republican Governor Richard Yates closed down the legislature.

In Ohio, the Democratic Party nominated Clement Vallandigham for Governor after the House of Representatives expelled him and President Lincoln deported him to the Confederacy for giving pro-rebel speeches. New York Governor Horatio Seymour, who would become the Democrat presidential candidate in 1868, spoke out in support of Vallandigham, as did former Democrat President Franklin Pierce, who called him "a noble martyr of free speech." Seymour also vehemently denounced Lincoln for issuing the Emancipation Proclamation.

The Republican Governor of Indiana, Oliver Morton, blocked a Democrat ploy to withdraw the state militia from the Union army by having the Republican minority in the legislature walk out, preventing a quorum. For the next two years he funded the state government with contributions from Republican counties and the War Department. Governor Morton described the Democratic Party as "a common sewer and loathsome receptacle into which emptied every element of treason, North and South." Of course, notwithstanding the Clinton administration's sale of nuclear weapon secrets to Communist China, many Americans today would disagree with that assessment.

New Orleans, the most pro-Union city in the South, had as its counterpart, New York, where there was more pro-Confederate sentiment than in any other city in a free state. In July 1863, the city exploded in a four-day killing spree by opponents of the military draft. Addressing the mob as "my friends," Governor Seymour at first encouraged the rampage as a blow to the Lincoln administration. Dozens of policemen were slain, and many Republican-owned businesses and newspapers were burned down. Numbering in tens of thousands, immigrant Irish and other malcontents descended on black neighborhoods and slaughtered hundreds of innocents. One crippled black man was dragged through the streets by his genitals, and his body chopped up and parceled out to the crowd. Black churches, schools, and an orphanage went up in flames. Not until the arrival of 10,000 Union soldiers, who had just fought at Gettysburg, was the insurrection suppressed. The death toll from the worst rioting in U.S. history exceeded 500 and may have been more than 1000.

The two factions of the northern Democratic Party, the War Democrats and the Peace Democrats, reached a compromise. The 1864 presidential candidate would be a War Democrat, while the Peace Democrats would get the second spot as well as the opportunity to write the platform. The Party nominated 39-year old General McClellan for President. His running mate would be Representative George Pendleton, who just had led the Democrats' successful drive to block passage of the 13th amendment. Pendleton announced that a Democrat victory would restore white-supremacist rule in the South. He also criticized our Republican Party for defending in the South "a semi-bar-

barous race of blacks who are worshippers of fetishes and polygamists" who want to "subject the white women to their unbridled lust."

The platform, largely written by Confederate sympathizer Clement Vallandigham, called for an immediate cease-fire, followed by negotiations. If McClellan had won the election, and taken office just a month before Appomattox, he probably would not have permitted Confederate independence however. In all likelihood, McClellan would have assumed direct command of the Union army, as Lincoln had considered doing after the Battle of Gettysburg, so as to be in position to accept General Lee's surrender. The Union would have survived but with slavery more or less intact, a situation not much different than what actually happened with that other Democrat, Andrew Johnson, in the White House.

Bouyed by the Union army's capture of Atlanta, Lincoln defeated McClellan by 55% to 45% in the popular vote and 212 to 21 in the Electoral College. Republicans won the governorships and legislative majorities in all but three northern states. In congressional races, results were equally good. The House of Representatives went from 103 Republicans and 80 Democrats, to 145 Republicans and only 46 Democrats, giving our Party a 3-1 edge. The next Senate would be 42-10, more than 4-1 Republican. Tragically for the country, however, according to a provision of the Constitution not amended until the 1930s, this overwhelmingly Republican Congress elected in November 1864 did not convene for another thirteen months, not until December 1865, by which time a racist southern Democrat had been President for eight months.

In January 1865, the House of Representatives approved the 13th amendment by a vote of 119 to 56, just over the two-thirds requirement. Every Republican voted for it, and most Democrats voted against but not enough to prevent passage. Speaker of the House Schuyler Colfax broke precedent by voting, in order to participate in our Party's victory over slavery. Ratification by the states was completed before yearend.

There was no sharp dividing line between Radical and conservative Republicans, but our Party was definitely becoming even more

radically opposed to slavery. Conservative Republicans found themselves complaining that Lincoln was becoming too Radical. The
President had pushed hard, for instance, for the Party convention's
endorsement of the 13th amendment, a Radical measure. He also
publicly backed the Radical Republican Roscoe Conkling, who would
later figure prominently in national politics, for nomination to the
House of Representatives over his conservative Republican rival. Not
to be overlooked is the fact that nearly all blacks sided with the Radical
Republicans. Another promising factor for our Party's future was that
younger voters tended to vote Republican.

In February 1865, as the war was drawing to a close, Lincoln met
with the Confederate Vice President, whom he had known while both
were in the House of Representatives years before. Lincoln advised
the rebel leader to ask the Georgia legislature to withdraw state troops
from the war. No problem there, but where the President made a serious error was in suggesting that the state send new Representatives
and Senators to Washington. Since Senators in those days were elected by state legislatures, Lincoln was by implication recognizing the
legitimacy of Confederate state-level regimes. Two months later, he
compounded this mistake by granting permission for the Confederate
legislature of Virginia to meet in order to withdraw state troops from
the war. This time, fortunately, on April 12th he quickly rescinded
the order, having been convinced that dealing with rebel civilian
authorities so late in the war would lead to a series of peace negotiations with the seceded states, greatly complicating postwar
Reconstruction.

Just the night before, Abraham Lincoln had given the last speech
of his life, in which he hinted at a major shift in his thinking about
Reconstruction. The President displeased the Radicals by not guaranteeing the vote to former slaves, but overall he made substantial
movement toward their position – he admitted that his "10%" state
governments might not be the way to go and that Congress should
have a role in Reconstruction. He said a major policy announcement
could be expected soon. That afternoon, Lincoln had reacted favor-
ably to a report to the Cabinet by Secretary of War Stanton that called

for military government to be imposed on the conquered South. He had already appointed military governors for conquered regions, so this step would not have been much more than formalizing a situation that already existed.

Ever the master of timing, the President could have been waiting for all the Confederates to lay down their arms before siding in this way with the Radical Republicans, with whom he had been drawing closer. Right after surrendering, the rebels would have been so relieved there would be no executions or other reprisals that they might have gladly acquiesced to Stanton's approach. Certainly, the horrible massacres of former slaves by former rebels in the late spring and early summer of 1865 would have forced Lincoln to abandon any expectation for southern autonomy in the near term.

What President Lincoln should have done was call Congress back into session in order to develop a Reconstruction plan. Of course, the debate would have been acrimonious and might have resulted in laws not to his liking, but after all, "government by the people" means that the people's representatives make the laws. Exactly what Lincoln had in mind for the postwar South we will never know, but listening to his last speech, John Wilkes Booth thought he had a pretty good idea. "This means n____r citizenship," he told his co-conspirators as he put into action his plan to prevent it.

Chapter Six

(1865-1875)

BATTLING THE NEO-CONFEDERATES

Andrew Johnson, the man who would be President for the first four years after the Civil War, was born dirt-poor in Raleigh, North Carolina. He learned to read as an adult and first worked as a tailor. Always a Democrat, his political career in eastern Tennessee took him from small town mayor, to state legislator, to U.S. Representative, to Governor, then Senator in 1856. Railing against the slave-holding plantation lords on behalf of poor whites, though he himself owned slaves, in ideological terms Johnson could be described as a populist. Once in power, as populists often do, President Johnson hurried to ingratiate himself with his former enemies.

The only southern Senator to remain loyal to the United States Government, Johnson pleaded with his constituents not to go with the Confederacy, several times facing down secessionist crowds with a pistol in his hand. Before President Lincoln appointed him military governor of Tennessee in 1862, Johnson served on the Joint Committee on the Conduct of the War. To President Lincoln, Andrew Johnson appeared to be solid presidential material when he had him nominated for Vice President. Others who knew him better totally disagreed. Thaddeus Stevens, his colleague on the Joint Committee, warned Lincoln that Johnson was a "demagogue" and a "damned scoundrel."

Embarrassingly drunk when he took the oath of office as Vice President, Johnson stumbled through an incoherent speech in the

Senate chamber just prior to President Lincoln's second inaugural address. A mortified Lincoln ordered a guard not to allow Johnson outside to speak in public. The new Vice President was whisked off to Silver Spring, Maryland to sober up, while several Senators introduced a resolution calling on him to resign. The night of the tragedy at Ford's Theater, a few days after General Lee's surrender at Appomattox, one of Booth's co-conspirators had crept up to Johnson's boardinghouse door with a pistol but lost his nerve at the last minute. A third man did gravely wound Secretary of State Seward with a knife.

Grateful that Lincoln's Reconstruction policies so far had had little effect on the slave system, most southerners regretted Lincoln's death. They also feared retribution at the hands of Andrew Johnson, who unlike most Radical Republicans, had demanded the gallows for many rebel leaders. Southerners were relieved when the new President proved just how much of a "damned scoundrel" he really was. In his three-minute inauguration speech, Johnson referred to himself more than twenty times, but did not mention Abraham Lincoln once. He may have envied the plantation lords to the point of hatred, but the bitterly racist Andrew Johnson hated blacks much more and would do all in his power to keep them down. Lincoln's friend Charles Sumner, who had arrived at his deathbed accompanied by the President's eldest son Robert, soon observed: "By assassination of Lincoln the rebellion has vaulted into the Presidential chair."*

When Johnson became President in April 1865, Congress was out of session, not to return until that December. Stevens and others asked him to call Congress back into session, but the new President refused, preferring instead to exercise complete control over the Reconstruction process until then. His Republican Cabinet stayed on, fearing being replaced by Democrats, but Andrew Johnson ran as partisanly Democrat an administration as Lincoln's had been Republican and saw to it that the Democratic Party regained power in

---

* There exists a photograph of a six-year old Theodore Roosevelt and his sister watching President Lincoln's funeral procession pass below their window in New York City, and an eight-year old Woodrow Wilson caught a glimpse of Jefferson Davis under arrest after the fall of Richmond.

the South. Overlooked by so many histories of the Reconstruction era is the fact that until 1867 the white supremacist Democrat regimes of the pre-Civil War era were back in business.

Johnson did insist that legalized slavery had to go, but other than that southern leaders were completely on their own, unrestrained by any Republican policy, Radical or otherwise. He pardoned thousands of rebels, starting with General Lee, who set an example for other rebels by asking the President for clemency, thereby acknowledging the authority of the United States Government.

The southern state governments which arose under President Johnson's protection were nearly indistinguishable from their Confederate predecessors. The first postwar Governor of Mississippi, for example, was a Confederate general, and the first postwar Governor of Georgia was a Confederate Senator. Nearly all the congressmen elected by these southern state governments were ex-Confederates.

In Mississippi, black people were to be paid only once a year. Plantation lords could fire them just before their last day so as not to have to pay them anything. In Virginia and Louisiana, blacks who refused any offer of work, under any conditions, were to be flogged and then hired out in chain gangs. In Alabama, blacks could be forcibly hired out for six months at a time. In South Carolina, blacks had to be either farmers or servants. In Florida, any black person who so much as resisted when a white jostled him could be sentenced to 20 years at hard labor for assault and battery. Not one black person was permitted to vote or hold political office, and not one was taught to read or write in a school administered by a southern Democrat state government during the Andrew Johnson administration.

Here was a major turning point in American history. What could have been simple and quick – reconstructing the South into a constitutional, free market society – became instead a wrenching, 100-year ordeal. Our country would have been immeasurably better off had the governmental structures in place in the seceded states been completely swept away right after the Confederate collapse. During the debate on the Confiscation Act of 1861, Thaddeus Stevens had advocated that as Union armies advanced, the seceded states should be treated like conquered provinces. By this he meant that in reestablishing government institutions in the South the federal government should disregard any pre-existing state and local authorities, as the United States had done after conquering California and Arizona. To do anything else, he said, would leave the South under "subjugation by traitors and their Northern allies."

Abraham Lincoln had in fact gone a long way down this road by appointing military governors to administer conquered areas. One problem many Republicans had with the conquered province approach is that it implied that the Confederate states had actually seceded from the United States. They also disliked tolerating military rule for any longer than was strictly necessary to establish order.

Charles Sumner and some other Radical Republicans had a much better idea. In their view, the Confederate states had never left the Union, but by voting to secede the state governments had in effect abolished themselves. In their place, the federal government could establish territorial governments, just as it had for Nevada and Colorado, or indeed for Alabama and Arkansas decades earlier before they were states. During the war, many Louisiana Unionists had asked the federal government to do just that. Several bills to establish territorial governments for the seceded states were actually introduced into Congress, but conservative Republicans, not to mention the Democrats, were reluctant to take so bold a step.

Had territorial governments been set up there would have been, for example, no worries about letting ex-Confederates vote before they had repented or concerns about letting illiterate slaves vote before they were educated, because federal law would have applied exclusively during the transition period. There already was a law against slavery in federal territories by then, so this and other reform legislation would have come into force immediately, with none of the arduous complications that afflicted the nation during the decade of Reconstruction.

Though President Johnson falsely claimed he was following the Reconstruction policies of his Republican predecessor, Republicans were justifiably outraged that after four years of sacrifice the Democrats were so quickly subverting our Party's objective for "a new birth of freedom." In early 1866, Johnson helped defeat Thaddeus Stevens' bill for black suffrage in the District of Columbia. In August, the President issued a proclamation that the rebellion was over, implying that everything should go back to normal – precisely the pre-Civil War situation that our Republican Party had been struggling since 1854 to change.

As early as the summer of 1865, the unrepentant southern leaders reestablished their state militias, commanded in many cases by officers wearing Confederate uniforms. Federal army officers who tried to stop them were overruled by the President. In August 1865, President Johnson removed almost all black soldiers from the South, and within two years there were hardly any at all left in the army. Any officer in the occupying federal army who exerted himself too much in defense of blacks or white Unionists was out of a job. For this reason, Johnson dismissed the conscientious Phil Sheridan from command in Texas and Louisiana and replaced him with General Winfield Hancock, who then allowed white supremacist thugs a free hand. So impressed were former rebels with the performance of Hancock, the Union general who had repulsed Pickett's charge, that he got the support of the Solid South when he was the Democratic Party presidential nominee in 1880.

The neo-Confederates in charge of the South right after the war would have little cause for complaint about later Radical Republican Reconstruction policies given the brutal revenge they exacted upon southern blacks and whites who had fought to defend the United States Government. Those southerners who had rallied to the U.S. flag during the war learned to keep a very low profile. White Republicans in the mountains of eastern Tennessee and western North Carolina tried for a while to defend themselves with their own militias, but these proved ineffectual against the Democrat state militias. Many white southern Union army veterans fled to the North or West. Patriotic organizations of southern Union veterans such as the Heroes of America were stamped out, leaving later generations with the impression that the South had been solidly Confederate.

The myth that the Radical Republicans were bent on personal vengeance is absurd. On the floor of the House of Representatives, Stevens and other Radicals denounced the idea of prosecuting anyone. In any event, there would have been no rebel punished whom Lincoln or Johnson could not have pardoned. President Lincoln had hoped Jefferson Davis would escape to Europe, but it was Andrew Johnson, not some congressmen, who had him imprisoned for two years.* In the aftermath of any other failed rebellion, there would have been mass arrests and executions; in fact, not one Confederate leader lost his life, and very few lost any liberty or property. Rebels laid down their arms so readily because they had no fear for their lives. They knew the most that could possibly happen in a restored Union would be the abolition of slavery. At Appomattox, General Joshua Chamberlain, a Republican soon thereafter elected Governor of Maine, ordered his troops to salute the surrendering Confederates. General Sherman was similarly magnanimous in accepting the surrender of the last rebel army two weeks later.

While the northern economy boomed during the war, the economy of the South deteriorated. The South, a region much poorer than the North to begin with, had poured four years of production into the war effort and lost some two hundred thousand men. Little was imported all this time. Slave-holders saw emancipation wipe out most of their capital, and Confederate bond-holders were also wiped out. To be sure, Union soldiers did wreck whatever war-related facilities they could get their hands on, but there was hardly any looting. The Union army's most destructive campaign, Sherman's march to the sea, it should be noted, was confined to a 60-mile wide stretch of land between Atlanta and Savannah. Confederate apologists would blame northern depredations for a South in ruins, but in truth the rebels had done it themselves.

After the fighting stopped, private charity poured into the South, where northern philanthropists established several major universities,

---

* Davis refused to ask for a pardon.

including Fisk, Rice, and Tulane. The Union army rebuilt the southern railroad system, but apart from this there was no federal government economic assistance to the South, as the concept that the government should tax money from some people in order to give it to others was still completely unknown to Americans. Another reason the southern economy remained so impoverished for the first years after the war was that few crops were planted in the spring of 1865. Most ex-slaves, understandably enough, refused to work for their former masters. Tens of thousands hit the road to see places far from their homes, and also to seek loved ones who had been sold away. As blacks were released from the slave system, family units began to emerge.

This socioeconomic dislocation transformed the plantation system. Unable to coerce blacks into working in gangs as before, landowners were forced to apportion individual plots for each family of black farm laborers. Landowners supplied the seeds and other requirements, and the "sharecroppers" were typically entitled to a third of the harvest. At first, blacks in the sharecropping system had some bargaining power with plantation owners, but soon they became mere serfs, bound to the land by having to borrow the money on which they lived against the next year's crop. Moreover, a plantation owner was usually the sole judge of whether a black sharecropper had kept his part of the deal and would be paid his share. Somewhat better off were the tenant farmers, whites mostly, who rented the land they worked.

This sad situation would have been avoided had the Radical Republicans had their way. In the place of vast plantations worked by oppressed black and white laborers, they wanted thousands of small farms owned by the people who actually worked the land. And these farmers would have been free to raise whatever crops they wanted, not just the cotton favored by plantation lords. Inspired by Representative Julian's Homestead Act, which was extending the free market system to the Plains states, Thaddeus Stevens proposed in 1864 to confiscate plantations from rebellious landowners and distribute the land among the emancipated slaves. Earlier in the war, Andrew Johnson had advocated much the same thing, saying plantation lords were fortunate not to be paying for their treason with their lives.

Carl Schurz, Lincoln's ambassador to Spain before becoming a Union army general, traveled throughout the South in the summer of 1865. His report to Congress on conditions under the Johnson state governments shocked the North. The defeated Confederates exhibited little loyalty to the federal government, Schurz stated, and could be expected to rebel again.

Schurz's accounts of how barbarously whites were treating blacks brought tears to the eyes of many readers: "The former masters exhibit a most cruel, remorseless, and vindictive spirit toward the colored people. In parts where there are no Union soldiers I saw colored women treated in the most outrageous manner. They have no rights that are respected. They are killed, and their bodies thrown into ponds or mud holes. They are mutilated by having their ears and noses cut off... Dead bodies of murdered Negroes were found on and near the highway... Gruesome reports came from the hospitals – reports of colored men and women whose ears had been cut off, whose skulls had been broken by blows. Whose bodies had been slashed by knives and lacerated by scourges." Other sources reported mass hangings of blacks, in one instance two dozen who had taken refuge in a church. On the Senate floor, Charles Sumner, who had denounced "The Barbarism of Slavery" before the Civil War, criticized President Johnson for condoning atrocities against blacks once again.

When the Congress elected in November 1864 convened for the first time, in December 1865, Republicans were in no mood to recognize the legitimacy of a ruling class which could perpetrate such cruelties. Among the southern congressmen who showed up at the Capitol were four Confederate generals, five colonels, six Cabinet secretaries, and several dozen members of the Confederate Congress. The new Georgia state legislature, much the same as the Confederate one, had elected the rebel Vice President to the Senate. Worse, once each black was counted as a whole person, not just 3/5 of one, for apportioning Representatives, there would be more southern Representatives than before the Civil War to fully represent the one-third of southerners who were black, though not one could actually vote. Nearly every congressman from an ex-Confederate state was a Democrat, and they were already reestablishing links with the northern Democratic Party in order to reverse or at least block the Republican free market agenda.

Thaddeus Stevens knew what to do. He had the House of Representatives clerk omit the names of congressmen from ex-Confederate states when calling the roll for the first time. The House was organized without the neo-Confederates, who took the hint and went home. The Senate also refused to seat the 22 ex-rebel Democrats. Our Republican Party, from Radicals to moderates to conservatives, was not about to let the rebels snatch victory from the jaws of defeat. Each of Johnson's southern state governments had refused to ratify the 13th amendment to free the slaves, but with the seceded states no longer recognized as part of the Union, the number of states ratifying the 13th amendment thus reached the required three-quarters and the amendment became part of the Constitution in December 1865.

The following April, Republicans in Congress overrode President Johnson's veto to enact the Civil Rights Act of 1866, anticipating the 1964 Civil Rights Act by nearly a century. The law declared that blacks were citizens whose constitutional rights had to be respected, no matter what those seven Democrats on the Supreme Court had come up with in the Dred Scott case. A measure which only the Radicals would have backed before the war was now mainstream Republicanism. In the South, protecting constitutional rights mainly involved eliminating, not creating, a government program – that is to say the black codes and their enforcement mechanisms. Since President Johnson did not enforce the Civil Rights Act in the South, it had little effect there but many racially discriminatory laws in the North were repealed or struck down as a result.

As usual, Thaddeus Stevens foresaw clearer than most anyone the fate of the emancipated slaves: "To trust to the tender mercies of their former masters and to the protection of State legislation, without giving them any voice in making the laws, is simply to turn them over to the torture of their enemies. To turn them loose unaided and unprotected is wholesale murder." Several hundred thousand emancipated slaves are estimated to have died in the months immediately following the Civil War. Previously, slave-holders had cared, however inadequately, for sick or elderly slaves, but once freed, southern blacks were on their own, and Democrats back in charge of southern state governments did not lift a finger to alleviate disease and malnutrition. Before the war, whites were reluctant to kill blacks because they were valuable slaves, but again, once they were freed, any white could prey on them.

At the end of the war, there were in the South four million ex-slaves, nearly all illiterate and ill-prepared for freedom. Most had never left the plantations where they had been born. What would they do? Where would they go? To assist southern blacks in their transition to freedom, the Republican Congress established the Bureau of Refugees, Freedmen, and Abandoned Lands in March 1865. Senator Sumner thought the Bureau's mission so important that he wanted it created as a Cabinet department. Prudence, however, dictated that the Bureau be part of the War Department, so that its activities could be protected by soldiers from hostile southern whites. The first head of the Freedmen's Bureau, appointed by President Lincoln, was General Oliver Howard, who would later found Howard University in Washington to educate former slaves.

The Bureau also helped displaced whites, but its main objective was to protect southern blacks. Civilian employees of the Freedmen's Bureau fed the hungry, built hospitals and schools, and tried to protect blacks from the nastiest excesses of the black codes. In its first twelve months, the Bureau established throughout the South over four thousand schools, which were also open to whites though few attended. Wherever military protection proved inadequate, the Bureau's teachers and health workers were often brutalized or even killed, and their schools and clinics burned down.

Originally, the Freedmen's Bureau was to last one year, but the black codes and other atrocities convinced Republicans that the Bureau's tenure should be extended three years. No southern jury would convict a white person for crimes against a black, so under the New Freedmen's

Bureau Act, the Bureau could prosecute violations of a black person's constitutional rights in military courts. Johnson vetoed the Act in February 1866, and Republicans used their large majority to override the veto in July. Republicans rightly took Johnson's veto as a declaration of war against blacks and our Republican Party.

Angry that blacks no longer had to bow and scrape to them, whites lynched more blacks in 1865-66 than in any year since. In May 1866, Memphis policemen killed six black Union soldiers in their camp, then led a white mob into the black section of town for a rampage of burning, looting, and rape. City officials admitted to a body count there of 40 civilians, but several hundred blacks may have died. Two months later in New Orleans, a Republican Party convention was attacked by a mob of whites led by the chief of police, who was the local head of the Knights of the White Camellia, a terrorist organization similar to the Ku Klux Klan. Dozens of blacks and several whites were killed. President Johnson cost himself what little Republican support he had left by blaming the Republicans for holding the convention rather than the Democrats who attacked it.

For evidence that the preponderant motive for secession was to maintain white dominance over blacks in the South, one need look no further than rebel reaction to losing the Civil War. Unlike the aftermath of most other defeated rebellions, a guerrilla movement did not spring up against the occupying army. Throughout Reconstruction, in fact, there were hardly any incidents of attacks on white federal soldiers. Instead, former Confederates focused their ire on the emancipated slaves and those whites who tried to elevate their condition.

To keep blacks down, discharged rebel troops started to form armed bands such as the Knights of the White Camellia, the Knights of the Rising Sun, the Regulators, the Pale Faces, and the Constitutional Guards. The most successful of these groups was the Ku Klux Klan, named for "kuklos," the Greek word meaning "circle" plus the alliterative "Klan." Goofy titles for high-ranking Klan commanders, such as Wizard, Dragon, and Cyclops, were intended to conceal the fact the

KKK was a paramilitary terrorist organization.

Founded in December 1865 in Pulaski, Tennessee by a handful of Confederate veterans, the Ku Klux Klan started off with pranks such as dressing up like ghosts to intimidate the freedmen, but soon turned to whipping, arson, castration, and murder. Within a year, the Ku Klux Klan had several thousand members. At an organizational meeting in Nashville in 1867, Nathan Bedford Forrest was chosen the national leader, or Grand Wizard, at the suggestion of General Lee, who said: "I hope he will succeed." The head of the Georgia Klan was John Gordon, the Confederate general who had led the surrender procession at Appomattox.

In most areas of the South, leadership of the Ku Klux Klan and the Democratic Party were indistinguishable, and the white-supremacist Democrats used the Klan to eliminate Republican opposition, assassinating many Republican officeholders and intimating countless others. A favorite target of the terrorists were the Union Leagues, lodges set up by our Party in an effort to form an alliance between blacks and poor whites, and to protect their constitutional rights. Thousands of southern blacks died at the hands of KKK killers.

In the fall of 1868, a mob of white Democrats followed up an attack on a Republican Party meeting in rural Louisiana with a massacre of some two hundred blacks in the area. This and other such assaults during the 1868 election campaign – and the threat of more if necessary – essentially wiped out our Republican Party in Louisiana for the next one hundred years. Mission accomplished, Wade Hampton, the former Confederate general and future Governor of the state, called on the Democratic Party not to carry out any more assassinations. Political murders did taper off there, but elsewhere Democrats kept up their devastating attacks on our Party.

The army was of little help in battling the Klan, since contrary to another popular misconception, there never were many federal occupation troops in the South. Perhaps 20,000 men in 1865, they stayed in their barracks and hardly ever patrolled the countryside. By yearend 1866, the entire U.S. army amounted to fewer than 40,000, and most of them were in the West. By 1871, the occupation force was down to about 5,000.

In 1870 and 1871, Congress passed three Enforcement Acts to stamp out the Ku Klux Klan. One law made denying someone's constitutional rights a federal crime. A second law expanded federal government control over the election process. This measure also had the effect of curbing vote fraud perpetrated by Democratic Party machines in the North, so the Democrats repealed it as soon as they won back the White House in 1884. A third specifically outlawed the Ku Klux Klan and similar terrorist organizations, and gave sweeping enforcement powers to the federal government. Within a year, the Klan was virtually gone. Law enforcement played a role in eliminating the postwar Ku Klux Klux, but primarily the Klan disappeared because once Democrat regimes replaced the Reconstruction state governments there was no longer any need for the white supremacists to carry out violent acts covertly when government authorities could again do so openly.

———

Andrew Johnson shared none of Lincoln's compassion for black people. Referring to Frederick Douglass, whom Lincoln had called "one of the most meritorious men in America," Johnson said: "I know that damned Douglass. He's just like any n____r." "White men alone must manage the South" declared President Johnson. In a message to Congress opposing black suffrage he said blacks have less "capacity for government than any other race of people. No independent government of any form has ever been successful in their hands. On the contrary, wherever they have been left to their own devices they have shown a constant tendency to relapse into barbarism." This from a man whose political party was overseeing the mutilation and murder of countless black people in the South.

At a February 1866 reception, the President said Thaddeus Stevens and Charles Sumner were as much traitors as the Confederate leadership. In one speech lasting an hour, the pompous and crude Andrew Johnson referred to himself more than two hundred times. In an August 1866 speech, Johnson went so far as to imply that the murder of Abraham Lincoln had been part of God's plan to make him

President. On a September 1866 Democratic Party campaign tour of the Midwest, he told one crowd that Thaddeus Stevens and Wendell Phillips deserved to be hanged. After he compared himself to Christ on one occasion, his remaining speeches, mostly in favor of the old states rights argument or opposed to Republican efforts to assist the freedmen, were drowned out by hecklers. State government officials refused to be seen with him.*

Had the Democrats won control of Congress in the November 1866 elections slavery would have been reestablished in all but name, and the Republicans' progressive economic agenda would have been repealed as well. Fortunately, Johnson and his state governments in the South had done such a good job of discrediting his party that Republicans held on to their veto-proof majorities in both houses of Congress and control of nearly all northern state governments. Opponents discredited Johnson further by publishing his earlier speeches in which he had said the federal government should administer the seceded states like conquered provinces – precisely the position of Thaddeus Stevens that he was now denouncing.

To Republicans, the Democrats' states rights arguments to defend racial discrimination in the South made no sense. How could it be constitutional for the federal government to free the slaves by force of arms but unconstitutional to preserve their freedom by force of law? Republicans pointed to the black codes as evidence that southern Democrats could not be trusted to uphold the Constitution they had so recently fought to destroy. Due to widespread revulsion at Democrat policies, most of the Republicans elected to Congress that year believed that radical measures against the slave system were in order.

Republican candidates were proud that our Party had enacted the Civil Rights Act and the 13th amendment, over the opposition of President Johnson, and their major issue during the election campaign was the vow to eradicate the slave system in the South. In April 1866,

---

* Voting to keep this wretch in the White House was what a future Democrat President, John Kennedy, termed a "Profile in Courage."

after hearing witnesses recount the horrors of the black codes, Republicans on the Joint Committee on Reconstruction determined that the only way to overcome the Democratic Party's defense of the slave system and keep the country safe from any future Democrat majority in Congress once the southern states were readmitted was to amend the Constitution again. Once part of a 14th amendment, the precepts of the Civil Rights Act could not be repealed by the Democrats or struck down by the Supreme Court. Congress would also be able to protect constitutional rights without having to rely on state courts or the military, or worrying about another Johnson veto.

The Joint Committee on Reconstruction, on which Republicans held twelve of fifteen seats, drafted the 14th amendment in the spring of 1866. Attorney General James Speed, brother of Lincoln's old friend Joshua Speed, resigned in protest against President Johnson's opposition to the amendment; he later chaired our Party's national convention that September. Though it was a Radical Republican team effort, Ohio's Republican Representative John Bingham was principal author of the amendment, and once again, Thaddeus Stevens was in charge, overseeing the entire process from drafting to ratification. In the Senate, Charles Sumner added some key language which made safeguarding all constitutional rights more a part of the amendment, a change which would have enormous effects on American jurisprudence in the 20th century.

Section 5 of the 14th amendment empowered Congress to enact enforcing legislation for the anti-slavery system and anti-Confederate provisions of the other sections. Section 4 forbade any southern state government from honoring the debts of the Confederacy or any incurred by the state during the rebellion. It also made sure that no future Democrat majority in Congress could repudiate the debts of the U.S. Government incurred to suppress the rebellion. And, neither the federal government nor any state could reimburse slave masters for their emancipated slaves. Section 3 effectively overruled the thousands of pardons which President Johnson had handed out to leading rebels. Military and civil officers of the U.S. Government who joined the rebellion, Confederate officials, and members of rebellious state governments would be excluded from postwar politics until Congress, not the President, said otherwise. All but five hundred rebels affected by this provision had their political rights restored by Congress by the Amnesty Act of 1872. Section 2 abolished the constitutional practice of counting black people as only 3/5 of whites for apportioning Representatives, and ensured their right to vote but in the indirect and regrettably unenforceable way of reducing the House seats of any state by the proportion of residents not permitted to vote. The 1965 Voting Rights Act was a much better way of safeguarding black suffrage.

Section 1 of the 14th amendment overruled the Supreme Court's Dred Scott decision that said blacks were not citizens and had no constitutional rights: "All persons born or naturalized in the United States and subject to the jurisdiction thereof, are citizens of the United States and of the State wherein they reside." State governments could not abridge any citizen's "privileges and immunities" (that term again taken from the Articles of Confederation); deprive any person of "life, liberty, or property, without due process of law" (a term repeated from the 5th amendment); or deny to any person "the equal protection of the laws."

Forcing state governments to comply with all provisions of the U.S. Constitution, not just the amendments known as the Bill of Rights, was what the Radical Republicans intended. The 14th amendment applied nationwide of course, sweeping away many racially discriminatory laws in the North as well and enabling blacks to vote in several northern states for the first time. Bingham and the other drafters also had in mind safeguarding the constitutional rights of the poor oppressed southern whites, most of whom could not vote either prior to Radical Reconstruction. However, in 1883, with Chief Justice Chase dissenting, the Supreme Court would rule that the 14th amendment did not mean much beyond protecting the constitutional rights of black people, and that even in this respect, this protection was sharply limited. Not until 1925 (Gitlow v. New York) would the Supreme Court recognize that the 14th amendment extended any federal constitutional right to state governments. Since then, many other constitutional provisions have been specifically incorporated, via the due process and equal protection clauses, into the 14th amendment's mandate to the states, thereby narrowing the range of issues on which majority rule applies.

Congress passed the 14th amendment in June 1866 by margins of 120-32 in the House and 33-11 in the Senate, all votes in favor being Republican and all votes against, Democrat. To Thaddeus Stevens Americans owe the 14th amendment, since it never would have passed had he not kept all those neo-Confederate Democrats out of Congress the year before. Radical Republicans were of the opinion that, as was the case with the 13th amendment, the 14th amendment could be ratified by three-fourths of the states then in the Union, but Secretary of State Seward (using one of his office's residual non-foreign affairs powers) delayed ratification by two crucial years by submitting it to the legislatures of the eleven seceded states as well.

Tennessee promptly ratified the amendment, and so was readmitted to the Union. The other ten refused, so Congress made ratification of the 14th amendment a condition for readmission. In 1868, six southern states relented, and ratified the amendment. They were then readmitted, just in time to vote in the 1868 elections. Georgia, Mississippi, Virginia, and Texas held out until 1870, by which time they were required to ratify the 15th amendment as well.

The 39th Congress had determined that the day after it expired in March 1867, the 40th Congress would convene, to minimize the time President Johnson would be left alone in Washington, and that month the Joint Committee on Reconstruction met to formulate policy for the South. Congressional Republicans then used their veto-proof majorities against the neo-Confederate Democrat regimes. They banned "peonage," or enslavement for debts, a measure Democrats soon learned to evade by instead sentencing blacks to lifetime servitude for intent to defraud creditors. Republicans also extended black suffrage to the federal territories. So accustomed did Congress become to maneuvering past President Johnson that its dominance over the presidency would last until Woodrow Wilson's first term.*

In a March 1867 speech to the House of Representatives, Thaddeus

---

* In 1885, Princeton's Professor Woodrow Wilson wrote a book criticizing congressional dominance.

Stevens again outlined his famous "40 acres and a mule" proposal, according to which the federal government should confiscate from the plantations belonging to rebels all lands more than 200 acres and give it to the former slaves. He calculated that this land, plus lands seized from the Confederate and state governments, would provide a million 40-acre farms, more than enough for each black family. In addition, the federal government would grant to each family, not a mule but $50, a sizable sum in those days. The rest of the confiscated land could be sold off at discounts to landless whites, and to pay war debts and soldiers' pensions. At the time, Radicals noted, the federal government was giving away farms in the Plains states, to immigrants even, but not providing for black citizens in the South.

This was one fight Stevens did not win. His proposal lost 126-37 in the House of Representatives. Democrats of course were opposed, but most Republicans did not like it either. They were uneasy about confiscating anybody's property, even as punishment for treason, especially in peacetime, and some pointed out that the Democrat state governments could easily evict the black farmers by imposing exorbitant property taxes on them. This objection could have been dealt with by providing that the federal government hold title for five or ten years and it would have been better to compensate the landowners with U.S. government bonds, but the main reason "40 acres and a mule" did not happen was that it came five years too late. Despite Lincoln's objections, land confiscation and redistribution should have been part of the wartime Confiscation Act of 1862.

Republicans, appalled by the suffering of blacks and white Unionists at the hands of the southern Democrats, concluded that they had tolerated Johnson's neo-Confederate state governments long enough. In March 1867, Congress overrode a presidential veto of the Radical Republicans' Reconstruction Act, introduced into the House of Representatives by Thaddeus Stevens.

The Act abolished Johnson's southern state governments and their militias, and just as Secretary of War Stanton's plan would have done, reimposed military rule on the South and divided the former Confederacy (except for Tennessee, readmitted in 1866) into five military districts. To avoid any further trouble from Andrew Johnson, army commander General Ulysses Grant, not the President, was empowered to appoint district commanders. Able to dismiss any state or local official, these five generals were to see to it that the southern states drafted new constitutions guaranteeing the constitutional rights of blacks and white Unionists. Unfortunately, this crackdown on the neo-Confederates came in 1867, not 1865.

All northerners who moved South after the war, even the missionaries, were known to rebel sympathizers as "carpetbaggers," after the cheap luggage they supposedly carried. Most were idealistic teachers and health workers employed by the Freedmen's Bureau or working on their own. Some southern whites did work with the new state governments or join our Republican Party. Usually, they were Unionists who had fought against the Confederacy or had remained loyal throughout the war in another way. Others, such as General Longstreet, were Confederate veterans who accepted the verdict of defeat. "Scalawag" was the neo-Confederate term for these groups of southern Americans.

The slavery system had nearly extinguished any entrepreneurial spirit, so northern business people were doing a tremendous service by filling this void. Abraham Lincoln would have been all for it, stressing as he did that we were one nation. Many of the iron, lumber, and other industries that would later flourish in the capital-starved South were started by northerners, who also strengthened commercial links with the North and with foreign countries. Some of the recent arrivals, to be sure, were opportunists, but by no stretching of the facts can northerners be considered to have exploited anyone as much as the plantation lords had exploited the slaves and poor whites before the war.

Northern politicians played no role at all in the South during the first two postwar years that southern Democrats were completely in charge, but they were prominent in the Reconstruction state governments set up in 1867. The bulk of the former ruling class was ineligible to hold public office and many other whites refused to participate in elections for these new governments, so the majority of state officials were northerners who had moved South after the war, elected mainly by black Republicans. Some were Union army veterans, including Joshua Chamberlain's first commanding officer, Adelbert Ames, who became the Governor of Mississippi.

Hundreds of blacks were elected to state government during Radical Reconstruction, but it would be an overstatement to say they controlled any administration. Ill-prepared or corrupt black politicians were much less common than white supremacist legend would have us believe. Most in fact were conscientious, and educated at least as well as the average southern white.

Every black person elected to Congress during Reconstruction was a Republican. Our country's first black Senator, former army chaplain Hiram Revels, was elected in 1870 to Jefferson Davis' old seat. Representative John Lynch, an ex-slave from Louisiana, later chaired the 1884 Republican National Convention. It was a speech seconding his nomination that marked 25-year old Theodore Roosevelt's entrance onto the national stage. Many blacks served on police forces or in the reconstructed state militias. To their credit, black state legislators or officials never sought vindictive measures against the white populace.

The first order of business for the Radical Reconstruction state governments was to repeal the black codes and all other vestiges of the slave system. Next, they drafted new constitutions guaranteeing the right to vote to blacks and also to the several million poor whites who had been unable to meet property qualifications imposed when the Democrats had been in power. Far superior to the documents they replaced, these constitutions had enforceable bills of rights, more efficient and impartial judiciaries, and fairer tax systems.

Bringing the Whig economic agenda to the South, Republican administrations spent heavily on railroads, roads, bridges, schools, and hospitals. Plantation lords complained about the higher taxes and mounting debts needed to fund these infrastructure projects because they could see little benefit for themselves. Ironically, improving transportation links to Appalachia and other hinterlands weakened our Republican Party in the South by facilitating the expansion of cotton-growing into these marginal areas.

Searching for a cause of their troubles other than themselves, southern Democrats accused the Republicans of all sorts of corruption, but none could accuse them of any crime approaching that of enslaving another person and whipping him into picking cotton. Legend also has it that bitterness over this Radical Reconstruction is why Republicans were so scarce in the South until recently, but of course slave interests knew since 1854 that our Party was their mortal enemy.

—⟫⟫⟩—

For three years, Republicans endured President Johnson's defense of the slave system. He had authorized neo-Confederate state governments in the South, opposed the 13th amendment, vetoed the Civil Rights Act, opposed the 14th amendment, disgraced his office, and failed to protect the emancipated slaves and white southern Unionists from rebel vengeance. By 1868, congressional Republicans had had quite enough of Andrew Johnson. That year he at last gave our Party a legal pretext for impeachment – it was not much of a pretext, but it would have to do.

In March 1867, Congress had passed over Johnson's veto a law forbidding the President from dismissing anyone from the Cabinet without Senate approval. The drafters of the Constitution had considered including this provision but decided against weakening the presidency so much. Nevertheless, the Tenure in Office Act was passed so that Johnson could not prevent Secretary of War Stanton from administering the Reconstruction Act which so closely resembled his own plan that he had presented to Abraham Lincoln. When in February 1868 President Johnson went ahead and dismissed Stanton anyway, the House of Representatives immediately impeached him for this and ten other alleged offenses, by a strictly party-line vote of 128 to 47.

The 75-year old Thaddeus Stevens was no longer able to walk and had to be carried to the Senate trial every day, so the lead prosecutor was Representative John Bingham, principal author of the 14th amendment. Chief Justice Chase, presiding over the trial, ruled consistently against the prosecution, though not for any devotion to some lofty principles. Through intermediaries, the Chief Justice was actively seeking the Democratic Party nomination for the fall election. Among the defenders of President Johnson, Clement Vallandigham figured prominently. During the trial, important southern Democrats conveyed to the President through his private secretary offers to raise troops in his defense. Johnson refused, but the offers do indicate the lengths to which many of his supporters were willing to go.

In the end, the May 1868 vote to remove Johnson fell one vote short of the required two-thirds, with all twelve Democrats backing their man. Seven Republican Senators also voted to acquit. Their refusal to rid the country of President Johnson is often described as a matter of principle, but a closer look reveals much more. According to the presidential succession law at the time, Johnson would have been replaced by the President pro tempore of the Senate, Ben Wade. The cantankerous Senator had just lost his reelection bid, and many Republicans were not eager to see him President for the last ten months of Johnson's term. Though radically against slavery, he held some other views unpopular with many in our Party. He was a "greenbacker," for instance, in favor of using inflation as way of easing debt burdens. Also, putting Wade in the White House might needlessly imperil the nomination of General Grant for President at the 1868 Republican National Convention less than a week later.

The seven Republican Senators who voted with Johnson were more inclined to tolerate white supremacist hegemony in the South than were the Radicals. Though every one campaigned for Grant in the fall, those who ran for reelection were all defeated. In 1872, their wing of our Party would split away as the Liberal Republicans, and twelve years after that became the "Mugwumps," who shifted over to the Democratic Party in support of Grover Cleveland.

Thaddeus Stevens died in August 1868, with Lydia Smith at his bedside. An honor guard of black Union army veterans stood at attention while his body lay in state at the Capitol. In an unprecedented tribute to their beloved leader, Republicans renominated him for another term, and in death he would win a nearly unanimous victory.

Once back in session, both houses of Congress would devote the entire first day to speeches in his honor. Some 20,000 people, half being freedmen from the South, attended his funeral in Lancaster. The chaplain of the U.S. Senate delivered this graveside eulogy: "God give to Vermont another son; Lancaster, another citizen; Pennsylvania, another statesman; the country, another patriot; the poor, another friend; the freedmen, another advocate; the race, another benefactor; and the world, another man like Thaddeus Stevens."

By 1868, the northern and southern wings of the Democratic Party had pulled themselves together to form a national party again. For President, though Johnson sought the nod, Democrats nominated Governor Horatio Seymour, New York's chief Copperhead during the Civil War. This was a man who had denounced the Emancipation Proclamation as "a proposal for butchery of women and children." In December 1860, he had written to the former Democrat President Franklin Pierce: "The Union is already gone...we have deferred cutting throats long enough... I should like to begin with the Abolitionists at once."

During this campaign, Democrats began referring to theirs as "The White Man's Party." Georges Clemenceau, the future premier of France, was a journalist in the United States at the time and observed: "Any Democrat who did not manage to hint in his speech that the negro is a degenerate gorilla, would be considered lacking in enthusiasm... That is the theme of all the Democratic speeches." The Democrat platform demanded that the southern states be returned to how they had been before the war, minus slavery as a legal institution. Ominously, it called for repeal of a law according the federal government authority over state militias during peacetime, which would have enabled southern states to rebuild their armed forces which had fought against Union troops less than four years earlier.

Republican convention delegates unanimously nominated the not very politically-inclined General Grant for President. To balance the moderate Grant, the vice presidential nominee was the Radical,

Speaker of the House Schuyler Colfax. His successor as Speaker would be Maine Representative James Blaine, whose contention with the faction of our Party headed by Roscoe Conkling would divide Republicans for the next twenty years.

Public opinion in the North having begun to turn against continuing the fruitless efforts to radically reconstruct the South, the Republican victory did not come easy. Grant won 214 to 80 in the Electoral College but only 53% to 47% in the popular vote. The half million blacks in the South able to vote for President for the first time provided Grant's margin of victory. Horatio Seymour narrowly carried his home state and won seven others, including Louisiana and Georgia. Reconstructed state governments in the South did their best to combat vote fraud, but Democrats managed to carry Georgia, for example, by keeping most blacks from voting. Voting in Appalachia was also significantly suppressed from 1866 levels.

White supremacist Democrats starting winning back control over southern state governments less than two years after passage of the Reconstruction Act of 1867. In Georgia, the administration of Governor and Klan leader John Gordon expelled all blacks from the state legislature, and Democrats took power in Texas and Tennessee as well. In Clinton, Mississippi, Democrats attacked a Republican event and killed several dozen black people. In Colfax, Louisiana, during the 1872 election campaign, after a three-week siege a white mob slaughtered more than 200 blacks defending the county courthouse from a Democrat takeover. With no fear of prosecution, another white mob slaughtered some 300 blacks in an attempt to oust a black Republican sheriff from office in Jackson, Mississippi in 1874.

By the mid-1870s, the number of murders committed by the Klan-Democrats was declining due to a shortage of potential Republican victims. As white Democrats regained control, most blacks were disenfranchised and the Republican vote dwindled to almost nothing. In many states, Democrats drew electoral district lines to concentrate blacks into just a few districts – just as they do today. Once back in power, the Democrats tended to repudiate debts of the Reconstruction state governments; so it was actually the northern bondholders, not southern taxpayers, who ended up paying for the capital improvement programs.

By 1876, only Florida, Louisiana, and South Carolina had Reconstruction governments. The establishment white Democrats who took control as Reconstruction state governments fell vowed to restore the South to the way it had been before the Civil War. They called themselves "Bourbons," after the kings of France who returned to power after Napoleon was overthrown. Most had fought in the Confederate army. William Oates, for example, who commanded the rebel regiment that attacked Joshua Chamberlain's famed 20th Maine at Little Round Top in the Battle of Gettysburg, was a seven-term U.S. Representative from Alabama before being elected Governor in 1894.

The power bases of the Bourbons were electoral districts with black majorities, where only the whites could vote. As industrialization came slowly to the South in the 1880s, the Bourbon ruling class kept themselves in power by exploiting the poor whites as well as the blacks. They made sure banks had little presence in the region, so that in a comparatively cashless economy farmers and factory workers could be controlled through contractual obligations directly to their employers. Bourbons opposed any hint of government regulation of their businesses, and kept state government expenditures to a bare minimum. They did away with much of the public school system that the Republicans had established and also closed down private schools staffed by northern teachers. By 1880, they had succeeded in holding down black literacy to 30%, compared to a national average of 80%. Literacy of southern whites suffered too. In Louisiana, for example, illiteracy among whites actually increased from 1880 to 1900.

In sharp contrast to the Lincoln administration, our nation's second Republican President did not appoint prominent Republicans to high office. Though a lion on the battlefield, having spent most of his adult life in the military, Ulysses Grant found politicians intimidating, and so surrounded himself with army buddies and nobodies whom he thought he could control. One notorious example, Secretary of War Belknap, who would be impeached for bribery, had previously been an obscure federal government employee along the frontier.

Grant himself was honest, but his administration earned its reputation for corruption. There was nothing particularly Republican that made it so, just that our Party was in office at a time when legal and ethical standards were yet to catch up with the new business methods then emerging, such as corporations, trusts, business consolidation, and long-distance coordination of activities. The worst scandal of the Grant administration involved a scheme to skim off millions of dollars from the federally-subsidized Union Pacific Railroad by arranging for the railroad to pay exorbitant fees to a sham construction company, Credit Mobilier. Vice President Colfax ended his promising career by accepting shares in Credit Mobilier. Corruption was not confined to the federal government. The first Democrat state treasurer of Louisiana after Reconstruction stole $1 million. And then there was "Boss" Tweed's Tammany Hall organization, which plundered a staggering $100 million from New York City taxpayers.

In an effort to counteract the Democrats' disenfranchising southern blacks, the Radical Republicans again introduced an amendment to the Constitution. The 15th amendment stated clearly: "The right of citizens of the United States to vote shall not be denied or abridged by the United States or by any State on account of race, color, or previous condition of servitude." The amendment was passed in February 1869, by the Congress elected in 1866, and was ratified in February 1870. Congressional authority to enforce this provision did not mean much once the Democrats were in control of the House of Representatives (1875) and the Senate (1879). Not until the Voting Rights Act of 1965 would the 15th amendment be enforced.

By 1872, seven years after the Civil War ended, many Republicans were ready to concede that the Democratic Party had defeated their efforts to extend the free market society to the South. They believed that after four years of warfare and then Reconstruction there was nothing more our Party could do to protect southern blacks from their white oppressors. They wanted civil service reform, lower tariffs, less government infrastructure spending, hard money (that is, not inflating the money supply with greenbacks), and other policies that required Democrat support to be enacted. Rejecting the Radical Republican focus on reconstructing the South, they opposed further attempts to build a racially-integrated Republican Party in the South. It was time, they said, to move on. In Congress, they voted with the Democrats to oppose the Enforcement Acts against the Ku Klux Klan, out of concern that military involvement in the southern political process might spread to the North and West.

In May 1872, calling themselves Liberal Republicans, these dissident Republicans met at a national convention in Cincinnati to nominate their own presidential candidate. They hoped that our Republican Party would then be forced to follow suit. Missouri Senator Carl Schurz headed the movement, but his German birth made him ineligible for the presidency. Delegates chose Horace Greeley. Upset about Grant administration corruption and favoring the new party's economic agenda, Charles Sumner endorsed the Liberal Republican standard-bearer, but soon regretted his decision. At their convention two months later, Democrats seized on what looked like a golden opportunity to defeat our Party by also nominating Greeley. Too late for the Liberal Republicans and the Democrats did it become apparent that Horace Greeley had become a crackpot. "Root, Hog, or Die!" was his advice to impoverished emancipated slaves. He had no political experience and made a terrible candidate.

Republicans renominated Grant for President. Replacing Colfax as the vice presidential nominee was another Radical, Senator Henry Wilson. While the 1872 Republican platform firmly backed equal rights for blacks and denounced Klan violence, Wilson lamented waning enthusiasm for the Radical cause. To mollify critics, the Republican Congress passed the Amnesty Act and reduced tariffs somewhat. Grant beat Greeley 55% to 44% in the popular vote, and 286 electoral votes to 80. In Congress, Republicans won even bigger, capturing 203 House seats to just 88 for the Democrats. Horace Greeley died a few weeks after the election.

The main event of Grant's second term was the Panic of 1873, the financial crash that abruptly ended the post-Civil War economic boom. The subsequent depression lasted five years, and the American people found themselves confronting a whole new batch of troublesome issues that had nothing to do with Reconstruction. In northern cities, urban workers began organizing unions to offset the growing power of the factory owners. Falling agricultural prices devastated the heavily-mortgaged farmers of the Midwest and Plains states. Miners out West complained when in 1873 Congress stopped the minting of silver coins in recognition of the fact that soaring output had lowered silver prices to the point that gold was the only practical monetary standard.

In the North, Democrat urban machines were smoothly integrating immigrants into their party during the depression, while many Americans believed that Republicans were devoting too much attention to Reconstruction and not enough to economic issues. In the South, Democrats were completing the eradication of our Republican Party. The 1874 congressional elections shifted the House of Representatives from 70% Republican to 62% Democrat. In a sign of their complete victory in the postwar South, Democrats in Tennessee elected Andrew Johnson to the Senate. One positive development was that as the Radical Republican movement faded, the Democratic Party toned down its anti-black rhetoric. By the mid-1870s, the Democrats' traditional Solid South-New York axis was putting an end to Republican majorities at the national level. The Reconstruction era ended in every meaningful sense in 1874, when the Democratic Party won a majority in the House of Representatives.

During the Civil War, Charles Sumner had been of great service to his country. As chairman of the Senate Foreign Relations Committee, it was he, not Secretary of State Seward, who was instrumental in keeping Britain and France from intervening on the Confederate side. His contacts developed the many years he lived in Europe proved especially useful after the Trent affair, in which a U.S. warship boarded a British ship to arrest two rebel envoys. A grateful Massachusetts legislature reelected Senator Sumner by a large majority in 1863 and nearly unanimously in 1869. Sumner's greatest achievement was his Civil Rights bill, which anticipated the 1964

Civil Rights Act by ninety years with its ban on racial discrimination in public accommodations.

Sumner had been pushing for the bill for years when he died in March 1874. The day he died, he told a former Attorney General: "You must take care of the civil rights bill – my bill, the civil rights bill – don't let it fail." A year later, Congress finally passed his Civil Rights Act. Though it came a decade too late to have much of an impact on the South, the law did eliminate many discriminatory practices in the North until the Supreme Court ruled it unconstitutional in 1883. The majority opinion declaring that 14th amendment guarantees did not extend to acts by private citizens and businesses was the reason the 1964 Civil Rights Act would have to be based more tenuously on the federal government's authority to regulate interstate commerce.

Chapter Seven

(1875-1916)

LINKS IN THE CHAIN OF EVENTS

The death of Charles Sumner cost our Republican Party its last effective spokesman for radically reconstructing the South into a free market society. By then, the Grant administration was easing up on its enforcement of constitutional rights protection for southern blacks. The white supremacist Democrats had won, the reasoning went, so what was the point of antagonizing them further with its ineffective federal government intervention on behalf of southern blacks? Despite our Party's best efforts to build a racially integrated political organization in the South, most whites refused to have anything to do with the Republicans as long as they defended the blacks, and they certainly were not going to sit down with black people at political meetings or listen to their speeches.

It was wishful thinking, but some Republicans thought that per- haps advocacy for blacks was counterproductive. They hoped that many southern whites might abandon the Democratic Party if the Republicans stopped pressing for racial equality.

For several decades after the Civil War, southern blacks revered our Party for having fought to save the Union and free the slaves, and local Republican social clubs, where permitted to exist, were an important part of their lives. They knew that even among Democrats who stayed loyal, most opposed emancipation. Those too young to remember the war, however, grew up with little sentimentality for our Party, and all southern blacks were angered by various Republican attempts to build a party organization in the South without their participation. Over time, our Party's failure to provide black Americans with land or to protect them from Democrats weakened their devotion to the Republicans just as our Party was turning away from its devotion to them.

By the late 1870s, the Republican vote in the South had declined from 20-40% to single digits. At the national level, however, convention delegates continued to be allocated on a basis more proportional to overall population, so most Republican delegates from southern states came to represent no one except the party bosses who appointed them. This concentration of political power in the hands of Republican Party bosses would shape national politics into the Taft administration and beyond. Another enormous implication of the failure to reconstruct the South was the discrediting of federal government measures on behalf of individuals. As industrialization progressed in the North, politicians remembered just how ineffectual federal government protection of southern blacks had been.

White supremacy was a common campaign promise of Democrat candidates in the South. No matter what their political views, southern whites stayed loyal to the Democratic Party, out of fear that if "The White Man's Party" lost power, blacks might be able to reenter the political process. Even a "yellow dog," so the saying went, would get a Democrat's vote before a white Republican or a black person would. Return of the South's prewar one-party system made the Democratic Party powerful nationwide, because to win the presidency or a congressional majority, a decent showing in the North and West was all the additional help the Democrats required.

⁂

In 1876, the Democratic Party expected to win the White House, and once again, linking New York with the Solid South seemed to be the way to do it. The Democrat presidential candidate was another New York Governor, Samuel Tilden, who, unlike Seymour, was not tainted by collaboration with the Confederates. Tilden had a reputation as a corruption-fighting reformer, which appealed to an electorate tired of the Grant administration's corruption scandals. President Grant backed the Radical leader Roscoe Conkling, but Republicans instead nominated Ohio Governor Rutherford Hayes for President. His wartime service as a Union general made him acceptable to the Radicals, while his record as Governor impressed Carl Schurz and most other Liberal Republicans, who had largely returned to our Party. For the third time in a row, a Radical Republican, New York's Representative William Wheeler, was named as the presidential candidate's running mate.

By 1876, Reconstruction had been over for several years in most areas of the South; and the monetary system, the tariff, and civil service reform had replaced the North-South divide as the main election issues. Before then, neither of the two major political parties had ever mentioned the rights of women, but the 1876 Republican platform called for more progress in that regard. Hayes was on record in favor of women voting, as they were already doing in several territories in the West. In another first for either party, a woman addressed the Republican National Convention. Democrats made no mention of women at all in their campaign. An issue closely linked to the early women's movement, prohibition, began to be debated seriously at the national level.

There were actually few policy differences between Hayes and Tilden, so the main theme of our Party's campaign was contrasting the patriotism of Republicans during the Civil War with the sorry record of perfidious Democrats. "Waving the bloody shirt" later became a metaphor for frank appeals to war veterans, but in 1876 Republicans did it literally, displaying Union army uniforms stained with blood from war wounds. At the convention that year, one speaker declared: "Every man that shot Union soldiers was a Democrat! The man that assassinated Lincoln was a Democrat! Soldiers, every scar you have got on your heroic bodies was given you by a Democrat!" True, true, and true – but would this approach sway many voters eleven years after the war? Referring to more recent outrages, sometimes the bloody shirt was of a southern Republican killed or whipped by the Ku Klux Klan.

Throughout the South, the Democrats' standard operating procedure was to prevent most blacks and many white Republicans from voting. In some instances where Klan violence proved insufficiently intimidating, a public ceremony was made of burning Republican ballots before they were counted. Vote totals recorded in areas which had been Unionist strongholds were down significantly from the already-low numbers from previous years. By 1876, of the eleven former Confederate states only in Florida, Louisiana, and South Carolina were there Republican Governors. In those three states, while Republican administrations could do little to ensure that their supporters could vote, they did prevent most of the ballot box-stuffing perpetrated by Democrats in neighboring states.

For the presidential election that year, both Republicans and Democrats claimed victory in the three states. The Democrats pointed to their figures showing small majorities for Tilden. Republicans countered by noting that almost no blacks had been allowed to vote there and that Hayes would have carried the states easily had they been allowed to do so. Not until two days before President Grant left office did a commission set up by Congress decide the dispute in favor of Hayes. Tellingly, the 1880 Democratic platform accused the Republicans of having stolen the electoral votes of only two disputed southern states, tacitly admitting that Hayes had indeed won at least one of the three in question four years earlier.

Tilden received some 260,000 more popular votes nationwide, but with the three disputed states in the Republican column Hayes won 185 to 184 in the Electoral College. This would be the last time for decades that our Party won a former Confederate state. In the House of Representatives, Democrats lost some ground but held onto their majority, and in the Senate, Democrats came to within three seats of the Republicans.

Another civil war might easily have broken out in 1876, especially if the Democratic Party had previously succeeded in setting up state militias under neo-Confederate control. In fact, the 1880 Democratic Party platform claimed that the party had accepted Hayes as President only to avert civil war. Governor Tilden, however, was unwilling to go that far. A deal was struck. Hayes would become President in return for recognition of Democrat claimants as Governors of Florida, Louisiana, and South Carolina. Hayes also agreed to appoint a former rebel to the Cabinet. So anxious was the new President to conciliate the South, he even considered naming Confederate General Joseph Johnston as Secretary of War.

The few federal troops left in the South were withdrawn from occupation duty, and the federal government discontinued its role as protector of the constitutional rights of southern blacks. Of course, if Tilden had become President, this would have happened anyway. Further gestures toward foes of the Radical Republicans included naming Andrew Johnson's last Attorney General as Secretary of State and the Liberal Republican, Carl Schurz, as Secretary of the Interior. The President did appoint Frederick Douglass U.S. Marshall for the District of Columbia. In 1879, faced with eighteen former Confederate generals in the Senate, Hayes had to veto several bills passed by the Democrats to repeal some Enforcement Act measures.

Once the Republicans gave up hope of protecting southern blacks from the Democrats, the Radical Republicans no longer had an issue. After the Reconstruction era, they dropped the label "Radical" in favor of "Stalwart," to emphasize their commitment to our Party, in contrast with the Liberal Republicans. What survived of their movement were their personal allegiances and dependence on federal patronage for advancing Republican policies, a practice learned from the master of patronage, Abraham Lincoln. The leader of the Stalwarts was New York's Roscoe Conkling, protégé of Lincoln and Thaddeus Stevens. Elected to the Senate in 1867, Conkling turned down Grant's offer to replace Chase as Chief Justice in 1873, preferring instead to exercise political power.

No longer ideological, the Stalwarts viewed politics solely as a means of winning and keeping power. Key to this was control over the federal bureaucracy, so they adamantly opposed any effort to weaken their power by establishing an independent civil service or reducing government spending. They also became firm proponents of a high tariff, which generated campaign contributions from protected industries and afforded them plenty of opportunity to boost their power by playing off one group seeking favors against another. They valued party loyalty above all else, and had a knee-jerk reaction against just about any reform.

Does this resemble any political movement we know today? Yes, there is a strong parallel between the Stalwarts and another group which held on to power long after its cause was gone. In the same way that the Radicals became the Stalwarts, the 1960s civil rights movement degenerated into a wing of the reactionary and corrupt Democratic Party we know today. Early accomplishments convinced both groups that whatever was best for themselves was best for the country. For example, just as the Stalwarts benefited from a high tariff, today's Democrats appreciate a complex tax code as their font of power. We see the same obsession with maintaining themselves in power through control over the federal bureaucracy and other patronage, the same self-righteousness lingering past their time of righteousness, that irritatingly brazen "My party (and President), right or wrong" solidarity especially when they know they are wrong.

Now we come to an issue which, along with the tariff, succeeded ratification of the Constitution, the Bank of the United States, slavery in the territories, the Civil War, and then Reconstruction as the defining issue of the day. For the rest of the 19th century, people argued for and against "the free coinage of silver," just as much as we Americans today debate health care or Social Security. It all started with the greenbacks that the U.S. Government used to finance the Civil War. In 1867, George Pendleton, the Democrats' former vice presidential candidate, proposed redeeming some war bonds with greenbacks (that is, paper money) instead of paying them off in gold. More paper money would cause inflation, which be to the advantage of farmers who had borrowed money at fixed rates.

The issue cut across party lines and would one day cause a major realignment of the electorate between the two major parties. Some Democrats, including standard-bearer Horatio Seymour, were not thrilled about it, but Pendleton's greenback plan became part of the

1868 Democratic Party platform. Even though our Party had come up with the greenback idea in the first place, most Republicans regarded redeeming the Civil War bonds in gold as a sacred obligation. In 1875, Congress put the country on the gold standard with a law requiring that within four years the federal government begin redeeming the greenbacks with gold. As the Hayes administration put the law into practice, the money supply contracted and exports of agricultural and other products declined precipitously.

First calling themselves the Independent Party in 1876, the Greenback Party was the only significant third party to emerge since our Republican Party was founded in 1854. The Greenbackers wanted paper money to completely replace gold and silver-backed currency. They elected fifteen Representatives to Congress in 1878, giving them the balance of power in the House during the second half of Hayes' term. The party began to fade two years later as prosperity returned, the price level rose, and as so often happens with third parties, the major parties shifted their positions to accommodate third-party backers. Within a few years, the greenback issue would be reborn as the free (that is, unlimited) coinage of silver, a policy which combined increasing the money supply to help farmers of the Plains states with boosting demand for silver as a means of assisting the miners of the Rocky Mountains.

His party having won control of the House, Democrat Representative Richard Bland introduced a bill to require the government to mint sixteen silver dollars for every gold one. The Republican majority in the Senate, led in this instance by Iowa's William Allison, managed to weaken the bill considerably, retaining the 16:1 ratio but replacing the free coinage of silver with a sharp limit on the number of silver dollars to be minted. The Bland-Allison Act was passed over President Hayes' veto in 1878. Initially, there was no problem, but requiring the federal government to redeem coins made of plentiful silver with scarce gold set a terrible precedent with disastrous consequences later on.

Somewhere about halfway on the ideological spectrum between Conkling's Stalwarts and Schurz's Liberal Republicans were the Half-Breeds, as supporters of James Blaine were known. The 1880 Republican National Convention deadlocked between Blaine, a Senator since 1876, and Grant, whom the Stalwarts wanted for a third term. The popular Rutherford Hayes could easily have been nominated and elected to a second term, but he had promised during his campaign to serve only one. Falling ill right before the convention weakened Blaine's prospects and Grant's record had been less than stellar, so delegates turned to a dark horse candidate. Abraham Lincoln's son, Robert,* was considered, as was Treasury Secretary John Sherman.

After sixteen ballots, the convention nominated Ohio's Senator-elect James Garfield, Sherman's campaign manager. During the Civil War, Garfield had been chief of staff to the general who had earlier commanded Rutherford Hayes' regiment. Elected to the House of Representatives in 1863, he was at first a Radical close to Salmon Chase but later backed Blaine's more moderate approach to Reconstruction. To balance one of Blaine's Half-Breeds at the top of the ticket, for Vice President Republicans nominated one of Conkling's Stalwarts, Chester Arthur.

As late as 1880, there was still considerable friction among northern Democrats between those who had been collaborated with the Confederates and those who had opposed them. That year, the party sought to erase its treasonous reputation by uniting behind Union army hero Winfield Hancock, whose bias toward the white supremacists during Reconstruction made him acceptable to southern Democrats. On a states rights platform, Hancock carried every former slave state plus California, Nevada and New Jersey, but lost to James Garfield. In the popular vote, Garfield won by fewer than 10,000 votes nationwide, but his margin in the Electoral College was 214-155. The 300,000 votes cast for the Greenback Party had cost the

---

* He would be Secretary of War during the next administration and later, ambassador to Britain.

Democrats the presidential election as well as their majority in the House of Representatives.

Appointed Collector of Customs for the Port of New York several years before, a post which gave him vast abilities for patronage and fundraising, Arthur had been dismissed by President Hayes for neglecting his official duties. To replace Arthur, Hayes nominated Theodore Roosevelt Sr., father of the future President, without first checking with Roscoe Conkling. Senator Conkling was so angry at this challenge that he resigned from the Senate in protest. He expected the New York legislature to reelect him in triumph, but legislators chose otherwise, and that was the end of Roscoe Conkling's political career. Nonetheless, the Stalwarts ensured that Roosevelt lost his bid for Senate confirmation, a stressful ordeal blamed for his death soon thereafter. Revulsion at this vindictive cronyism would shape the political beliefs of Theodore Roosevelt Jr., making him an early proponent of civil service reform and leading him on the path toward more progressive policies.

The Stalwarts fell into further disrepute when in July 1881 a deranged man shot President Garfield, shouting "I am a Stalwart! Arthur is now President!" There was no evidence that the murderer had links to any politician or political movement, but the new President, Chester Arthur, was shocked into reversing many of his Stalwart positions. He became a fervent supporter of civil service reform and signed George Pendleton's Civil Service Reform Act of 1883.

The other significant development during Arthur's presidency was the grave threat to the economy posed by the enormous federal government surpluses. The tariff had been pouring so much revenue into the Treasury that the money supply was shrinking. Worse, since national banks had to hold a certain portion of their capital in the form of U.S. Treasury bonds, extinguishing the federal government debt would in effect shatter the banking system. Reducing the surplus by cutting the tariff was unacceptable to Washington power-brokers (as cutting taxes is to most of their modern-day counterparts), so Congress looked around for something to spend money on in a big way. The project of choice was building an all-steel navy. The economy was saved, and the United States took its first step toward becoming a world power.

The Democrats regained a large majority in the House of Representatives in 1882 and looked to win the presidency for the first time since 1856. In 1884, their candidate was once again a Governor of New York, Grover Cleveland, who had recently won the office by defeating Chester Arthur's Treasury Secretary in a direct repudiation of Republican economic policy.

Our Party nominated James Blaine, and to balance this professional politician gave second place on the ticket to a former general who served under Ulysses Grant's command, Illinois Representative John Logan, head of the Union army veterans organization and creator of Memorial Day. The Republican platform called for hard money (that is, no more greenbacks), regulation of the railroads, and an 8-hour work day. Our Party agreed to lower the tariff somewhat, but not as much as the Democrats wanted. Though he was never accused of any specific crime, Blaine suffered from a reputation for corruption. Democrats gleefully reprinted a questionable letter of his that concluded: "Burn this letter."

Cleveland beat Blaine by only 23,000 votes nationwide, and won in the Electoral College only by carrying his native New York state. This he did by just 1047 votes. Shortly before the election, Blaine lost thousands of Catholic voters there by failing to disavow a remark by a speaker at a dinner he was attending who said the Democratic Party was the party of "Rum, Romanism, and Rebellion." For the first time ever, blacks voted Democrat in appreciable numbers, as they too turned to other issues besides Reconstruction.

Third parties also bled away Republican support. The Greenback Party ran Ben Butler, the former Union army general and Radical, while the new Prohibition Party attracted voters disappointed with the intemperate Senator Blaine. The worst blow to the Blaine campaign was the desertion to the Democrats by Carl Schurz and his Liberal Republicans. Known as the Mugwumps, they were reformers unhappy that the

Republicans had nominated an old-line politico such as Blaine. Their idealism clouded their judgment about the Democrats, as most were also of the opinion that southern blacks might benefit if Republicans abandoned them entirely – supposedly, southern whites then might not feel as threatened and might not oppress them quite so much.

As President, Cleveland disregarded Mugwump pleas, and replaced most Republican office-holders with Democrats. He opposed federal aid to drought-stricken farmers: "Federal aid in such cases encourages the expectation of paternal care on the part of the government and weakens the sturdiness of our national character." A hard money Democrat, Cleveland did what he could to counter the Bland-Allison Act.

For twenty years, Republican administrations had been spending billions of dollars on pensions to Union veterans of the Civil War as a way of ensuring their support. Such payments would eventually far exceed the actual cost of the war and amount to more than a quarter of the federal government budget. President Cleveland vetoed many bills to increase these pensions, preferring to spend federal government surpluses on the steel navy begun under his predecessor. In any case, this Republican vote-getting mechanism had to come to an end, because unlike the Democrats' later ploy with Social Security payments, as the original Civil War pensioners died off they could not, of course, be replaced by newborn pensioners. The next Republican administration would enact a big increase in the Union military pensions to spend another federal government surplus.

In 1884, the Democrats at last accepted the Whig internal improvements policy, and a centerpiece of their campaign was the promise of lower tariffs. Their party platform even included this gem: "We are opposed to all propositions which upon any pretext would convert the General Government into a machine for collecting taxes to be distributed among the States, or the citizens thereof." Just as today's Democratic Party thrives off the federal government's wealth transfer schemes, the late 19th-century Republicans were doing the same with the pensions to Union veterans and with tariffs, which transfer wealth from consumers to protected producers.

By Cleveland's first term, the nation's attention was drawn to the problem presented by the railroads' strong grip on the economy, especially in the West. Early on, farmers saw railroads as a godsend, enabling them to get their crops to market. Over time, as farmers became dependent on the railroads, often on a single line of track with no competition, the railroads were able to charge very high rates. These powerful businesses also exerted tremendous influence over state legislatures, and in many states had considerable say in their selection of U.S. Senators. There was no constitutional impediment to state governments regulating railroads within their borders – Illinois had begun doing so a decade earlier – but until the Supreme Court reversed itself in 1886 the federal government was unable to regulate railroads using its interstate commerce authority.

The first federal regulatory agency, the Steamboat Inspection Service, had been set up in 1838, but not until 1887 would federal government regulation have an impact on the general economy. That was the year Congress passed the Interstate Commerce Act, in order to regulate the railroads. Promoting competition, not control for its own sake, was the original purpose, but the Interstate Commerce Commission soon fell under the control of the railroad and later the trucking industries it attempted to regulate. The ICC became a powerful force against competition, and not until the 1990s would Congress be able to abolish this tool of monopolist interests.

Ironically, around this time, the 14th amendment began to be used to strike down many state and local economic regulations as unconstitutional infringements of the right to due process. Before then, there would have been no basis for mounting a constitutional challenge – except for obstructing interstate commerce – to just about any economic regulation a state government might wish to impose, such as the nation's first worker protection laws, enacted by Massachusetts in 1874. Now, any such regulation could be challenged as a violation of somebody's right to due process, a quandary federal courts later resolved by recognizing that government regulations could be constitutional if due process is followed in a nebulously-defined "substantive" way.

For the 1888 elections, Carl Schurz returned to the Republican camp, but most of the other Mugwumps stayed with the Democrats permanently. Cleveland was renominated, though he had angered many Union army veterans by returning captured Confederate battle flags to the southern states. Republicans nominated Indiana Senator Benjamin Harrison, a grandson of President William Harrison, who had commanded a Union regiment during the Civil War. He was also an ally of James Blaine. Harrison campaigned for a higher tariff and for "demonetizing" silver. Blacks were almost completely shut out of the political process in the South by then, and Republican references to their plight trailed away to nothing in the 1888 campaign.

Winning the presidency had become a difficult proposition for the Republicans given the Democrats' Solid South, which in 1888 accounted for 156 electoral votes out of the 201 needed to win. A successful Republican presidential candidate would have to win more than 80% of the electoral votes everywhere else in the country. To attract voters in crucial New York, our Party's vice presidential nominee was New York's former Representative and ambassador to France, Levi Morton. In the popular vote, Harrison actually received 100,000 fewer votes than Cleveland, but Harrison won New York and so the presidency, by 233 to 168 in the Electoral College.

Blaine became President Harrison's Secretary of State. Republicans also won control of both houses of Congress. It was around this time that Republicans began to refer to ours as "The Grand Old Party" in recognition of the return of our Party to power. Since Lincoln's day, "Republican" had been virtually synonymous with "Patriot," but as the Civil War generation aged and millions of immigrants arrived with no memory of the war, popular allegiance in the North to "the Party of Lincoln" began to wane. Nonetheless, the GOP retained its dominance over national politics until the Franklin Roosevelt administration.

In those days, political parties were a mechanism for social integration to an extent far greater than they are now. People often wore

Republican or Democrat badges and watch chains, and would belong to various organizations sponsored by one or the other party. Even the poorest person could feel a bond with the high and mighty, who in turn would actively solicit his support.

Unlike today, vote fraud then was not an entirely Democratic Party phenomenon. There was no secret ballot until the late 1880s, and voters would cast their votes publicly. The term "party ticket" dates from this period. Before then, voters usually wrote their preferences on an ordinary piece of paper. As secret balloting was introduced, the political parties supplied their supporters with pieces of paper, or tickets, on which were already printed "the straight party ticket," which could then be dropped in the ballot box. Pre-printed official ballots were later introduced and then voting machines replaced paper ballots, but the concept of "the ticket" endures.

The Republicans, in control of both houses of Congress for the first two years of Harrison's presidency, had little inclination to do much of anything except increase pensions for Union veterans and implement other spending programs to entrench their power, with the result that the federal government surplus turned into a deficit. In 1890, the chairman of the House Ways and Means Committee, William McKinley, drafted the Tariff Act of 1890, which boosted tariffs from an average 38% to 50%, so high in fact that revenues from the tariff actually declined.

To secure enough votes in the West for the higher tariff, Republicans replaced the Bland-Allison Act with the Sherman Silver Purchase Act of 1890, as a concession to the "free silver" sentiment prevalent in that region. The Act made national bank notes, the legal tender currency, redeemable in either silver or gold. Naturally, people preferred gold over silver. Government gold reserves plummeted, as did confidence in the creditworthiness of the federal government, both at home and abroad. The Silver Purchase Act was repealed in Cleveland's second term, but not before gold reserves were so low that the federal government had to buy gold from a consortium of New York banks at an exorbitant premium. This vulnerability of federal government finances would lead to the creation of the Federal Reserve System.

The Harrison administration enacted the Sherman Anti-Trust Act of 1890, which prohibited any "restraint of trade" of interstate commerce. Terms were undefined and the law proved unenforceable, but the precedent had been set for subsequent measures against monopolies and other unfair business practices. Another of President Harrison's more positive moves was to appoint a young Theodore Roosevelt Jr. to the U.S. Civil Service Commission in 1889.

In 1890, the Republican majority in the House passed a Federal Elections Bill intended to guarantee the right of southern blacks and also southern white Republicans to vote in federal elections. Federal election supervisors were to oversee registration and voting in federal elections nationwide, and federal courts were to be empowered to enforce compliance. Acting at the direction of the Republican congressional caucus, the drafter of the legislation was Massachusetts Representative Henry Cabot Lodge. With all House Republicans voting for it and all House Democrats voting against, the bill passed the House of Representatives but was blocked in the southern Democrat-dominated Senate.

This measure was our Party's – and the nation's – last effort to implement the Radical Republicans' Reconstruction program until the 1960s. The constitutional rights of black Americans would not resurface as a national issue until the Brown v. Board of Education decision in 1954. Had it become law, the Federal Election Act would probably have been overturned by the Supreme Court. Henry Cabot Lodge was elected to the Senate in 1893 and eventually became Majority Leader. His grandson, Henry Cabot Lodge Jr., would be Richard Nixon's running mate in 1960.

In reaction to the higher tariff, the Federal Elections Bill, and the economic uncertainty stemming from the Silver Purchase Act, Republicans were clobbered in the 1890 midterm congressional elections. The House of Representatives went from 52% Republican to just 26%, while the Democrats won a two-thirds majority. William McKinley lost his House seat, but was elected Governor of Ohio the next year. Only the admission of six largely Republican states in the West preserved Republican control of the Senate.

Ever since the relatively issue-less 1876 election campaign, the major parties were ignoring the real issues of the day. Having moved past Reconstruction, the Republican and Democratic parties argued endlessly about tariff rates for particular products and the proper ratio between gold and silver coins, but had little to say about problems arising from the adjustment to a rapidly industrializing society. Often, Congress debated hardly anything but the tariff for weeks at a time.

Out of this void emerged Farmers Alliances and the Grange, farmers organizations which would later form the nucleus of the Populist Party. Squeezed between high railroad freight charges and low crop prices, farmers demanded that the government somehow solve both these problems. An East-West political divide was opening up, largely supplanting the century-old North-South fault line. In the West, people tended to be greenbackers (and later "free silverites"), while most easterners were for hard money.

Another example of the growing need for political realignment was an 1873 bill for federal regulation of the railroads; western and southern Democrats and Republicans were for it, and eastern and northern Democrats and Republicans were opposed. Urban workers also began to organize. In 1869, an incipient union movement arose, the Knights of Labor, followed by the American Federation of Labor in 1881.

In the second half of the 19th century, prices fell as often as they rose. This deflation was due to burgeoning production in the factories, mines, and farms. Economic growth was particularly hard on the farmers. Demand seemed limitless for manufactured goods, but after all, people could eat only so much food. Crop prices fell relentlessly. Blind to such harsh economic reality, many farmers saw their panacea to be a greater supply of money to match the greater supply of goods.

At a meeting of various farmers organizations held in Cincinnati in 1891, a new political party was born, the People's, or Populist, Party. Women figured prominently in the Populist movement, and it was a female Populist who said famously: "What you farmers have to do is to raise less corn and more Hell." They appealed to factory workers to join them, but city-dwellers felt they did not have much in common with the farmers. The Knights of Labor and the American

Federation of Labor refused to ally themselves with the Populist Party, preferring to remain independent of any political organization.

Composed mainly of dissident Democrats upset by their former party's hard money stance, the Populists were prone to anti-Catholic, anti-Jewish, and anti-immigrant rants. The party held its first national convention in Omaha and nominated the former Greenback standard-bearer, former Union army general James Weaver, as their presidential candidate for the 1892 election. Unfortunately for their cause, they concentrated on the free coinage of silver to the detriment of the rest of their reform agenda, which included a graduated income tax; direct election of Senators; government ownership of the railroads, telephones, and telegraphs; breakup of monopolies; and an 8-hour workday.

While in the North the Populists formed a separate political party, southern populists remained Democrats, for fear of allowing blacks and the Republican Party back into the political process. In the South, the populist movement turned into a battle with the Bourbon establishment for control of the Democratic Party. Since black people did not at all threaten their dominance, Bourbon leaders had not gone out of their way to oppress them, aside from keeping most from voting. As a result, some southern blacks began to prosper by the 1880s, and a few even made it into the middle class.

This comparatively mild interregnum ended when political power was won by populist leaders representing the poor whites, who regarded prosperous blacks as competitors and enemies. Typical of the new generation of southern leaders were nasty demagogues such as South Carolina Governor "Pitchfork" Ben Tillman, Mississippi Governor James Vardaman, and Georgia Representative Tom Watson.

The Jim Crow laws, named for a popular minstrel character of the day, were enacted during this period of southern populist ascendancy. There had been some racial segregation before, but these laws made it official and in some ways were harsher than the black codes. In some southern states, Jim Crow went so far that in court black witnesses had to swear on separate Bibles. The purpose of these laws was to keep blacks down economically and socially, so that poor whites could have other people to look down on.

In the 1880s, the Interstate Commerce Commission ruled that any racially segregated facilities in trains had to be equal. This was actually intended as a step up for blacks, since facilities in the South were already segregated and the ones for black people were terrible, but the effect was to legitimize Jim Crow. The Supreme Courts' infamous Plessy v. Ferguson decision of 1896, during Cleveland's second term, gave constitutional sanction to "separate-but-equal."

Lynchings became more numerous than at any time since right after the Civil War, and often were public spectacles of black people being tortured, mutilated, and burned alive. Not being deferential enough to the lowliest white, no matter how illiterate or uncultured, could get a black person killed. White men in the South said they were against blacks and whites mixing socially, but what they really were against was black men having sex with white women, as most were all for the reverse. Another consequence during the Jim Crow era of the failure to radically reconstruct the South was that the lynching mania began to infect northern states too.

Not satisfied with unofficial measures to prevent as many blacks as possible from voting, southern populist state governments enacted outright legal bans. The new constitution of Mississippi effectively disenfranchised blacks in 1890, followed by Georgia, South Carolina, Louisiana, and Alabama. They got around the Radical Republicans' 15th amendment with voter registration trickery, legal reprisals, all-white primaries, poll taxes, literacy tests, and other devices. At the turn of the century, some southern populists even advocated repeal of the 15th amendment. By 1900, virtually no blacks could vote in the South, a violation of the Radical Republican amendments which the Supreme Court upheld on various technicalities.

The Democrats enabled illiterate whites to vote, despite the literacy tests, by providing that any man could vote whose grandfather had been eligible to vote – the origin of the term "grandfather clause." There were at the time literacy tests for voting in many northern states as well; the difference in the South was that the tests provided the Democratic Party with added incentive to prevent black people from being educated. The literacy rate for blacks in the North improved from 20% in 1870 to 55% in 1900, but decreased in the South. Reacting to this tragedy, the Republican Congress passed a law in 1890 for a federal government program to establish schools to educate southern black children, to which Democrat Governor Vardaman said: "What the North is sending South is not money, but dynamite; this education is ruining our Negroes. They're demanding equality."

Booker T. Washington and W.E.B. Du Bois exemplified the varying ways in which blacks responded to Jim Crow. Both men were educated at institutions of higher learning established by Radical Republicans after the Civil War, Washington at the Hampton Institute and Du Bois at Fisk University. Washington, an admirer of Frederick Douglass, emphasized vocational training for blacks in order to prepare them to be better farmers and artisans. The Tuskegee Institute, which he founded, rejected the curriculum of northern schools – Latin, geometry, and such – as absurdly unsuited to southern reality. His bottom-up approach advocated incremental personal advancement for all blacks through self-improvement and moral rigor.

As a southerner, Washington recognized the futility of challenging the white supremacist Democrats, that struggling for political rights was not only pointless but could be suicidal. In 1895, at the height of the lynching mania, he gave an important speech that advocated acceptance of Jim Crow restrictions on southern blacks' political rights as the price of securing their social autonomy. Modern readers may sneer at Washington's acquiescence unless they understand that his strategy was calculated so as not to provoke a devastating reaction by southern whites, at a time when a black person could be lynched for as little as looking a white person in the eye.

Though at the time he congratulated Washington for his speech, the northern-born Du Bois broke with him in 1903. He and many other prominent black leaders shifted from this gradualist approach out of concern that it was cementing an inferior status for blacks. In contrast to Washington's emphasis on primary and secondary education, Du Bois advocated his "Talented Tenth" strategy to create an educated southern black elite which could be the vanguard for political agitation, as impossible as that would have been in the Jim Crow South, where a 1960s-style protest march, say, would have resulted in the mass slaughter of the demonstrators, followed by hangings of whatever leaders were left to be hunted down. Du Bois was one of the founders of the northern-dominated National Association for the Advancement of Colored People, which was established in 1910. Over the years, the NAACP would mount many successful legal challenges to illegal and unconstitutional racial discrimination.

In the 1892 rematch between Harrison and Cleveland, Republicans ran another New Yorker, Whitelaw Reid, owner of Greeley's New York Tribune and former ambassador to France, for Vice President, while the Democrat running mate was former Illinois Representative Adlai Stevenson, grandfather of the 1952 and 1956 Democratic Party presidential nominee. The Republican platform once again demanded voting rights for southern blacks and condemned inhuman "Southern Outrages" against them.

Former President Cleveland defeated the Republican incumbent 46% to 43% in the popular vote and 227 to 145 in the all-important Electoral College. Democrats won majorities in both houses of Congress. For the first time since before the Civil War, a third party won electoral votes; Weaver, the Populist Party nominee, received 9% of the vote and garnered 22 electoral votes in the western states. For a time, there would be several Populist Senators and Representatives, as well as three Governors.

Returned to the White House, President Cleveland called Congress into special session to repeal the Silver Purchase Act, angering Democrats in the western mining states, but the damage was already done. A run on gold reserves was still underway, and capital was fleeing abroad. The stock market crashed a month after the second Cleveland administration took office, and there was a wave of bank failures. Financial trouble overseas compounded this disaster, and the U.S. economy would remain in a depression from 1893 to 1896. Though it did not last as long as the Great Depression, farm prices plunged, unemployment soared, and businesses collapsed just as would occur less than forty years later. In contrast to the 1930s, there was no government relief at either the state or federal level and some people actually starved to death. President Cleveland refused to consider any federal government relief measures, even spending projects proposed by Republicans.

In 1894, Cleveland sent in the army to crush a widespread railroad workers strike which started when the Pullman company in Chicago slashed wages at the depth of the depression. The Governor of Illinois, Democrat John Altgeld, protested that such federal intervention was unconstitutional since he did not request it, but the President used the pretext of keeping the U.S. mails going, even though the strikers were careful not to interfere with mail trains. Around this time, the federal government began using court injunctions – as opposed to prosecutions and jury trials – as a way of forcing compliance with government edicts.

The Democrat majority in Congress reduced tariffs in 1894, and to make up for the lost revenue, reestablished a federal income tax. The Supreme Court struck it down the following year, citing the constitutional provision in effect at the time that direct federal taxes must be levied proportionately to the population. This logic could just as easily have been used against the previous federal income tax, but the Supreme Court of the 1860s had not dared rule against a law with which the federal government was financing the Union war effort. Just four years after the Democrats won their two-thirds majority in the House of Representative, the 1894 midterm elections held during the economic depression handed the Republicans a two-thirds majority in the House and a five-seat edge in the Senate. Our Party expected to win the presidential election in 1896.

<hr />

The Democratic Party that year was sharply divided between Cleveland's "hard money" faction and those Democrats who leaned toward the Populist Party's inflationary "free silver" policy. Four years before, positioning themselves between the Republicans and the Populists had brought victory, but in 1896 the Democrats veered toward the Populists and thereby lost the election. What happened was, convention delegates handed the presidential nomination to 36-year old William Jennings Bryan, a former Representative from Nebraska, after he delivered an eloquent speech in favor of the free coinage of silver, concluding: "You shall not crucify mankind upon a Cross of Gold."

Such magnificent rhetoric was necessary to obscure the fact that the free silver position did not make much sense. A lack of silver coins was not the reason for bad times down on the farm, or in mining towns, or among factory workers. The Democrats' claim that it was the reason discredited the rest of their economic agenda and handed the policy initiative to our Party for the next sixteen years.

Along with free silver, the Democrats adopted the bulk of the Populist Party's platform, just as the Populist movement was fading in response to improving conditions for farmers. At their subsequent convention, the Populists had little choice but to nominate Bryan as well, thereby in effect merging their party into the Democratic Party. Political allegiances dating back to the Civil War and Reconstruction were losing meaning, and in what became known as the "Great Realignment," millions of "silverite" Republicans joined the Democratic Party and millions of Democrat "gold-bugs" joined the Republicans.

The 1896 Republican presidential candidate was that proponent of high tariffs, William McKinley, who while in the House of Representatives had been one of Blaine's Half-Breeds and during the Civil War had risen to the rank of major in the regiment commanded by Rutherford Hayes. Our Party downplayed its high tariff stance but did come down squarely for hard money. Another theme was the contrast between the poor, backward South controlled by the Democrats and the prosperous North, where the Republicans were largely in charge; Republicans asserted that only they were in favor of industrialization and progress. The Republican platform condemned the Democrats for oppressing southern blacks, and also was far ahead of the Democrats in advocating a greater role in politics for women.

The enthusiastic Bryan ran an impassioned campaign and was the first major party presidential candidate to travel around the country.

His campaign was also the first in U.S. history to make an overt appeal to class consciousness, with fiery rhetoric against the wealthy and powerful. McKinley responded with an innovation of his own, the "front porch" campaign; he would remain at home looking presidential, speaking to Republican groups from across the country who came to see him.

Bryan won the Solid South and much of the West, but McKinley carried the North, where most of the electoral votes were. McKinley won 51% to 47% in the popular vote and 271 to 176 in the Electoral College. Republicans did lose their two-thirds majority in the House of Representatives but retained a majority, and would not lose control of the Senate until 1912.

Investment, scared off during the campaign by Bryan's threats, recovered as soon as McKinley was elected. The McKinley administration immediately raised tariffs higher than ever, so that certain protected industries, such as steel and sugar, prospered at the expense of the rest of the economy. President McKinley soon learned the political cost of making even the slightest gesture on behalf of southern blacks. The appointment of just one black man to a federal government post in New Orleans sparked huge protests across the Jim Crow South. McKinley further incurred the wrath of southern Democrats by giving a speech at Booker Washington's Tuskegee Institute in Alabama. Southern patriotism received a boost from the Spanish-American War, as the attacks on Cuba and Puerto Rico were launched from Tampa, Florida, and many top army officers were Confederate veterans. The swift and overwhelming victory over Spain in the summer of 1898 also gave McKinley excellent prospects for reelection in 1900.

McKinley's first Vice President having died in office, Republicans found an ideal vice presidential candidate in Theodore Roosevelt Jr. Roosevelt's political career had begun with election to the New York legislature in 1881 at the age of twenty-three. His reformist attitude garnered him the appointment by President Harrison to the U.S. Civil Service Commission in 1889, and six years later the mayor of New York named him to the city's board of police commissioners. On the strength of a book he had written about sea battles in the War of 1812, incoming President William McKinley named Roosevelt Assistant

Secretary of the Navy.

Just prior to the outbreak of hostilities with Spain, Roosevelt took advantage of the Secretary of the Navy taking an afternoon off, and cabled an order to Commodore Dewey's fleet, then at Hong Kong, to prepare to steam to Manila Bay at a moment's notice. As a result, the U.S. ships were able to catch the Spanish ships there unprepared once Congress declared war. When the war started, Roosevelt resigned from the Navy in order to be second in command of a cavalry regiment known as the Rough Riders. One charge up San Juan Hill later, Roosevelt was an army as well as naval hero of the "Splendid Little War." That November, he was elected Governor of New York.

As Governor, Roosevelt supported a broad range of reforms, including a bill to desegregate the state's public schools. His drive against corruption within the state bureaucracy earned the wrath of Senator Thomas Platt, party boss and one of Roscoe Conkling's Stalwart cronies from way back. Wanting to get his nemesis out the way, it was Platt who convinced the Republican National Convention that Roosevelt would be perfect as McKinley's running mate. And he was! War hero, popular enough to carry New York state, anti-corruption crusader, energetic campaigner, young enough to appeal to the post-Civil War generation but with ties to the Blaine camp – Roosevelt had even worked for two years in the Dakota Territory as a rancher and deputy sheriff.

Democrats again nominated Bryan, who campaigned for free silver once more as well as lower tariffs. The rest of their party platform was the reform agenda of the Populist Party, which by then had largely been absorbed by the Democratic Party. The Republicans campaigned for the gold standard and higher tariffs. Their platform called for enforcement of the 15th amendment in the South and denounced the southern Democrat state governments for condoning lynching. Military success overseas and a roaring economy at home handed McKinley a bigger margin of victory than in 1896. He won 52% to 46% in the popular vote and 295 electoral votes to Bryan's 155, nearly all of which were from the Solid South. The next House of Representatives would be 55% Republican and the Senate, 62% Republican.

Six months into his second term, William McKinley was murdered by an anarchist, making Theodore Roosevelt the youngest President ever, at the age of forty-two. Breaking with our Republican Party's Whig tradition of congressional leadership, the dynamic new President regarded himself as the nation's leader and soon learned just how effective his "bully pulpit" could be. Aside from his relative indifference about the tariff issue, he was a devotee of Alexander Hamilton, so much so that he made no secret of despising Thomas Jefferson as much as Hamilton did.

President Roosevelt's first significant public act would have angered Jefferson as much as it did southern Democrats. A month after taking office, Roosevelt invited a black person to dinner at the White House. Of his guest, the President said: "I do not know a white man of the South who is as good a man as Booker T. Washington today." The fury with which southern Democrats reacted to this one gesture of respect for a black person astonished Roosevelt. Some of the protests sweeping across the South went so far as to demand that the President throw away whatever silverware and china Washington used. The purpose of the meeting had been to discuss reviving our Republican Party in the South, a goal which Roosevelt was forced to abandon.

Fierce Democrat opposition also forced him to stop appointing black people to federal posts in the South, after southern Senators filibustered against his nomination of a black man as Collector of Customs in Charleston. The Democrats finally relented after the persistent Roosevelt nominated him for a fifth time.*

Our Party did, nonetheless, crack down hard on the practice common in many areas of the South under Democrat control of forcing blacks to sign abominable labor contracts and then holding them under guard permanently at work camps. The Roosevelt administration emancipated these captives through rigorous enforcement – states

---

* President Taft later appointed this man, Dr. William D. Crum, ambassador to Liberia.

rights arguments be damned – of the federal law against imprisonment for debt enacted by the Radical Republicans in 1867.

As the nation's first President of the post-Civil War generation,
Roosevelt was a major transitional figure in our political history. For
his first year or so in office, the new President followed McKinley's
policies, but in 1902 the reform-minded Roosevelt began speaking
publicly about a "Square Deal" for the American people. The Populist
movement had been the agrarian sector's reaction to its decline relative to urban industry, and now it was the cities which grappled with
new problems arising from industrialization. Though Roosevelt was
not the founder of this "Progressive" movement, he made himself its
national spokesman.

Progressives believed that the economy had become too complex
for old legal structures to handle, so government had to assume a more
activist role. State governments were to do what they could on local
concerns such as education, but insofar as this new economic activity
took on the nature of interstate commerce, the federal government
was to meet the growing need for regulation – for example, a consumer in, say Ohio, needing to be protected from a faulty product
manufactured in Massachusetts. Similarly, monopolies were recognized as a public menace that in many cases only the federal government could defeat.

In contrast to the bloated regulatory bureaucracies of today,
Progressive regulation was intended to compensate for any lack of
competition and other failures of the free market, not to supplant the
free market. The Progressives were just as mainstream Republican as
the Radicals had been, but just as the 1860s abolition movement and
the 1960s civil rights movement mutated into their very opposites, the
vast regulatory machinery we contend with today, particularly at the
federal level, bears little resemblance to what Progressives such as
Theodore Roosevelt had in mind a century ago. Protecting the individual from the arbitrary exercise of power was their objective, so in
many respects opposing unwarranted government power over individuals today is in the best of the Progressive tradition. Government regulation was for the Progressives a means of empowering people, not,

as the modern Democratic Party sees it, a means of controlling them. While in office, President Roosevelt denounced socialism every chance he got.

The rise of Theodore Roosevelt to power absorbed most of the Progressive movement into our Republican Party, as the Democrats had done with the Populist Party by nominating Bryan. Progressives and Populists had many reform goals in common, and Roosevelt appropriated for our Party the truly progressive elements of the reformist agenda, without that backward-looking free coinage of silver nonsense. The Progressives effected many political reforms, such as electoral primaries and referendums. Campaign donations by corporations were banned in 1907, and disclosure of campaign finances for federal elections became mandatory in 1910. To curb monopolistic abuses by the railroads, the Interstate Commerce Commission was strengthened in 1903 and again in 1906. The Pure Food and Drug Act was passed in 1905, followed by the Meat Inspection Act of 1906. In its 1905 Lochner v. New York decision, the Supreme Court slowed the Progressive regulatory surge by ruling that a legal maximum on the length of the working day violated the 14th amendment guarantee of due process. Three decades later, this precedent would cause many early New Deal measures to be overturned.

In 1903, the Roosevelt administration established the Department of Commerce and Labor in order to, as the name implied, referee between Big Business and Big Labor. The Department was also to investigate corporate abuses, not to create so many of them as the Commerce Department does today. In 1904, the federal government secured Supreme Court approval to use the Sherman Anti-Trust Act to break up a railroad trust (a type of monopolistic business combination). Roosevelt accepted that there can be legitimate reasons of coordination and economies of scale for consolidation, but his administration indicted more than two dozen trusts it believed to be merely scams.

Efforts to conserve natural resources had first gained strength in the 1870s – Yellowstone National Park was established during the Grant administration and Yosemite National Park during the

Harrison administration – but Theodore Roosevelt made conservation, particularly in his beloved West, a top priority. Under authority of a law dating back to 1890, the President withheld millions of acres of federal government land from sale to the public, a policy which has remained a fixture to this day. Indeed, the federal government still owns half the land west of the Mississippi.*

Theodore Roosevelt was immensely popular – at last a President who was doing what the country wanted and was not getting side-tracked by the tariff or free silver issues. The classic 1902 novel The Virginian, for example, is dedicated to Theodore Roosevelt, "the greatest benefactor we people have known since Lincoln." In the 1902 midterm elections, our Republican Party retained its majorities in both the House of Representatives and the Senate, and the President headed toward an easy reelection. Henry Cabot Lodge was the keynote speaker at the 1904 Republican National Convention. The platform condemned the Democrats for their crimes against southern blacks, and also denounced a trend toward socialism within the Democratic Party.

No major Democrat wanted to face certain defeat, so that party's 1904 presidential nominee was a nonentity, former federal judge Alton Parker. With his candidacy the Democratic Party sought to allay uneasiness within the business sector about "Bryanism." Parker abandoned free silver completely, but was duly crushed by Roosevelt 56% to 38% in the popular vote and 336 to 140 in the Electoral College. All of Parker's electoral votes came from the Solid South. The Socialist Party candidate, Eugene Debs, won 3% of the popular vote. Our Party increased its majority to 64% in both houses of Congress.

During his second term, President Roosevelt's approach toward the South underwent a major change. In a bid for southern white support, no longer would he side with the oppressed blacks. While

---

* but relatively little in Texas, because the state, not the federal government, inherited the property of the Republic of Texas.

touring the South in 1905, he praised the valor of surviving Confederate veterans and pointed out that many of his ancestors had fought with them against the United States Government. That November, the President ordered the dishonorable discharge of 167 black soldiers in Brownsville, Texas on suspicion, but no proof, that several of them may have committed crimes. Southern whites cheered, but blacks throughout the country resented him for the grave injustice. Nor would they forgive the Secretary of War who carried out Roosevelt's order, William Howard Taft.*

For the 1908 presidential election campaign, the Democratic Party turned for a third time to William Jennings Bryan. Forgetting all about free silver, Bryan tried to position himself as the person who could best continue the Progressive policies of Theodore Roosevelt, who had appropriated the more sensible elements of his Populist agenda. Bryan went well beyond Roosevelt's policies, however, by calling for the nationalization of the railroads, for example. The short-lived but severe economic recession after the Panic of 1907 provided him with another major issue. Organized labor's pro-Democrat stance dates from the endorsement of the 1908 Bryan ticket by the American Federation of Labor.

The Republican nominee was Roosevelt's hand-picked successor, Secretary of War Taft, who previously had been a federal judge and military governor of the Philippines. While the Democrats asserted their states rights doctrine, the Republican platform called for equal rights for blacks, a plank which for Republicans would not again appear in their party platform until 1932. The Republican platform also called for full disclosure of all campaign contributions.

Taft was the first Republican presidential candidate to campaign in the South, which nonetheless once again proved solidly Democrat. Bryan carried just three other states. In the popular vote, Taft won 52% to 43%, and 3% for the Socialists' Eugene Debs. The Electoral College result was 321 for Taft and 162 for Bryan. Republicans won 56% of the

---

* Also in 1905, Theodore Roosevelt was the guest of honor at the marriage of his niece, Eleanor, to his fifth cousin, Franklin Roosevelt.

House of Representative and held on to 64% of the Senate seats.

Aiming to rebuild our Republican Party in the South but this time without blacks, President Taft completely ignored our Party's platform, not only abandoning the oppressed black people of the region but dishonoring the legacy of the Radical Republicans. In his inaugural address, he informed the white southern Democrats that as long as they did not overtly violate the 13th, 14th, and 15th amendments, they could do whatever they wanted to the southern blacks. He later even sided with the Democrats in opposing a federal anti-lynching law on states rights grounds.

Presumably, Taft believed that since southern blacks could not vote anyway, it would be best for our Republican Party to write them off politically. This strategy proved to be a mistake of colossal proportions. Very few white southerners responded by becoming Republicans, and even more significantly, as black people began leaving the South in substantial numbers in 1915 many arrived in northern cities with no allegiance to the political party which had emancipated their grandparents.

Taft was a conservationist. On economic policy, though he actually did more trust-busting than Roosevelt, President Taft was less of a reformer. He angered the Progressive wing of our Party by signing a Republican bill that raised tariffs after he had promised to reduce them. One notable Progressive measure was enacted, authorizing the Interstate Commerce Commission to regulate telecommunications. Rather more progress was achieved by amending the Constitution. The income tax amendment was ratified during Taft's term, and the 17th amendment, for the direct election of Senators, passed Congress, though it was not ratified until after he was out of office.

***

As the economy worsened and the new tariff raised consumer prices, the Democrats won a majority in the House of Representatives in the 1910 midterm elections. Leading up to the 1912 presidential election, Democrats looked for someone who could appeal to the three components of their party: the Solid South, urban machines, and western populists. Convention delegates had to cast forty-six ballots before set-tling on a southerner recently elected Governor of a northern state. Born in Virginia, Woodrow Wilson had been President of Princeton University before being elected Governor of New Jersey in 1910. Though not as extreme as Bryan, Wilson had solid reformist credentials. The Democratic Party platform again endorsed states rights, but for the first time Democrats campaigned actively for the votes of black people, though of course only in the North.

On the Republican side, things were even more complicated. Wisconsin Senator Robert La Follette, who had formed the National Progressive Republican League to promote the Progressive cause within our Party, contested President Taft for the nomination. La Follette's campaign disintegrated when in February 1912 former President Roosevelt, having spent much of Taft's term in Europe and Africa, announced he wanted a third term. Most Republicans preferred Roosevelt – still only 53 years old – over Taft, but the incumbent President had the party apparatus and was able to round up a majority of the convention delegates.

At Roosevelt's command, his supporters stormed out of the con-vention and formed a new political party, the Progressive Party, also known as the Bull Moose Party for their leader's supposed vigor. His running mate was the Governor of California, Hiram Johnson. Taft was not as much of a Progressive as Roosevelt had expected, but the former President's decision to divide our Party was mostly motivated by jealousy and personal ambition. During his presidency, one observer had famously summed him up: "What you have to remem-ber is, the President is about six." The Bull Moose platform was for every Progressive reform then under consideration, including women's suffrage, a ban on child labor, and a federal income tax. These were all sensible ideas, but the Progressives also went in for class warfare rhetoric and other ill-conceived emotionalism. In fact, Roosevelt the Bull Moose ran a campaign that was more stridently socialist than he had accused Bryan of being twelve years before.

In the South, the Bull Moosers were a strictly whites-only organ-ization, in the hope of avoiding the race issue altogether, but the Solid

South stayed with the Democrat nominee. The Electoral College result was a huge victory for Wilson. Capturing 40 of 48 states, he received 435 electoral votes, to 88 for Roosevelt and 8 for Taft, whose campaign suffered a big setback when his running mate died shortly before election day. In the popular vote, Wilson came in first with 42%, followed by Roosevelt with 27%, Taft with 23%, and Debs with 6%. It would be an oversimplification to say Roosevelt split the Republican vote. Running alone, either Roosevelt or Taft* probably would have won, but Roosevelt attracted many Democrats away from Wilson, who consequently received fewer votes than Bryan ever did. The Democrats won a two-thirds majority in the House of Representatives, and the Republicans lost their majority in the Senate.

Woodrow Wilson was the first President since John Adams to deliver his State of the Union message in a speech before Congress, leading Theodore Roosevelt to exclaim: "Why didn't I think of that!" Among Wilson's first official acts was something Roosevelt would never have done – fire nearly every black federal government employee in the South. The new Democrat President ordered all federal government offices and facilities racially segregated, and during his first term, Wilson appointed just two black people to a federal government post. Such malice toward all blacks helped keep them solidly Republican for another generation. Referring to Haitians, his first Secretary of State, William Jennings Bryan,** was heard to say: "Imagine, n_____s speaking French." President Wilson did not lift a finger against his fellow Democrats who were lynching thousands of southern blacks; in Georgia in 1918, for example, a pregnant black woman was burned at the stake, and the fetus cut out alive and stomped to death.

At the height of Democrat terrorism against blacks in the Jim Crow South, the Ku Klux Klan, which had disappeared toward the end of Reconstruction, was reborn. Just days after seeing the movie The Birth of a Nation in November 1915, a Georgia salesman,

---

* Taft was appointed Chief Justice by President Harding in 1921.
** In 1925, Clarence Darrow made history by cross-examining him about the Bible during the Scopes Monkey Trial.

William Simmons, accompanied by fifteen followers, set a wooden cross ablaze atop Stone Mountain and declared himself the leader of a new KKK. The movie, featuring a couple of villains caricaturing Thaddeus Stevens and Lydia Smith, had been based on the 1905 novel The Clansman: A Historical Romance of the Ku Klux Klan.

From the Sir Walter Scott novels so dear to the South, the author had adopted rituals such cross-burning, reminiscent of the calling of the Scottish clans. This novel was one of several vicious literary attacks on black Americans popular then, including the bestsellers The Negro, A Beast and The Negro, A Menace to American Civilization. Within a few years the KKK had nearly a million members and many more millions of supporters. Many Democrats proudly declared their allegiance to the Klan, and hundreds of office-holders were members. Five Senators were present or former members of the Ku Klux Klan, including Hugo Black, whom Franklin Roosevelt later appointed to the Supreme Court. Alongside blacks on the enemies list of the new Klan were Jews, Catholics, and foreigners, especially those with socialist politics. These Klansmen played down their Confederate heritage and made themselves out to be jingoistic super-patriots.

During the Wilson administration, the Democratic Party abandoned its traditional laissez-faire economic policy. President Wilson and the Democrat majority in Congress implemented a series of economic reforms with the theme the "New Freedoms." The best of these measures was the Federal Reserve Act of 1913, a huge policy shift for Democrats considering that their party had been founded by opponents of the Bank of the United States. The Panic of 1907, when the banking system nearly collapsed because of a liquidity crisis which a central bank could easily have averted, convinced most Democrats that Alexander Hamilton may have been onto something. Unlike Hamilton's Bank, however, the Federal Reserve would not engage in commercial banking. Moreover, there would be no central bank; instead, the country would be divided into twelve districts, each with its own Federal Reserve Bank so that regional views – not just Wall Street's – would be taken into account. Monetary policy would be set by periodic meetings of the Federal Reserve Board.

President Wilson was right to denounce tariffs as "the mother of trusts." The Underwood Act of 1913 lowered tariffs to an average 29%, their lowest levels in fifty years. To compensate for the lost revenue, the same Act instituted a small graduated income tax. The Clayton Anti-Trust Act of 1914 strengthened the Sherman Anti-Trust Act, and exempted union activity from prosecution as illegal restraints of trade. The Federal Trade Commission was established that year to require disclosure by corporations and to prevent unfair competition.

The Federal Highway Act of 1916 began as an incentive for state government spending on highway construction but later evolved into a mechanism for permanent federal government control. Similar fund-matching schemes for agriculture, vocational training, and urban programs further blurred the delineation between state and federal government responsibilities. Still, it must be said that overall, Wilson's New Freedoms were intended more to promote competition than to impose federal government control. Control for its own sake would not become a Democratic Party goal until the New Deal.

<hr/>

Having rebounded in the 1914 midterm congressional elections, Republicans had good prospects for defeating Wilson's reelection bid. Our Party's 1916 presidential candidate was a former Governor of New York, Charles Hughes, whom President Taft had named to the Supreme Court. Hughes resigned upon accepting the nomination. With his excellent reformist record, Hughes would have been an invincible candidate four years earlier, but this time, with the chief election issue being the war in Europe, it was more difficult for the Republican standard-bearer.

Nonetheless, Hughes only narrowly lost to Wilson. The popular vote Wilson won by 49% to 46%, and the Electoral College tally was just as close, 277 to 254. Hughes lost California, and so the election, by just 3773 votes. What proved decisive there was that the Republican Governor, former Bull Mooser Hiram Johnson, so resented not getting the nomination himself that he refused to campaign for

Hughes. The Progressive Party faded away soon after former President Roosevelt publicly backed Hughes, though most voters who considered themselves Progressives preferred Wilson. In the House of Representatives, Republicans won six more seats than the Democrats, but a Democrat was elected Speaker with the support of the handful of Representatives elected as Progressives that year.

Chapter Eight

(1916-1952)

SLIDING INTO SOCIALISM

During World War I, demand for American industrial and agricultural goods surged as Europe devoted its own production to armaments. Prior to about 1915, nearly all black Americans lived in the South; but over the next ten years, attracted by plentiful factory jobs, more than a million southern blacks moved to northern cities. Decades of Democrat rule since Reconstruction meant that these new arrivals were far less educated than the average northerner. Most of these migrant blacks took bottom-rung manual labor positions, but others were able to fill some of the tens of thousands of private and public sector clerk positions being created at the time.

Across the North, whites responded to this "Great Migration" by imposing segregation laws that were in many cases even stricter than Jim Crow. Unions tended to exclude blacks, and government regulations kept them out of many trades. "Race riots," a euphemism for mobs of whites assaulting black neighborhoods, erupted across the North. One of the deadliest of these occurred in East St. Louis in 1917. The chief motive, resentment by poor and lower-middle class whites toward black people competing for work, intensified when a postwar economic slump set in.

In the North, these southern-born blacks could vote, and throughout the 1920s they voted overwhelmingly Republican. Over time, however, the arrival of so many black people into the cities, which were always strongholds of the Democratic Party, spurred Democrats into doing what they did best. While southern Democrats did whatever they could to keep blacks out of politics, urban Democrats in the North regarded black migrants as just another immigrant ethnic group of voters to be integrated into the party machines. Most older blacks remembered Democrat oppression in the South too well to be lured away from the GOP, but younger blacks viewed the Democratic Party in this entirely new context. Their generation would be the one to become predominantly Democrat in the 1930s.

After President Wilson's "war to end all wars" there was tremendous disillusionment in the United States. The conflict had resolved nothing, and our country had very little to show for the deaths of a hundred thousand soldiers. Theodore Roosevelt had backed the war enthusiastically, and so the Progressive movement he personified was discredited in the backlash. "So this is what comes of the urge to interfere in other people's lives!" thought millions of Americans.

When Wilson returned from the Versailles peace conference in July 1919 touting his League of Nations idea, most Republicans were in no mood for anything that might drag our country into future foreign squabbles. Hughes and Taft, to name two moderately Progressive Republicans, favored the League, but to salvage their movement's reputation, the Progressives Robert La Follette and Hiram Johnson joined with more traditional Republicans in the campaign to defeat Senate ratification of the League of Nations treaty. Wilson's massive stroke in September 1919 sidelined him for rest of his presidency.

Among the foremost domestic concerns of the day were prohibition and women's suffrage. The two were closely related and were predominantly Republican issues. The Prohibition Party, established in 1869, was a Republican splinter group. Founded in 1874, the Women's Christian Temperance Union opened the door for political involvement by women with the argument that liquor ruined family life – if women could vote, the WCTU asserted, they could protect their children and their husbands too by getting alcoholic beverages banned.

Many states had already banned alcoholic beverages by the time the 18th amendment was ratified in January 1919. President Wilson had his veto of the Volstead implementing legislation overridden by

Congress in October 1919. Women's suffrage was a logical extension of the Radical Republican drive to allow black men to vote, for if black men could vote then why not women, white and black? Starting with Wyoming in 1869, women could already vote in six western states when the 19th amendment was ratified in August 1920, in time for the 1920 general elections.

Another development during World War I to prove tremendously significant later on was the vast expansion of federal government control over the economy. In 1917, the federal government established the War Industries Board and five other such production boards that exercised virtually limitless power to decide what private industry, farms, and mines would produce; while price controls, rationing, and other regulations sharply curtailed consumer freedom.

Republicans and many other Americans came to bitterly resent government activism in all its manifestations. Bureaucrats governing the economy might be a war-winning strategy, but it had disastrous long-term results. For example, the Dust Bowl of the 1930s is directly attributable to overplanting first mandated by the federal government during the war. Americans tolerated this unprecedented government interference while the war lasted, but once peace was restored they hungered for their freedom to be restored too – what Warren Harding would call "normalcy."

The Democrat presidential candidate in 1920 was Ohio's lackluster Governor James Cox. Mainly to link their party to the legacy of Theodore Roosevelt, who had died the year before, the convention named as his running mate Franklin Roosevelt, who was the Assistant Secretary of the Navy, just as the other famous Roosevelt had been.

On the Republican side, the Progressive Governor of California, Hiram Johnson, pushed hard for the nomination, but too many delegates remembered his betrayals of our Party in 1912 and 1916. By 1920, most Republicans, as well as many Democrats, were tired of Progressivism. There being no other major contender, the Republican National Convention turned to a relative unknown, Ohio Senator

Warren Harding. Hiram Johnson declined the second spot on the ticket (Imagine how different the 1920s would have been had that Progressive war horse accepted!), so the nomination went to Massachusetts Governor Calvin Coolidge, who had recently gained fame by ending a Boston police strike.

During the election campaign, Republicans called for lower taxes and the total elimination of all remaining wartime federal government interventions in the economy. They denounced as socialist any inclination by the federal government to extend its economic war powers past the November 1918 armistice. Women had a much more active role in the Republican convention than in the Democrat convention. The constitutional rights of blacks were not mentioned in the Democrat platform, but the Republican platform condemned lynching and called for federal legislation to stop it.

Harding's victory was one of the biggest in our Party's history. He won 60% of the popular vote to Cox's 34%, and the Electoral College result was 404 to 127. All of the states carried by the Democrats were in the South, which for the first time in forty-four years was not quite Solid – the Republicans narrowly won Tennessee. Harding was especially popular among women and blacks. The Socialists' Eugene Debs, whom the Wilson administration had imprisoned for opposing the war, won 3% of the popular vote while sitting in his prison cell. In the House of Representatives, Republicans increased the majority they won in the 1918 midterm elections to 69%, and their Senate majority grew to 62%.

The new Republican President soon pardoned Eugene Debs and others imprisoned during the "Red Scare" orchestrated by Woodrow Wilson's hard-line Attorney General, A. Mitchell Palmer. He made a few good appointments, such as Charles Hughes as Secretary of State, but overall Warren Harding filled top government posts with cronies. The worst of the many scandals which inevitably erupted was when some businessmen bribed the Secretary of the Interior to lease them the federal government's Teapot Dome oil reserve without competitive bidding.

The severe economic recession following the war ended in 1921, but prosperity did not return to the agricultural sector. As European grain production recovered after the war, U.S. farm prices slumped, and the higher tariffs enacted by the Republican Congress in 1922 made things worse.

Apart from the occasional speech condemning southern Democrats for lynching black people, President Harding himself did not respect our Party's heritage of defending the constitutional rights of black Americans. Neither he nor Coolidge nor Hoover undid the racial segregation imposed within the federal government by Woodrow Wilson. At the dedication of the Lincoln Memorial in 1922, there were separate seating areas for whites and blacks, an outrageous insult to blacks and to the memory of the Great Emancipator. In contrast to the callous President Harding, many Republicans in Congress were touched by "the better angels of their nature." In 1922, the Republican major-ity-House of Representatives passed a bill to make lynching a federal crime, but a Democrat filibuster killed it in the Senate.

After World War I, the Ku Klux Klan spread to the North and West, and not just among Democrats; outside the South, many Republicans joined the new Klan. For several years, the Klan was par-ticularly powerful in Oregon and Oklahoma. In Tulsa in 1921, sev-eral hundred people, mostly blacks, were killed in fighting which erupted when a group of black men tried to stop a lynching. Indiana was where the Klan actually gained control over the state government. Even worse, it was a Republican administration. The Republican Governor elected in 1924 was a Klansman as were the majority of the state legislators, giving the leader of the Indiana Klan, David Stephenson, cause to say: "I am the law in Indiana."

The Indiana Klan was destroyed in March 1925 when Stephenson, a self-proclaimed defender of American womanhood, raped a woman, savagely biting her lip while doing so. In this case, the victim took poi-son and died. Stephenson was sentenced to life in prison, but not before releasing documentary evidence of corruption that swept hundreds of Klansmen out of political office and some, including the Mayor of Indianapolis, into prison. Nationwide, the second Ku Klux Klan was already in decline, and would be formally disbanded in 1944.

President Harding died in August 1923 and was succeeded by his Vice President, Calvin Coolidge. Coolidge cleaned house, and there were no more scandals. He appointed 29-year old J. Edgar Hoover to head the new Federal Bureau of Investigation. His first message to Congress defended the constitutional rights of blacks, but he did little for them. He was, however, the first President to show real concern for Native Americans.

Calvin Coolidge was a very popular President, who was giving the public what it wanted: cautious, pro-free market policies just as they had wanted Progressivism a generation earlier. He secured the 1924 Republican presidential nomination on the first ballot. The platform once again advocated greater protection for the constitutional rights of blacks, but Coolidge (as well as the Democrats) refused to denounce the Ku Klux Klan.

For the 1924 Democrat presidential nomination the leading contender was New York Governor Al Smith, but because the Ku Klux Klan could not accept a Catholic as the party's standard-bearer they deadlocked the convention by throwing their support to President Wilson's son-in-law, former Treasury Secretary William McAdoo. After an incredible 103 ballots, convention delegates finally nominated West Virginia Senator John Davis, a former Wall Street lawyer with economic policies to match Coolidge's. To appease the still-formidable Bryan wing of the party, Democrats handed the vice presidential nomination to his younger brother Charles, who was Governor of Nebraska.

Warren Harding would probably have lost a reelection bid, but the honest and able President Coolidge won easily in the three-candidate race of 1924. That year, Senator La Follette was nominated by a new progressive party he had founded, the Conference for Progressive Political Action. Among the policies advocated by La Follette's party was federal government ownership of railroads and many utilities. La Follette carried his native Wisconsin and Davis won the South, but Coolidge captured the electoral votes everywhere else. The economy was booming and most Americans preferred to "Keep Cool with Coolidge."

In the popular vote, Coolidge received 54%, Davis 29%, and La Follette 17%, a third-party tally not exceeded until Ross Perot won 19% of the vote in 1992. The Conference for Progressive Political Action faded quickly after Senator La Follette died in 1925, and most of his supporters returned to the GOP. In Congress, the Republicans increased their majority in the House of Representatives to 57% and in the Senate to 56%.

In 1928, New York Governor Al Smith succeeded in winning the Democrat presidential nomination. Counting against him in the eyes of many voters, especially in the South and West, were his Catholicism, opposition to Prohibition, ties to Tammany Hall, even his New York accent. Smith did favor somewhat more federal government intervention in the economy than did his Republican opponent, but generally his policy proposals were very similar. In a significant reversal, the Democrat platform called for higher tariffs. The two parties were reflecting a broad consensus within the electorate which would end abruptly during the Great Depression.

Republicans nominated Commerce Secretary Herbert Hoover, a former mining engineer who came into prominence for administering U.S. economic assistance programs in Europe after World War I. His running mate was Kansas Senator Charles Curtis, an Osage Native American. The Democrat platform did not mention black Americans, but the Republican platform at least repeated its call for a federal anti-lynching law.

Once again, victory went to the Republican presidential candidate. Hoover defeated Smith 58% to 41% in the popular vote and 444 to 87 in the Electoral College. The Republican ticket actually carried five southern states. Republicans won 61% of the House of Representatives and their majority in the Senate was 58%. An Illinois Republican elected to the House, Oscar De Priest, became the first black person in Congress since 1901.

The hatred for black people which southern Democrats displayed when Theodore Roosevelt invited Booker Washington to dinner in 1901 had not abated by the time President Hoover took office. In 1929, the legislatures of several states in the South passed resolutions censuring the President for including Mrs. De Priest in a White House luncheon for the wives of Republican congressmen.

A year later, Hoover's nomination of a southerner to the Supreme Court was defeated in the Senate because of a mildly racist remark he had made a decade earlier, illustrating the dilemma faced by our Party at the time of finding many prominent white southerners who had not said as much or worse. As a Democrat, in contrast, Franklin Roosevelt was later able to secure Senate approval for Hugo Black, the former Klansman. To succeed Chief Justice Taft, who retired in 1930, President Hoover named Charles Hughes, the former presidential candidate and Secretary of State. Hughes is perhaps best remembered for his observation that "the Constitution is what the judges say it is."

Seven months after President Hoover took office, the stock market crash of 1929 marked the beginning of the Great Depression. As had happened in previous depressions, banks collapsed and unemployment soared, but several factors made this economic downturn especially devastating. This time, the depression was a world-wide phenomenon. Also, demand for both industrial and agricultural products slumped simultaneously. American farmers, not having shared in the prosperity of the Roaring Twenties, were caught helpless. The Federal Reserve made a bad situation worse by decreasing the money supply, repeating the monetary tightening by the Bank of the United States which set off the Panic of 1819 and Andrew Jackson's misstep which triggered the Panic of 1837. Just as the Democratic Party had been blamed for economic depressions during the Van Buren and Cleveland presidencies, popular support dropped precipitously for the party in power.

To deal with the crisis, President Hoover called Congress into special session. Far from being passive, the Republican majority was quick to take action. Unfortunately, what our Party decided to do was precisely the wrong thing. The Hawley-Smoot tariff, signed into law in June 1930, raised tariffs to their highest levels ever. Some

Democrats voted for it and some Republicans voted against, but the GOP deserves all the blame.

Contrary to the advice of hundreds of economists, our Party believed that domestic factories and farms would somehow benefit from the federal government charging higher taxes on foreign imports. Of course, foreigners do not pay these taxes – Americans do, in the form of higher prices for consumer goods and for imported components of goods that domestic industry exports. And inevitably, foreign countries retaliated against the higher U.S. tariffs with high tariffs of their own, further reducing American exports. The one positive outcome for our Party from this blunder is that free trade has been mainstream Republican policy ever since.

The steadfast refusal of Grover Cleveland to do anything at all about the depression of 1893-96 had occurred within the lifetimes of most American adults, and compared to that Democrat President, Herbert Hoover was a dynamo. Though President Hoover balked at getting the federal government directly involved in providing economic assistance to individuals, preferring state and local governments for that task, early on he asked Congress for sharp increases in spending on public works. The massive Hoover Dam is one such project he sponsored, but he did veto a bill for the federal government to establish power generation facilities in the area later developed by the Tennessee Valley Authority (TVA). The Hoover administration also increased assistance programs for the agricultural sector.

A mild economic upturn enabled the Republicans to stave off complete disaster in the 1930 midterm elections and hold onto the Senate, but control of the House of Representatives passed to the Democrats by the barest of margins. In an unprecedented effort to prevent total economic collapse, the new Congress created the Reconstruction Finance Corporation to prop up essential industries such as banks and railroads with cheap loans. The Home Loan Bank Act, allowing financial institutions to sell their mortgages, was passed in 1932 but did not become operational until the following year.

In evaluating the performance of the Hoover administration (except for the inexcusable Hawley-Smoot tariff) it ought to be borne in mind that the world had never experienced an economic depression of this magnitude. No one in the United States or in any foreign government knew what to do. To this day, scholars are uncertain just what caused the Great Depression, much less what the cure might have been.

Despite the disaster, President Hoover encountered little opposition to being renominated, mainly because most Republicans who considered themselves Progressives shifted over to support the Democrat presidential candidate, including Hiram Johnson; La Follette's son and successor in the Senate, Robert La Follette Jr.; and Nebraska Senator George Norris,* who would later draft the law creating the TVA. This was a political realignment as significant as that of 1896.

For the ninth time, the Democratic Party nominated a Governor of New York, Franklin Roosevelt, who had been elected to the office four years earlier. Though Governor Roosevelt had pushed for more public works to boost employment, other than that his performance had not been especially noteworthy, and he would not run on his record. Rather, his strengths as a candidate were name recognition, the ability to carry his native state, and his charismatic and dynamic style. To balance the northeastern Governor at the top of the ticket, the vice presidential nomination went to John Garner, a Texan and Speaker of the House.

Roosevelt broke tradition by flying to Chicago to accept the nomination in person. In his speech to the convention, he said the Democratic Party must be "the bearer of liberalism," a meaning of the term precisely the opposite of how it had been used in the 19th century. Everywhere else in the world, "liberal" still retains its original sense of "freedom from government coercion," but in this country the word came to replace "Progressive" as a label for proponents of federal

---

* Senator Norris led the drive that created Nebraska's unicameral legislature in 1934, a Progressive move to speed up government by reducing checks and balances. He also drafted the 20th amendment that, among other things, moved up the start of a new presidential term from March to January.

government-directed collectivism. "Socialist" would have been a more accurate term, but Americans had always regarded socialism as a foreign menace, which by 1932 it had indeed become in its Communist, Fascist, and Nazi variants.

However mislabeled, socialism has been the core ideology of the Democratic Party ever since. As Roosevelt implemented his policies, Democrats found "liberal" a more attractive label than "New Dealer." The change in the meaning of the word was not completed for another two decades; Senator Robert Taft, "Mr. Republican" and a firm opponent of all things socialist, called himself a "liberal" throughout a career that stretched into the 1950s.

During the campaign, Hoover had little new to say about the depression, and our Party had clearly run out of economic ideas. On social policy, the Republican platform did repeat its call for greater protection of the constitutional rights of black Americans. While Governor Roosevelt had not done anything in particular to assist blacks, black people appreciated that Hoover, as Commerce Secretary, had ordered his Department desegregated and prohibited racial discrimination in its operations. The majority of black voters backed the Republican nominee, the last time this would occur until Dwight Eisenhower ran in 1952.

Herbert Hoover lost by 472 to 59 in the Electoral College, though in the popular vote he did not do much worse than the Democrat presidential candidate had done four years earlier. The real landslide was in the congressional races. The Republicans' share of the House of Representatives fell from 49% to 27%, and from 50% to 38% in the Senate.

The 1932 presidential campaign was not fought on ideological grounds. Roosevelt knew that to win, his best strategy was to capture the middle ground by campaigning as only a moderate Progressive. Though Roosevelt advocated that the federal government assume responsibility for public relief and ending the depression, like Hoover he promised a balanced federal government budget, and said he would reduce federal government expenditures by 25%. The Democrat platform advocated "the removal of government from all fields of public enterprise except where necessary to develop public works and natural resources in the public interest," and for the first time included a nod to "equal rights to all." Due to this lack of specifics, in the five months before President-elect Roosevelt took office, the American public had no idea just what the new President would do.

Franklin Roosevelt was inaugurated on March 4, 1933. Two days later, he ended the wave of panic-induced bank failures by ordering all banks closed while the Treasury Department evaluated the fiscal soundness of each one. This "bank holiday" was an excellent move. Though it tightened federal government domination over the financial sector, the measure was nothing compared to what President Roosevelt could have done. So desperate were people for action – any action – that Congress would have permitted Roosevelt to nationalize the banking system.

In similar circumstances, tyrants use crises to seize power for themselves, but Roosevelt did no such thing. In his inaugural address, the President had hinted he might ask Congress for broad emergency powers over the economy, but he did not. He had no master plan other than to provide the nation with inspirational leadership at the depths of its worst crisis since the Civil War. Roosevelt is to be revered as much for what he did not do as for what he did. The President could have led the country right off a cliff had he been so inclined.

Consider the many democratic governments which were toppling at the time. Or consider the fate of our country if a power vacuum in Washington had led to the emergence of some home-grown fascist movement. The threat to our democracy posed by demagogues such as Louisiana's Huey Long, Democrat Senator and former Governor, show the path down which our country could have gone. Long had his good qualities – he built roads and schools and unlike most other populists was decent to blacks – but Senator Long found a large national audience disturbingly impressed with the dictatorship he established in his state. Murdered over a personal grudge in 1935, Long died with decades of mischief ahead of him, and had he lived, would have contested Roosevelt for the presidency in 1936, legally or otherwise.

In what became known as his "Hundred Days," President

Roosevelt proposed a flurry of legislative proposals, which congressional Democrats, and many Republicans at first, avidly supported. The "New Deal" was Roosevelt's name for this updated and expanded version of Progressivism. A month after taking office, to staunch the outflow of gold reserves the President proposed that the federal government no longer honor its promise to redeem its bonds in gold. Abandoning the gold standard and the subsequent devaluation of the dollar proved to be beneficial. As an emergency measure to stave off utter ruin for American farmers by subsidizing them indirectly at a cost to urban consumers and taxpayers, the Agricultural Adjustment Act of May 1933 had its merits, but it laid the foundation for federal government control over the agricultural sector.

The Act was a prime example of the contradictory nature of many New Deal programs, in this case raising food prices to help farmers at the expense of the urban poor. Sometimes the Roosevelt administration wanted more competition and other times saw more cooperation among producers as the answer. Two laws enacted in June, the Farm Credit Act and the Home Owner's Loan Act, provided for cheap loans to farmers and homeowners in order to forestall foreclosures. Again, these measures made sense given the dire circumstances but lacked any sort of justification once the worst of the crisis had passed. Much the same could be said for the Civilian Conservation Corps and the Works Progress Administration.

The Tennessee Valley Authority was created by Congress in 1933 as an enormous federal government program to develop the water resources of Tennessee and adjoining areas of six other states. It involved dam and power plant construction, and anti-erosion and flood control projects. The region certainly did benefit, but at the cost of taxpayer money extracted from elsewhere in the country. Moreover, government bureaucrats could not resist the temptation to impose on the populace a heavy-handed array of social engineering programs, a ploy which if unchecked would have converted the region into a vast federal government company town.

A nearby private power company sued the federal government for using subsidies to sell electricity at about half the cost of privately-generated electricity. The company's president, Wendell Willkie, pointed out that the federal government could use the same technique on any private competitors and thereby take over any industry. Willkie lost the court fight but won the political battle. President Roosevelt fired the over-reaching TVA chairman, and Congress refused to fund any more such economic development programs.

The worst of Roosevelt's proposals enacted without much consideration was the National Industrial Recovery Act of June 1933. The NRA was the most far-reaching and potentially revolutionary of all the New Deal programs. Out the window went half a century of anti-trust activity meant to promote greater economic competition. The federal government drafted "codes of fair practices" intended to become legally binding on entire industries, and enforceable by threat of fine or imprisonment. What would have been criminal collusion just the day before – price-fixing, carving up markets, and so on – became official government policy.

The law did ban child labor and create a 40-hour work week, but overall the NRA was a monster just hatching from the egg. The process of government bureaucrat rule-making for the private sector was completely open-ended and completely outside the normal system of checks and balances, and in time could have grown large enough to swallow the entire economy. Even if stopped before it got to this point, the NRA would have spawned monstrosities of corruption and inefficiency. In May 1935, the Supreme Court did everyone except the NRA bureaucrats a great service by striking down the core of the National Industrial Recovery Act.

Republican Party criticism of the New Deal is misguided and even counterproductive insofar as no distinction is made between its positive and negative aspects. The first of three types of New Deal programs were those intended to stave off imminent economic collapse. Roosevelt's expansion of the Reconstruction Finance Corporation, the Emergency Banking Act, the Federal Emergency Relief Act, the Home Owner's Loan Act, and various agricultural assistance programs fall into this category; as do the Civilian Conservation Corps, the Works Progress Administration, and other make-work projects. At their height, the CCC provided employment for half a million Americans and the WPA, four million – desperate people who otherwise might have been driven to political extremism.

Unlike the 1960s War on Poverty, the New Deal required the able-bodied to work. Another difference is that the federal government did not administer most New Deal economic relief; the federal government provided block grants to state and local governments, utilizing its greater creditworthiness, in effect, to borrow on their behalf. Given the economic catastrophe the nation faced in the spring of 1933, these measures were fully justified and even commendable.

The second type of New Deal programs were structural economic reforms, some good and some bad. Among the best were the Securities and Exchange Commission and the Federal Deposit Insurance Corporation. Congress strengthened the enforcement powers of the Federal Reserve System and extended its control to nonbank financial institutions. The Glass-Steagal Banking Act was right for its time. To counter the effects of Hawley-Smoot, the President was given the power to lower many tariffs without specific congressional authorization.

Standards were raised, pre-testing required, and enforcement improved when the Food, Drug, and Cosmetic Act of 1938 replaced the 1906 Pure Food and Drug Act. The Rural Electrification Administration, set up by executive order in 1935, brought millions of Americans into the 20th century, but as happens with so many federal programs, lasted decades after its mission was accomplished.

The New Deal greatly increased the power of the federal government over the states and also the power of the President relative to that of Congress. It was during the 1930s that the American people came to consider the federal government responsible for economic prosperity. Intentionally running federal government deficits to boost the economy was another innovation, to which the English economist John Keynes' 1936 "General Theory" gave academic imprimatur, however dubious. Federal taxes levied on corporate income in 1935 were a horrifically socialist measure aimed at draining pools of undistributed profits which The Rich were supposedly keeping from The People.

The third type of New Deal programs were the insidious schemes that had nothing to do with alleviating the Great Depression or stabilizing the economy. From the outset, their purpose was to strengthen the Democratic Party. For Republicans today, key to promoting the free market society is to disentangle in the public consciousness the partisan legacy of the New Deal from its nobler achievements.

The Social Security Act is a prime example. A bundle of disparate insurance and pension programs, it was enacted in 1935, several years after the economic nadir. Initially, only the aged and infirm were to receive payments, and these were to be mere supplements to other income. But the Roosevelt administration knew that promised benefits could be increased over time so that recipients would eventually become reliant on Social Security. In contrast to our Republican Party's 19th century Union army pension scheme, dependence on the federal government to provide Social Security payments could be extended to the entire population.

Government pension systems were nothing new – Germany's Otto von Bismark had created one in the 1880s – but the New Deal version was created as the ultimate patronage program. The Act established a payroll tax on employers and another on employees, and federal and state government funds would be mixed together. This confusing method of funding Social Security enhanced the centrality of the Democratic Party's handiwork in everyone's life while increasing the leverage of the federal government over the states. The federal government gained further ascendance over the states with dozens of programs that matched state and local government spending with federal government funds.

The wide array of new federal government agencies strengthened the Democratic Party tremendously. Prior to the New Deal, a political machine could hold people in its grip by providing or withholding specific government services, but through Roosevelt's foresight, the growth of government has made the traditional party machine obsolete. The New Deal converted the Democratic Party into the party of government and the federal government into one giant political machine, leading the millions of people on government payrolls or dependent on government expenditures to believe their interests are aligned with those of Democrat politicians. Today, integral parts of the Democrat organizational apparatus are the strong unions of government employees and their dwindling counterparts in the private sector.

A year and a half into Roosevelt's first term the Great Depression continued unabated and unemployment still hovered near 20%. Nonetheless, in the 1934 congressional races, Democrats increased their majority in both houses, a rare accomplishment for the party holding the White House. The Republican share of seats declined to 24% in the House of Representatives and 26% in the Senate. These midterm elections, not the ones in 1932, were the true national referendum on the New Deal. The bulk of the northern electorate (southern whites having been solidly Democrat since our Party was born) shifted away from the Republicans, and except for only a few years Congress would remain under firm Democratic Party control into the 1990s

Struggling to formulate an effective response to Roosevelt's popularity, delegates to the 1936 Republican National Convention were of two principal factions, the Progressives who favored the New Deal and the Hoover supporters who opposed it. The compromise presidential nominee was a former Bull Mooser, Kansas Governor Alf Landon, one of the few prominent Republicans to have held onto office over the previous four years. Landon accepted most of the New Deal but asserted that he would not go as far as Roosevelt.

The platform basically accepted the New Deal programs but said our Party could administer them better and without the partisanship. It accepted the need for lower tariffs and had many economic reform proposals that made more sense than what the Democrats were doing. Our Party saw right through the Democrat lies regarding Social Security, pointing out that the "reserve fund," what we today would call the "trust fund," does not exist, as it contains "nothing but the Government's promise to pay, while the taxes collected in the guise of premiums will be wasted by the Government in reckless and extravagant political schemes." Now there is a truth for the ages!

Republicans criticized Roosevelt for racking up a large federal government debt after having promised to balance the budget and denounced the Democrats generally for "appeals to passion and class prejudice." Concerned about their party's socialist drift, some Democrats, including Al Smith, the 1928 Democrat presidential candidate, endorsed the Republican ticket in 1936.

Landon was personally popular, but the shell-shocked Republicans were unable to mount much of a counterattack against the socialist onslaught. "The New Deal, but not so much, and better!" was hardly a winning campaign theme. The Harding-Coolidge-Hoover approach had been discredited and Franklin Roosevelt had appropriated his fifth cousin's Progressive mantle, so what was our Party to stand for?

While the platform heaped all sorts of valid criticisms on the New Deal, these lacked coherence because by then most Republicans had forgotten how during the 1860s the Lincoln administration had met an even greater challenge with its own vast expansion of the federal government. The key difference, however, was though the Republicans demobilized the Union army it had created, the Democrats were creating a standing army of millions of dependents in the federal bureaucracy. Moreover, the 1936 Republican platform barely mentioned black Americans, though Stevens, Sumner, and other early heroes knew that to defend the Constitution effectively, one cannot pick and choose which constitutional rights to uphold.

In the November 1936 elections, the Democrats won a victory even greater than their trouncing of the Republicans four years earlier. Roosevelt beat Landon* by 61% to 37% in the popular vote and 523 to 8 in the Electoral College. Our Party was left with just 20% of the House of Representatives and 18% of the Senate. Only six states would have Republican Governors.

Our Party looked to be heading into oblivion along with the

---

* Landon's running mate, newspaper publisher Frank Knox, would serve as Roosevelt's Secretary of the Navy during World War II, while the Secretary of War would be Henry Stimson, previously Taft's Secretary of War and Hoover's Secretary of State.

Federalists and the Whigs. Republicans rebounded strongly, however, in the 1938 midterm elections, more than doubling the number of House seats and picking up six seats in the Senate. This revival occurred for two main reasons.

Throughout his first term, President Roosevelt had seen the Supreme Court rule much of his New Deal agenda unconstitutional, along with many socialist measures taken at the state government level. In unanimously striking down the NRA, for instance, the Supreme Court had grasped just how far the socialists would go in order to get their way; if the interstate commerce clause was stretched limitlessly, then "the federal authority would embrace practically all the activities of the people and the authority of the state over its domestic concerns would exist only by sufferance." Indeed, this is just what has happened to our country.

Just a month after beginning his second term, Roosevelt over-reached himself by asking Congress for authority to appoint up to six additional Justices to the Supreme Court, so that his opponents among the original nine might be outvoted. Congress rejected this proposal. Resentment of the Supreme Court's authority could be traced back to Thomas Jefferson, but even most Democrats thought the President had gone too far. Over the next few years, opposition to Roosevelt's policies by the Supreme Court would weaken nonetheless, as the President had the opportunity to appointed several new Justices.

Another reason Republican prospects improved was that the economy deteriorated sharply in 1937. The stock market tanked again and unemployment rose to near-1932 levels. It was plain to Republicans, and to many Democrats as well, that five years of the New Deal had not ended the Great Depression. That would have to wait for Pearl Harbor.

❦

Several well-known Republicans vied for the 1940 presidential nomination, including Ohio Senator Robert Taft, son of the former President, and Michigan Senator Arthur Vandenberg, but most Republicans recognized the need for a completely new face for our

Party. Just as the Democratic Party opted for a relative unknown in 1904 to erase the stigma of its free silver folly, the Republican National Convention chose Indiana-born business executive Wendell Willkie, whose defense of the free market system had made him a national figure. Willkie, a Democrat who did not switch parties until after his nomination, supported most of the New Deal, though with greater respect for the Constitution and for the private sector. The Republican platform advocated a "square deal" for blacks, a use of Theodore Roosevelt's term, and called for racial integration of the armed forces.

Roosevelt saw to it that he was nominated for an unprecedented third term. He also had the convention hand the vice presidential nomination to his Agriculture Secretary, Henry Wallace. The 1936 Democrat platform had avoided the issue altogether, but in 1940 there was a strongly-worded plank on the rights of black people that cited the many employment and training opportunities afforded them by the New Deal, and a black minister offered a prayer before the convention. While the number of black people working in the federal bureaucracy quadrupled during his presidency, Roosevelt's sincere goodwill toward them was also an important factor behind the shift of most blacks toward the Democratic Party. The President made sure all New Deal programs were racially integrated, and he ended the racial segregation established by Woodrow Wilson within the federal government.

Black voters fondly remembered that a year earlier the Roosevelt administration had offered the Lincoln Memorial as a concert site to Marian Anderson* after the Daughters of the American Revolution had refused to allow her to perform at their Constitution Hall. Before an audience of 75,000 and millions over the radio, standing in front of the statue of the first Republican President, Ms. Anderson opened with "My country tis of thee, sweet land of liberty, of thee I sing." Within just one lifetime, our Party had let slip to the Democrats the aspirations of the Radical Republicans. Worse, as they found common cause with white southern Democrats who opposed the New Deal, some Republicans began to soft-pedal our Party's traditional

---

* In 1961, she would sing the National Anthem at President Kennedy's inauguration.

commitment to safeguarding the constitutional rights of blacks.

The energetic and charming Willkie ran a terrific campaign, but he did not really stand a chance even though some prominent Democrats, including Al Smith, campaigned for him. The main issue of the 1940 presidential campaign had nothing to do with domestic politics, but rather was how the United States should respond to the wars raging in Europe and Asia. With American entry into World War II likely, most voters were uneasy about electing a new President who had zero political experience. Another factor, as former President Hoover was quick to point out, was that the New Deal expansion of the federal government had, in effect, put millions of voters on the Democratic Party payroll.

Roosevelt defeated Willkie* by 55% to 45% in the popular vote. The South remained Solid for the Democrats, so the Electoral College tally was a lopsided 449 to 82. Still, the Republican ticket did much better than it had the last time, particularly so in the Midwest. In congressional races, our Party gained five Senate seats while losing only seven seats in the House of Representatives.

By the 1942 midterm elections, our Party had fully recovered from its near-death experience a decade earlier, almost winning a majority in the House of Representatives while gaining ten seats in the Senate. Republicans expected to win the presidency in 1944. The presidential nominee that year was the 42-year old Governor of New York, Thomas Dewey, who had risen to prominence as a gangster-battling district attorney. Dewey campaigned against New Deal abuses and excesses, but overall he accepted the immense expansion of federal government power which the New Deal entailed. The wing of our Party he typified would later become known as "Rockefeller Republicans," after a later New York Governor, though Dewey himself was much more devoted to the free market than was Nelson Rockefeller.

What cost Dewey the election was the common perception

---

* Willkie died in October 1944.

among the electorate that with the country at war it was no time for a change in leadership at the top. As in 1940, the war overshadowed all other issues; such was the Republicans' bad luck that their convention took place just after the invasion of Normandy. Earl Warren, who had been elected Governor of California two years earlier, was offered the vice presidential nomination, but he turned it down. Governor Warren did deliver the keynote address to the 1944 Republican National Convention, and slammed the New Deal repeatedly. The platform that year reflected a return to our Party's traditional concern for blacks, calling for a federal anti-lynching law and the elimination of poll taxes.

Dewey's 46% of the popular vote and 99 electoral votes were a bit better than Willkie had done, but the Republican standard-bearer did not even carry his own state. Considering the loss of the presidential election, results in congressional races could have been worse for Republicans. Our Party lost 19 seats in the House of Representatives but held its own in the Senate. Suspecting that President Roosevelt had little time to live, Democratic Party bosses had insisted that his Communist-leaning Vice President, Henry Wallace, be replaced on the ticket by Missouri Senator Harry Truman. A faithful New Dealer, Truman would, the bosses expected, continue Roosevelt's domestic polices while carrying out foreign policy in the interests of the United States, should he assume the presidency. In April 1945, three months into his fourth term, Franklin Roosevelt died and Harry Truman became President.

In the postwar 1946 midterm elections, Republicans won a majority in both the House of Representatives and the Senate – an impressive comeback for a political party on the verge of extinction a decade earlier. Having postponed the move until after the elections, Truman soon lifted the wartime wage and price controls. Wages and prices soared, but after five years of wartime strictures on the economy this readjustment of relative prices was inevitable. It was about this time that our Party took on strident anti-Communism as a major theme, even though the Truman administration had done little to merit criticism in this regard. The real reason for the Republican effort to outdo Truman in opposing Communism and other forms of socialism overseas was that most Republican leaders had given up hope of defeating socialism at home.

⁂

Confident of victory, the 1948 Republican National Convention renominated Governor Dewey over his chief rivals, the more pro-New Deal Harold Stassen, the former Governor of Minnesota; and the anti-New Deal Senator Taft. Dewey's running mate was California Governor Earl Warren, who had also vied for the nomination.

Our Party again called for an end to racial segregation in the military and denounced lynching and other mob violence. Having implemented many racially advanced policies in New York, the Republican standard-bearer faulted Truman for moving too slowly to guarantee the rights of blacks. Republicans denounced the Democratic Party as a marriage of convenience between self-described progressives in the North, who kept themselves in power through federal government patronage and bureaucratic muscle, and the viciously racist white supremacist regimes in the South. What these two groups of Democrats had in common was dedication to the socialist credo that the ignorant many should be governed by the enlightened few.

In Congress, most Republicans were very critical of the New Deal and the corruption it had engendered; while Dewey and his team, who drafted the platform, accepted most of it and even proposed some additional programs. On the campaign trail, Dewey* was complacent and overconfident, but more than anything else, this divide between congressional Republicans and the presidential nominee cost him the election.

During the election campaign, the astute President Truman called Congress back into special session. He challenged the Republican majority to enact the policy proposals of the 1946 campaigns as well as those outlined in their 1948 platform. Senator Taft, resentful of Dewey

---

* One of the oldest T-shirts with lettering printed on it known to exist dates from Dewey's 1948 campaign.

for getting the nomination again, and other New Deal opponents in the Republican caucus were reluctant to make enough concessions to Dewey's positions to pass anything. When Congress adjourned without having taken action on constitutional rights protection or the economy, Truman went on the offensive against the "do-nothing" 80th Congress, campaigning much more against congressional Republicans than against Dewey, with whom he had far fewer policy differences.

In July 1948, President Truman ordered the racial integration of the military. Of course, he or Roosevelt could have taken this step any time in the past fifteen years, but his purpose in doing so four months before the election was to signal to the electorate that under his leadership the Democratic Party would no longer be "The White Man's Party." Prior to assuming the presidency, Truman had not shown any particular sympathy for black people, but once in the White House he made clear where he stood. In 1947, he was the first President to address the NAACP national convention. During the campaign he agreed with Republican denunciations of lynching and poll taxes, and called for permanent Civil Rights and Fair Employment Practices commissions. At the urging of the Mayor of Minneapolis, Hubert Humphrey, the 1948 Democratic National Convention adopted a strongly-worded plank in support of the constitutional rights of blacks.

This was too much for many southern Democrats. Led by South Carolina Governor Strom Thurmond, several dozen southern delegates stormed out of the convention waving the Confederate flag. Calling themselves "Dixiecrats," they held a convention in Montgomery, Alabama, the first capital of the Confederacy, and nominated Thurmond for President. For Truman and the rest of the Democratic Party it was good riddance.

Another faction of the Democratic Party also split away. Former Vice President Wallace formed a new Progressive Party, which stood for even more socialist measures at home and appeasement of the Soviet Union abroad. At first glance, Truman appeared weakened by these defections, but actually the Thurmond and Wallace candidacies unburdened him from having to defend extremists in his party.

Dewey narrowly carried New York this time and Thurmond won the electoral votes of four southern states, but Truman won 50% of the popular vote to Dewey's 45%, and 303 of 531 electoral votes. In the congressional races, for which the Dixiecrats and the Progressives did not run independent slates of candidates, results were just as disappointing for our Party. The Democrats won back majorities in both houses of Congress, leaving Republicans with only 39% of the House of Representatives and 44% of the Senate.

In his January 1949 State of the Union address, Truman announced what he called the "Fair Deal," a continuation of the New Deal that was in many ways more socialist. The President got through the Democrat-controlled Congress an expansion of Social Security, a hike in the minimum wage, increased transfer payments to farmers, and more federal government spending overall.

Truman's attempts to establish a national health care system, one actually more expansive than the Great Society's Medicare and Medicaid, was blocked by Republicans and Democrats concerned that his real aim was to nationalize a large sector of the economy. Congress also refused to establish a Department of Public Welfare, for the same reason. Similarly, Truman's proposal for a massive federal government program to build housing went nowhere. Again for Republicans, forgetting their Radical Republican heritage proved damaging to our Party and the nation. Republicans did not pass a bill to protect the constitutional rights of blacks when they held a congressional majority, and now they compounded this error by voting with enough southern Democrats to defeat Truman's bill.

Truman also failed in his attempt to repeal the Taft-Hartley Act, passed over his veto in 1947 – a major achievement in fact of that so-called "do-nothing" 80th Congress. Recognizing that union bosses had converted their organizations into a branch of the Democratic Party, Taft-Hartley reduced the political power of organized labor by banning unions from making contributions to political candidates. Other provisions instituted a 60-day cooling off period before any strike and banned "closed shops," in which employees were forced to join a union.

Generally, Taft-Hartley repealed the 1935 Wagner Act, a New Deal measure based on outmoded notions of class warfare and enacted to salvage as much as possible from the notorious National Industrial Recovery Act. Truman favored the union bosses, but in many respects he was no friend of the average worker. Like President Cleveland, he came down hard on strikers, threatening to draft striking steel workers into the army and to seize coal mines to force striking miners back to work.*

---

* Compare this brutality to President Reagan's dismissal of striking air traffic controllers. These people were federal government employees, in contrast, who upon being hired had agreed never to strike.

Chapter Nine

(1952-2000)

REPUBLICANS AT A LOSS

To succeed Harry Truman, Democrats in 1952 nominated Illinois Governor Adlai Stevenson, grandson of Grover Cleveland's second Vice President and Bryan's 1900 running mate. Their vice presidential candidate was a prominent segregationist, Alabama Senator John Sparkman. The Democrat platform had a lengthy section on constitutional rights protection, but Stevenson and Sparkman avoided the issue as much as possible during the campaign. The platform also contained a long list of promised expansions of Fair Deal policies. Stevenson campaigned as Truman's heir on domestic economic policy, less so on foreign affairs, and not at all on respect for black Americans.

Our Party was again divided into those who accepted most New Deal programs and those who looked to reverse the socialist trend. As in 1948, opponents of the New Deal gathered behind the leadership of Senator Taft. Governor Warren and former Governor Stassen were also in contention for the nomination, but fortunately for Republicans a candidate with much greater voter appeal was on hand, General Dwight Eisenhower, who had been the Allied Supreme Commander in Europe during World War II. Considering that many Democrats had urged Eisenhower to be their presidential candidate four years before, the General could count on a broad base of popular support.

After the war, Eisenhower had headed Columbia University before being appointed by President Truman as the first military commander of NATO. In 1952, Eisenhower, a life-long Republican, resigned from the army and returned home to battle Taft for our Party's presidential nomination. Most Republican heavyweights favored Taft, but Eisenhower had both the firm support of Thomas Dewey and superb political skills. Another of his advantages over Taft was that the Senator's opposition to NATO and the Marshall Plan was clearly out of place in the postwar world. Taft* would probably have lost to Stevenson, but the magnetic Eisenhower proved to be a formidable standard-bearer for the Grand Old Party.

Governor Dewey was the person most responsible for California's Richard Nixon receiving the vice presidential nomination. Elected to the House of Representatives in 1946 and to the Senate in 1950, Nixon was only 39 years old when he became Eisenhower's running mate. He had gained national prominence for exposing the diplomat Alger Hiss as a Soviet spy after Truman had publicly defended him, a feat which made him especially popular among the more anti-New Deal Republicans. Nixon was in fact, as Dewey knew, a Progressive in the tradition of Theodore Roosevelt.** Back in 1948, Democrats had thought highly enough of Nixon to give him their party's nomination for the House of Representatives as well.

Americans had grown tired of twenty years of Democrat administrations. So many years after the Great Depression, plenty of New Deal programs had degenerated into the breeding grounds of corruption that Republicans said they would, and most people knew that a thorough housecleaning was in order. Eisenhower campaigned against the paternalist, free-spending, dependency-promoting Democrat ways, and he also promised to bring an end to the war in Korea.

The Taft wing of our Party believed that no laws could be passed to protect black Americans as long as southern Democrats were able to filibuster them in the Senate, but most Republicans were still willing to take on the Democrats. Dewey led the fight at the convention to

---

* He died in July 1953.

** In a farewell speech after resigning the presidency in 1974, Nixon said his woes were trifling compared to those of Theodore Roosevelt, who lost his wife, daughter, and mother within a few days.

include in the platform a lengthy section on protecting the constitutional rights of black Americans, which among other things promised to abolish poll taxes, prevent lynching, and desegregate the Democrat-controlled District of Columbia government. Eisenhower's campaign manager was grandson of the author of the 1890 Federal Elections Bill, Massachusetts Senator Henry Cabot Lodge, who himself would be defeated for reelection that year by Democrat Representative John Kennedy.

Campaigning fully in the South, much more than any previous Republican presidential candidate had done, paid off for Eisenhower, winning him six southern states. Nationwide, he defeated Stevenson 55% to 44%, and 442 to 89 in the Electoral College. In congressional races, Republicans built on their successes in the 1950 midterm elections to gain control of both houses.

In contrast with the previous career military man elected President, Eisenhower did not surround himself with army cronies, and he had no time for fuzzy-thinking academics either. He returned to the Whig tradition of deferring to congressional leadership on many policy issues. Determined to undo the federal government's militaristic orientation imparted by World War II, Eisenhower appointed business people to most top positions. His choice for Attorney General, who would play a crucial role in the incipient civil rights movement, was Herbert Brownell, former chairman of the Republican National Committee and key aide to Governor Dewey. Richard Nixon was the first Vice President ever to have a substantial role in an administration, this in consequence of Eisenhower's poor health as well as the growing demand for official representation overseas.

Eisenhower did reduce involvement by the federal government in the economy, but overall he had no problem with the New Deal legacy. Social Security was expanded under his presidency, and during his first year in office the Department of Health, Education, and Welfare was established. Even had he wanted to, with only narrow majorities in Congress at first and then Democrat majorities for the rest of his presidency, a root-and-branch eradication of the New Deal was out of the question. One of the Eisenhower administration's major initiatives was a Whiggish internal improvement, construction of the federal highway system.

Another achievement of President Eisenhower was helping to quash Senator Joseph McCarthy's persecution of alleged Communist sympathizers, a throwback to the Wilson administration's far worse Red Scare after World War I. In 1954, a large majority of his Senate colleagues voted to censure the Wisconsin Republican, but displaying his own kind of Profile in Courage, John Kennedy did not vote for the resolution against McCarthy, on whose Unamerican Activities Committee his brother Robert served as assistant counsel.*

Eisenhower had promised Earl Warren, who was close to Brownell, an appointment to the first vacancy on the Supreme Court, and when Chief Justice Vinson died in the fall of 1953 the President nominated him. Though he would not be confirmed by the Senate until March 1954, Governor Warren participated unofficially on the Supreme Court until then, and so was fully prepared for the first major decision of the Warren Court, Brown v. Board of Education.

The Supreme Court first heard arguments on the challenge to the Topeka, Kansas public school racial segregation policy in December 1952. In June 1953, the Court ordered the case reargued that fall to consider whether the 14th amendment had been intended to end segregation in public schools and whether the Supreme Court had the authority to order them desegregated.

The federal government was not a party to the case, but Attorney General Brownell filed a brief in favor of overturning the 1896 Plessy v. Ferguson decision which sanctioned "separate but equal." Arguing on behalf of Linda Brown was Thurgood Marshall, director of the NAACP's Legal Defense and Education Fund, who a decade earlier had succeeded in convincing the Supreme Court to strike down Texas' all-white Democratic Party primary. On the other side, the chief lawyer for the Board of Education was John Davis, the 1924 Democrat presidential candidate.

---

* In 1951, McCarthy was godfather to Robert Kennedy's first child, Kathleen Kennedy Townsend, currently the Lt. Governor of Maryland.

In May 1954, the Supreme Court ruled unanimously that racial segregation in public schools was unconstitutional, recognizing after nearly a century that the Radical Republicans' 14th amendment meant what it said.

On one occasion prior to the decision, the President urged Warren not to vote for desegregation. Dwight Eisenhower, a career soldier in a strictly segregated army, did not really know many black people and felt uncomfortable around them. Unlike Truman, he did not meet with any black leaders until June 1958. Eisenhower was not a racist, however, and had nothing but contempt for Democrat oppression of southern blacks.

His concerns were that southern Democrats would turn violent and that they would carry out their threat that if ordered to desegregate the public schools they would abolish them, as they had largely done after the Reconstruction state governments fell. He thought it would be futile for our Party to once again take on the entrenched white Democrat opposition in the South and in the Senate. Though Eisenhower favored equal rights for blacks in the abstract, basically he regarded a battle over public school desegregation as a huge hassle he would rather do without.

The ferocious reaction by white Democrats in the South shamed the nation and afforded our Republican Party a tremendous opportunity to reclaim its heritage, but President Eisenhower did not seize the moment. He let his chief of staff, Sherman Adams, talk him into distancing himself from the Brown decision, so that people would not blame the Republicans for it. What the Republican President should have embraced as one of the great accomplishments of his life, he merely said he would accept. Nonetheless, desegregation of public schools was now the law of the land, and Eisenhower wasted no time in carrying it out.

The very next day, Eisenhower told the District of Columbia government to integrate its schools immediately, even before a specific court order to do so. Unfortunately, not until the following year did the Supreme Court render a second decision in the Brown case on how desegregation was to be implemented. His years in the army had taught Eisenhower that one's opponents should not be given time to regroup after a defeat. He personally rewrote the federal government's brief for the second Brown case to argue that the Supreme Court should order immediate nationwide desegregation of the public schools, but instead the Justices opted for "all deliberate speed" on the part of individual federal judges.

Just as the two-year delay before implementing Radical Republican Reconstruction policies in the South was an immense error, so was leaving desegregation to district courts, with no timetable for implementation. It would take another two decades to accomplish what could have been done in 1954. Permitted to recover the initiative, southern Democrats intensified their legal oppression of blacks in the South. They dusted off their states rights arguments, and four state legislatures passed resolutions that the Brown v. Board of Education decision was not valid in their states. In 1956, 101 members of Congress (97 of them Democrats) signed the "Southern Manifesto" which declared, nonsensically, that the Brown decision and other measures to implement the 14th amendment to the Constitution were somehow unconstitutional.

The 1954 Brown v. Board of Education decision, marking the resumption of the civil rights movement first undertaken by the Radical Republicans, emboldened southern blacks to begin resisting their white Democrat oppressors. In December 1955 in Montgomery, Alabama – the original Confederate capital, appropriately enough – a black woman, Rosa Parks, was arrested after refusing to give up her seat on the bus to a white person, as required by city ordinance. A local minister, Martin Luther King Jr., whom Parks had nominated for the executive board of the Montgomery NAACP, was named to head a boycott of the bus company to force it to treat black commuters equally. King* and another local minister, Ralph Abernathy, warned protesters to be non-violent but determined.

The boycott lasted nearly a year, during which time King's house was firebombed, until the Supreme Court upheld a lower court decision

---

* a graduate of Atlanta's Booker T. Washington High School

striking down the discriminatory ordinance. One of the federal judges who had voted against the ordinance was Frank Johnson, a Republican hero of the civil rights movement. A native of Winston County, Alabama, that Unionist stronghold during the Civil War, Johnson had managed Eisenhower's 1952 campaign in the state. The President appointed him to the federal bench just prior to the bus discrimination ruling, which was actually his first case. Johnson would go on to be a resolute opponent of Democrat Governor George Wallace. Johnson spearheaded the drive to desegregate public schools and other state and local government facilities throughout the South.

For the 1956 presidential election, Democrats renominated Adlai Stevenson, but with the economy doing well and trouble brewing overseas, Republicans were confident that voters would prefer Eisenhower once more. The President offered to name Nixon Secretary of Defense, to get him off the ticket, but the Vice President would not budge, mindful of the added importance his position had gained since Eisenhower's heart attack in September 1955. The Republican platform had a long section supporting the constitutional rights of blacks, but, at Eisenhower's insistence, the convention dropped a plank claiming credit for Brown v. Board of Education.

Eisenhower made up for this error somewhat by agreeing to submit to Congress Attorney General Brownell's civil rights bill. Six times in the past decade, congressional Democrat opposition had defeated legislative attempts to implement the Radical Reconstruction political agenda in the South, but at the very least Brownell hoped to signal to the electorate that our Republican Party was firmly committed to black Americans. Even if the bill failed in Congress, thought Brownell, at least Republicans would get credit for trying.

Apprehensive that being too bold might hurt reelection prospects in the South, Sherman Adams made sure the bill came from Brownell, not directly from the President. Eisenhower admonished Brownell to be cautious: "Don't take the attitude that you are another Sumner," though of course, another Sumner was precisely what our Republican

Party and the nation needed.

Vice President Nixon campaigned much harder than Eisenhower did for protection of the constitutional rights of blacks, saying in a speech just before the election: "Most of us here will live to see the day when American boys and girls shall sit, side by side, at any school – public or private – with no regard paid to the color of their skin. Segregation, discrimination, and prejudice have no place in America."

Eisenhower defeated Stevenson by a popular vote of 57% to 42% and won all but seven states to gain a 457-73 margin in the Electoral College. For the last time up to the present day, the Republican presidential ticket received a majority of the votes of black people. At his second inauguration, the President signaled his decision to side with the civil rights movement by having a black administration official sit with him during the parade. This may seem trivial today unless one considers the volcanic Democrat reactions to similar overtures that Herbert Hoover and Theodore Roosevelt had made to blacks a generation and two earlier.

Early in 1957, Martin Luther King and dozens of other black ministers in the South formed the Southern Christian Leadership Conference, in order to be independent of the northern-dominated NAACP. Resentful of this challenge to the establishment NAACP, Thurgood Marshall denounced King as "an opportunist" and a "first-rate rabble-rouser."

One of King's first acts as president of the new organization was to send telegrams to Eisenhower, Nixon, and Brownell asking that the President make a major address in the South on race relations. Here was another historic opportunity for our Party, but again Eisenhower let it pass. Southern blacks were pleading for protection against violence by white segregationist Democrats, but the President put a stop to the drift of blacks back to our Republican Party with a curt "You can't legislate morality."

Still another opportunity for the Republicans presented itself at a March 1957 ceremony in Ghana celebrating that country's independence, where Martin Luther King and Ralph Abernathy met with Vice President Nixon to ask for his help. They again requested that President Eisenhower deliver a speech on improving relations between blacks and whites in the South. King and Abernathy added that if Brownell's bill guaranteeing voting rights for blacks was enacted, it could be followed up by a huge voter registration campaign, and that most blacks would vote Republican, as they themselves had the year before. Nixon agreed to confer with them back in Washington, and though the Vice President was enthusiastic, the administration took no action as a result of the meeting.

In his January 1957 State of the Union address, President Eisenhower resubmitted the civil right bill to Congress, where it had languished the year before. Brownell's original draft would have permitted the Attorney General to sue anyone violating another person's constitutional rights, but this powerful provision would have to wait until the 1964 Civil Rights Act.

The new Act established a Civil Rights Division within the Justice Department and a Civil Rights Commission, and authorized the Attorney General to request injunctions from federal courts against any attempt to deny someone's right to vote. Violations would be civil, not criminal offenses, and penalties were light, so the Act turned out to be ineffective and easily circumvented. Not until 1965 were more than a few southern blacks able to vote. Nonetheless, though it had been weakened considerably in order get congressional approval, the Civil Rights Act of 1957 was the first legislative action to reconstruct the South since Charles Sumner's Civil Rights Act of 1875.

From the beginning, the 1957 Act had overwhelming support in the House of Representatives. As ever, southern Democrats in the Senate were the chief obstacle, and Vice President Nixon played a key role in outmaneuvering them. In his capacity as President of the Senate, Nixon ordered the bill as approved by the House directly to the Senate floor, bypassing the Judiciary Committee, where Democrats would surely have bottled it up. Attorney General Brownell foolishly chose this critical time to be in London attending a conference, so it fell to a Democrat, Senate Majority Leader Lyndon Johnson, to be the person most responsible for passage of the Civil Rights Act of 1957.

Prior to 1957, Johnson had voted the segregationist party line, opposing various bills against lynching and poll taxes, but in securing passage of Brownell's bill he revealed his personal sympathy toward blacks. Previously, he had opposed efforts to weaken the ability of Senators to filibuster, fearing that Republicans would then be able to get a stronger bill through Congress. Once he recognized the 1957 Civil Rights bill as a way for the Democratic Party to obtain most of the credit for reducing racial discrimination, Johnson was all for it. To prevent a filibuster by his fellow southern Democrats, the Majority Leader deleted from the Senate version the provision for desegregating public schools. He also had to support an amendment disabling the injunction provision, a move Nixon criticized as "a vote against the right to vote." Not just most southern Democrats but some Republicans too wanted a weaker bill, so as to appeal to white voters.

Among the prominent opponents of the Civil Rights bill in the Senate were Tennessee Democrat Sam Ervin, of later Watergate fame, and Arizona Republican Barry Goldwater. South Carolina Senator Strom Thurmond, then a Democrat, set a record in filibustering 24 straight hours just before the final vote. In August 1957, the Senate approved the Civil Rights bill by 60 to 15. Attorney General Brownell, who could justly have chosen the moment to trumpet his bill as a tremendous achievement for our Party, instead resigned from the Cabinet shortly after the Act was signed into law. He was succeeded by William Rogers, Brownell's assistant and former prosecutor under Dewey.*

In September 1957, a few days after passage of the Civil Rights Act, Orval Faubus, the Democrat Governor of Arkansas, ordered the state National Guard to prevent the court-ordered integration of a Little Rock public school. President Eisenhower viewed the situation primarily as an armed insurrection, akin to Shays' Rebellion. At first he tried to negotiate with Faubus, but after several fruitless weeks the President lost patience with his Democrat foe. Eisenhower had not been afraid to take on the Nazis, and he certainly was not going to be fazed by Faubus or any other Democrat challenging the Constitution.

---

* Rogers would later serve as Nixon's first Secretary of State.

Under authority granted to the President by Reconstruction-era legislation, Eisenhower placed the Governor's soldiers under federal government control and ordered the 101st Airborne to Arkansas. Senators Johnson and Kennedy, among others, publicly criticized the move. Many Democrats compared this use of force to the Soviet invasion of Hungary, but of course a more apt comparison was the Grant administration's deployment of troops to protect southern blacks from white Democrats during Reconstruction.

In the 1958 midterm elections, Republicans lost heavily and saw their share of both the House of Representatives and the Senate fall to just 35%. An unfortunately-timed recession was mostly to blame, but unrest in the South due to the administration's defense of the Constitution also cost the Grand Old Party millions of votes. Eisenhower's timidity on constitutional rights guarantees for black Americans had been the wrong strategy. While progress the GOP had been making with southern whites halted completely, blacks gave the Republicans little credit for our Party's accomplishments.

In May 1960, after southern Democrats in the Senate filibustered for nearly a week, Congress passed another Civil Rights Act. At Eisenhower's insistence, this law improved enforcement of the 1957 Act, by among other measures making any obstruction of voting rights a federal crime. As had occurred in 1957, passage of the 1960 Civil Rights Act sparked protests across the South.

<hr/>

Amid another recession in 1960, Democrats had high hopes for victory in that year's presidential election. Not wanting to imperil their party's prospects, southern white Democrats put up with a long section of the platform which promised full implementation of the 1957 and 1960 Civil Rights Acts. This plank was not strong enough, however, for many black delegates, some of whom walked out of the convention in protest.

The presidential nominee was John Kennedy, a hawkish Democrat with a respectable voting record on guaranteeing constitutional rights for blacks. His chief rival for the nomination had been

Lyndon Johnson, who, having worked his way up from poverty, resented the multimillionaire from Massachusetts. Despite their personal differences, Kennedy offered him the second spot on the ticket, and Johnson wisely accepted. The two men made a superb campaign team, the Texan adding to the Kennedy glamour not only a big advantage in the South but an enviable legislative record.

Vice President Nixon was virtually unopposed for the 1960 Republican nomination, easily besting his two closest rivals, New York Governor Nelson Rockefeller and Arizona Senator Barry Goldwater. Knowing that a Nixon-Rockefeller ticket would have been tough to beat, Nixon asked the Governor to be his running mate, but the resentful Rockefeller refused and later would hardly campaign for him. Nixon then selected United Nations Ambassador Henry Cabot Lodge, grandson of the former Senate Majority Leader who was one of Theodore Roosevelt's oldest friends. Lodge was even closer to the civil rights movement than Nixon was, but the Vice President did not need any help on that topic or on foreign policy. Unlike Lyndon Johnson, Lodge brought nothing to the ticket and proved to be as bad a campaigner as he had been against John Kennedy in 1952. Worse, President Eisenhower did little to help Nixon's campaign.

The main issues of the 1960 presidential election campaign were national defense and foreign policy, and racial politics had an impact on the election only in the last few weeks. At the Republican National Convention Nixon had fought hard for our Party to take a firm stand on constitutional rights protection, and he and Rockefeller issued a joint statement to that effect. Much to his credit, the platform had a lengthy section of detailed policy proposals on racial issues and belatedly took credit for having argued for desegregation in its legal brief submitted to the Supreme Court for Brown v. Board of Education.

One plank denounced the Democrats for having weakened the 1957 and 1960 Civil Rights bills in Congress, and others promised further progress for blacks in education, voting rights, and employment. Unlike the Democratic Party's convention, none of the many black delegates attending the Republican National Convention walked out in protest. Ominously, Goldwater and his supporters among the delegates were the ones protesting, upset that Nixon and the majority of the convention were so supportive of fully extending constitutional rights protection to black Americans.

Martin Luther King Jr. attended both the Republican Party and Democratic Party conventions in 1960, and he refused to endorse either candidate. In October 1960, Kennedy asked for a meeting with King, who agreed only on condition that he also offer to meet with Nixon. Kennedy then backed out, fearing that Nixon would accept. Baseball great Jackie Robinson, the most famous black person in the United States at the time, campaigned for Nixon. On October 18th, King's father, Rev. Martin Luther King Sr., joined with most other prominent blacks ministers in Atlanta to endorse Nixon for President.

But then there was the famous incident which cost Nixon the close election. The very next day, October 19th, while leading sixteen blacks students in an attempt to eat at an Atlanta whites-only diner, Martin Luther King Jr. was arrested and quickly sentenced to four months in a chain gang. Nixon had done much more than Kennedy for black Americans, but Kennedy seized the moment and Nixon did not.

The Vice President suggested privately to Justice Department officials that they investigate the matter, but he felt he could not take a public stand because he hoped to get enough votes from whites in the South to carry several states there. Kennedy, the Democrat candidate with a southern running mate, had a bit more room to maneuver. He issued a statement that he was looking into the matter – vague, but more than Nixon was doing. Kennedy then placed a call to Coretta King to express his concern for her husband. The national media did not make much of it, either for or against Kennedy, but the effect on black voters of Kennedy's gesture was tremendous. Martin Luther King's father reversed himself and declared he would vote for Kennedy. In a deft move to appeal to black voters without angering too many whites, in black churches on the Sunday before the election the Kennedy campaign distributed two million pamphlets describing his call to Coretta King.

Four years before, three-fifths of blacks had voted for the Republican presidential candidate, but this time around a last-minute surge toward Kennedy gave the Democrat 70% of the black vote, a tally far in excess of Kennedy's 49.7% to 49.5% margin in the popular vote results and the probable margin of Democrat vote fraud that year. Nixon did carry four southern states, but he narrowly lost New York, Illinois, Missouri, and several other large northern states. In the Electoral College, Kennedy defeated Nixon 303 to 219. Nixon actually did much better than our Republican Party fared in congressional races. Though it picked up seats in both Houses, our Party ended up with just 36% of the Senate and 40% of the House of Representatives.

Clever strategizing had won him the support of most black voters, but it took President Kennedy nearly two years to make good on even one of his campaign promises to them. Neither his inaugural address nor his first State of the Union address contained any mention of constitutional rights protection for blacks. Not until November 1962 did he end racial discrimination in federal government public housing, though he had pledged to do so immediately.

Like Eisenhower, Kennedy sympathized with oppressed black Americans, but also, like his predecessor, Kennedy was reluctant to take on the southern Democrats in Congress, especially when he needed their support for policies he regarded as higher priorities, such as more spending on domestic programs and the military. Kennedy was also concerned that white Democrats might desert their party in the 1962 midterm elections, so nothing came of his campaign promise to submit to Congress a new civil rights bill soon after taking office.

Over the objections of southern Democrats, President Eisenhower had appointed to the federal bench his Solicitor General, who had submitted the anti-segregation brief on Brown v. Board of Education, and in the South Eisenhower had appointed federal judges regardless of the opinions of the Democrat Senators in their states.

In sharp contrast, most of Kennedy's appointees to the federal bench in the South were segregationists. That Democrat in the White House could boast of appointing no judge in the South of the stature of Frank Johnson. The President, to his credit, did appoint Thurgood Marshall to the federal bench, but that was to the Second Circuit of the U.S. Court of Appeals, far from the fray in the South. Kennedy refused to appear at a dinner commemorating the 100th anniversary of the Emancipation Proclamation. The most he would permit was for the Attorney General, his brother Robert, to attend but not deliver a speech – inexcusable lapses which Martin Luther King was quick to denounce.

Events in the South forced Kennedy into action. In September 1962, Mississippi's Democrat Governor, Ross Barnett, in defiance of two federal court orders, personally blocked a black man from enrolling in the University of Mississippi as he was escorted by Justice Department official John Doar, a holdover from the Eisenhower administration. After negotiating with the President, Barnett eventually backed down. The student was enrolled, but in an ensuing riot 160 federal marshals were injured and a bystander killed.

To quell this insurrection, Kennedy placed the Mississippi National Guard under his control and deployed 23,000 soldiers to the state for months. This use of military force to protect southern blacks from white Democrats was reminiscent of the Radical Republicans' use of soldiers for the same purpose during Reconstruction, though the Grant administration had far fewer of them at its disposal. At last, the Kennedy administration was turning its full attention to undoing the consequences of the Democratic Party's thwarting of Reconstruction a century earlier.

While the Kennedy administration was ignoring its campaign pledges, the Republican minority in Congress introduced many bills to protect the constitutional rights of blacks, including a comprehensive new civil rights bill. In February 1963, to head off a return by most blacks to the GOP, Kennedy abruptly decided to submit to Congress a new civil rights bill. Hastily drafted in a single all-nighter, the Kennedy bill fell well short of what our Party had introduced into Congress the month before. Nonetheless, given that the Democrats controlled the White House and both houses of Congress, the administration measure to improve enforcement of the 1957 and 1960 Civil Rights Acts stood a better chance of being passed.

A second outrage by fellow Democrats prodded Kennedy further toward moving to fulfill the Radical Republican vision for the South.

In April 1963, police in Birmingham, Alabama brutally attacked peaceful black demonstrators, using dogs, clubs, and high-pressure water hoses. Along with protest leaders, hundreds of black children were arrested. Abetted by Alabama's Democrat Governor, George Wallace, rioting by whites gripped the city for weeks. The even more vicious Democrat crackdown on the civil rights movement of a century before had gone comparatively unnoticed by the general public, but this time the crimes were televised across the nation and the world, and could no longer be ignored. The violence intensified after a federal court order to desegregate the public schools. Many blacks were killed, including four schoolchildren who died in a bombing of a local church.

Angered by the Birmingham violence and concerned that blacks were drifting back to our Republican Party, President Kennedy finally took the initiative. In June 1963, he gave a televised address to the nation decrying the violent oppression of black Americans and outlining his goal for a comprehensive civil rights bill. Though he left it unsaid, in its new version the bill would be much closer to the one Republicans had introduced back in January. Coming just a few hours after the President spoke, the murder of Mississippi NAACP official Medgar Evers heightened the resolve of Martin Luther King and other leaders of the civil rights movement that the time had come for them to take the initiative on the national scene as well.

In August 1963, well over two hundred thousand people gathered in Washington for the largest demonstration the capital had ever seen. There Martin Luther King delivered one of the masterpieces of American political discourse, his "I Have a Dream" speech. A jittery President Kennedy had 4000 soldiers standing by and another 15,000 on alert in North Carolina in case of violence, but his fears proved groundless. Concerned about stiffening southern Democrat opposition, he had declined an invitation to address the crowd. Meeting with King and other protest leaders that evening, Kennedy also expressed trepidation that they were moving too fast and refused their pleas that he use the March on Washington to launch an all-out campaign to pass a comprehensive new civil rights bill. Over the next several months, Democrat racists in Congress were indeed gearing up for a protracted filibuster of the civil rights bill. The bill was before a committee in the House of Representatives when John Kennedy was murdered in November 1963.

The new President, Lyndon Johnson, was much more a New Deal Democrat than Kennedy had been. Johnson began his career in 1935 as the head of the National Youth Agency in his home state and was elected to the House of Representatives in 1937. He was elected to the Senate in 1948. More so than Kennedy, Johnson sympathized with blacks, and he understood that racial segregation was keeping the South economically backward and was therefore bad for southern whites as well.

Invoking his slain predecessor, Johnson, the ace legislator, would be able to get a civil rights bill past congressional opposition that might have stymied Kennedy. He made passage of the bill his top priority, and in his first speech to Congress he urged Representatives and Senators to do "more for civil rights than the last hundred sessions combined." Just as "Only Nixon could go to China," it took a committed Democrat President to complete the work of the Radical Republicans. Though Nixon was even more committed than Johnson was to safeguarding the constitutional rights of blacks, if he had been in the White House then instead, Democrats in favor of segregation and those unwilling to see a Republican achieve the victory would have teamed up to block his legislative initiative in Congress.

The 1964 Civil Rights Act was an update of Republican Charles Sumner's 1875 Civil Rights Act. In striking down that law in 1883 the Supreme Court had ruled that the 14th amendment was not sufficient constitutional authorization, so the 1964 version had to be written in such a way as to rely instead on the interstate commerce clause for its constitutional underpinning. The 1964 Act guaranteed equal access to public facilities and banned racial discrimination by any entity receiving federal government financing, thereby extending coverage to most every hospital, school, and government subcontractor. Also banned was racial discrimination in unions and companies with more than twenty-five employees. Enforcement provisions were much more rigorous than those of the 1957 and 1960 Acts.

The summer of 1964 was known within the civil rights movement as "Freedom Summer." In June of that year, the attention of the nation was riveted by the murder in Mississippi of two white activists from the North and a local black colleague. A century before, southern whites had murdered hundreds of such "carpetbaggers" and "scalawags" whom the federal government could not protect from KKK terrorists, but now President Johnson ordered FBI Director J. Edgar Hoover to infiltrate and destroy the resurgent Klan. Attorney General Robert Kennedy oversaw the FBI's covert activities against the Klan while his Justice Department aggressively prosecuted Klansmen and their allies. In addition to rousing the federal government into declaring war against the Ku Klux Klan, the murders shamed many white southern Democrats into weakening their opposition to the civil rights bill before Congress.

Mindful of how Democrat opposition had forced the Republicans to weaken their 1957 and 1960 Civil Rights Acts, President Johnson warned Democrats in Congress that this time it was all or nothing. To ensure support from Republicans, he had to promise them that he would not accept any weakening of the bill and also that he would publicly credit our Party for its role in securing congressional approval. Johnson played no direct role in the legislative fight, so that it would not be perceived as a partisan struggle. There was no doubt that the House of Representatives would pass the bill.

In the Senate, Minority Leader Everett Dirksen had little trouble rounding up the votes of most Republicans, and former presidential candidate Richard Nixon also lobbied hard for the bill. Senate Majority Leader Michael Mansfield and Senator Hubert Humphrey led the Democrat drive for passage, while the chief opponents were Democrat Senators Sam Ervin, Albert Gore Sr., and Robert Byrd. Senator Byrd, a former Klansman whom Democrats still call "the conscience of the Senate," filibustered against the civil rights bill for 14 straight hours before the final vote. The House of Representatives passed the bill by 289 to 124, a vote in which 80% of Republicans and 63% of Democrats voted yes. The Senate vote was 73 to 27, with 21

Democrats and only 6 Republicans voting no. One of those 6 Republicans was Arizona's Barry Goldwater. President Johnson signed the new Civil Rights Act into law on July 2, 1964.

Overall, there was little overt resistance to the 1964 Civil Rights Act. The struggle was not yet over, however, as most southern state governments remained under the control of segregationist Democrats. Alabama's Governor, George Wallace, the man who had stood in the door of a public school to deny admittance to black students, was among the most notorious. In 1966, another Democrat, Lester Mattox, a restaurant owner who became famous for refusing to serve blacks, was elected Governor of Georgia. President Johnson did not ease up after this triumph, and set as his next goal an expanded version of the Republicans' Federal Elections Bill of 1890. During his presidency, Johnson appointed 18 blacks to the federal bench, most notably Thurgood Marshall to the Supreme Court in 1967.

Enforcing the Constitution was – along with the Kennedy tax cut and expanding the federal government's control over the economy – one of the three components of President Johnson's legislative program which he would later label "the Great Society." The three policies had nothing in common with each other except that Johnson favored them and had grouped them together in his May 1964 speech which launched the Great Society theme. President Johnson's first order of legislative business was to see that the Senate passed Kennedy's tax cut bill, which the House of Representatives had approved in September 1963. The Tax Reduction Act passed the House again and the Senate in February 1964, and more than any other economic policy proved to be responsible for America's tremendous prosperity in the 1960s

In his January 1964 State of the Union address, President Johnson called for a "war on poverty." He had nothing specific in mind yet, but in general terms his goal was a vast expansion of the New Deal. Averting economic collapse was Franklin Roosevelt's initial objective and only later did the New Deal focus squarely on strengthening the Democrats' grip on power. In contrast, Lyndon Johnson faced no economic crisis, and from the very first his aim was to extend the reach and power of the Democratic Party. Even he could not have believed his claims that the federal government would eliminate poverty within just a few years and at minimal cost to the taxpayer. Combating poverty by his trickle-down approach, from bureaucrats down to the needy, created millions of job openings for bureaucratic tricklers while the official poverty line could be adjusted upward endlessly to ensure a limitless supply of qualified recipients of taxpayer-financed government assistance.

President Johnson saw to it that millions more people were placed, if indirectly, on the Democratic Party payroll and that still more millions came to depend on government spending for some or all of their personal income. Increasing the American people's dependence on government was precisely the opposite of the goal of the 1964 Civil Rights Act, which was intended to liberate people from the unconstitutional exercise of power. This distinction is crucial: socialism is a policy which government officials are free to adopt or not, while protecting constitutional rights is the solemn obligation of everyone who swears loyalty to the Constitution of the United States.

Lyndon Johnson, like Franklin Roosevelt, had zero experience working in the private sector. To direct his War on Poverty, President Johnson named Sargent Shriver, Director of the Peace Corps, a choice that exposes the faulty reasoning behind the President's policy and explains why it was bound to fail to achieve its stated objectives. The 137 academics and bureaucrats who worked on the Task Force (a World War II military term) met at Peace Corps headquarters in the same messianic atmosphere of Hillary Clinton's health care task force three decades later.

Looking at poor countries overseas, it is readily apparent that the escape route from poverty lies down the path of free markets and the rule of law. This increases the power of the poor relative to the rich because without clearly established rules the powerful can always out-muscle the weak. Concentrating power in the hands of ruling elites, strengthening the ability of foreign bureaucrats to impose their will on a subject people, is of course the worst thing the U.S. Government could recommend for other countries. Here at home, governing elites, down deep, probably accept this truth, but presented with the opportunity to gain power over others, they choose self-interest over the common good.

Shriver called in Pentagon experts amenable to the militaristic tone laid down by Johnson's declaration of War on Poverty. To oversee the actual drafting of the implementing legislation, he appointed Adam Yarmolinsky, special assistant to the Secretary of Defense, Robert McNamara, who was architect of the nation-building exercise in a faraway land soon to become the Vietnam War.

The Economic Opportunity Act was drafted in just over a month and sent to Congress in March 1964. The law – a mishmash of various programs which included the Job Corps, the Office of Economic Opportunity, assorted monetary grants to urban and rural areas, and VISTA – had no coherence, as its components were modeled after the multitude of misguided foreign aid programs already underway. Yarmolinsky was soon forced out, and the President appointed another special assistant to Defense Secretary McNamara, Joseph Califano, as his new War on Poverty commandant.

The administration's rhetoric concentrated on the poverty problem to the exclusion of the proposed solutions. On July 23rd, the Senate approved the War on Poverty bill easily, by a 61-34 margin, but its fate in the House of Representatives was much less certain. Johnson's bill was more than a dozen votes short of passage until a convenient foreign crisis afforded the Commander in Chief the opportunity to rally the nation to war. On August 7th, three days after addressing the nation about the Gulf of Tonkin incident, President Johnson asked Congress for authority to use military force in Southeast Asia. Within hours, Congress endorsed nearly unanimously a war on Vietnamese communism. The very next day, swept up by Johnson's call to arms and again without thinking through the implications, the House of Representatives passed the Economic Opportunity Act, by 226 to 184. Both votes gave Lyndon Johnson a blank check to use however he wished.

The President could have had either the War on Poverty or the War in Vietnam, but he chose both. The same egotism and self-delusion gave us both. To illustrate, the mentality behind the strategic hamlet program – herding peasants into villages where they could be more easily controlled – at the same time inflicted upon our own nation the atrocity of herding hundreds of thousands of urban poor into wretched public housing projects, where again the Johnson administration hoped they could be more easily controlled so as to win their hearts and minds. We are amazed to read of Lyndon Johnson selecting particular enemy positions to bomb, though modern-day Presidents are no less foolish in micromanaging which domestic targets to attack with federal government dollars. U.S. involvement in the Vietnam War ended in 1973, but its domestic counterpart, the War on Poverty, drags on well into its fourth decade.

The War on Poverty was a framework to which no end of new federal government programs could be attached. Buried beneath the blizzard of new programs would be any means of assessing which agency was responsible for what, whether the tax money was being spent effectively, or how the delineation between federal, state and local government was supposed to work. With Republicans offering little resistance, 1965 brought the Elementary and Secondary Education Act, the Higher Education Act, federal tax money for Appalachia and the arts, and more. Congress set up the Department of Housing and Urban Development in September. To be sure, some of the laws passed during this flurry of legislative activity made perfect sense, such as the Water Quality Act. Medicare, the health insurance program for the elderly financed by younger federal taxpayers, was enacted in July, followed by Medicaid, a federal government program for the poor administered by state governments.

Johnson's 1966 State of the Union address would outline 113 new spending programs, but most of these items were measures less ambitious than those of 1964 and 1965. The Clean Water Restoration Act was the best legislative achievement of 1966. The Department of Transportation was established that year. The worst of the lot was the Model Cities Program, and control of most city governments by Democrats ensured that the nationwide urban decline would continue for at least two more decades.

Breaking with the Franklin Roosevelt approach, the Johnson

administration portrayed being on welfare as a noble calling and regarded welfare recipients almost as government employees, paid to stay poor and dependent on the Democratic Party. An underclass of the permanently poor – casualties of Lyndon Johnson's domestic war – arose for the first time in the history of United States.

Blacks had been making great strides in economic terms in the 1940s and 1950s, but this progress was halted abruptly by the War on Poverty. Just as had occurred under slavery, the formation of families within the black community was discouraged, by government programs aimed at displacing the black man as provider for his wife and children. Free enterprise was suppressed among the poor, making urban blight a commonplace feature of the American landscape. Crime rates soared in the cities, and blacks and other minorities were the chief victims. Public school education disintegrated for millions of blacks, just as it had when the Democrats crushed the Reconstruction state governments of the post-Civil War South.

Black people were no longer slaves, but their renewed degradation served the interests of the Democratic Party all the same. Dwight Eisenhower had warned about a "military-industrial complex," but it is Lyndon Johnson's "civilian-bureaucratic complex" which bedevils us to this day.

_____

President Johnson was very popular in 1964 and he looked unbeatable for reelection, so none of the major Republican contenders bothered to seek the presidential nomination. Some prominent Republicans even announced well ahead of time that they would vote for Johnson. New York Governor Rockefeller, who had earned an excellent reputation within the civil rights movement, did vie for the nomination, but his avid devotion to proposing a federal government program for seemingly every problem unsettled most Republicans. A messy divorce the year before also hurt his reputation. Henry Cabot Lodge won the New Hampshire primary as a write-in candidate, but his entry into the race came too late. After brushing aside a last-minute challenge by Pennsylvania Governor William Scranton, Arizona Senator Barry

Goldwater won the nomination. Rather than unite Republicans, the nominee wasted no time before insulting those in our Party who did not agree with him. His hand-picked vice presidential nominee, New York Representative William Miller, was even more obnoxious.

Goldwater had worked in the family business and been a military transport pilot during World War II before turning to politics. He had little higher education and gave the impression of loathing anyone who had read more than the few books he had. What Goldwater lacked in intellectual heft he tried to compensate with his ability to inspire his followers, and it was their enthusiasm which got him the nomination. Goldwater's zeal for the free market was sorely needed within our Republican Party, but lacking any appreciation for our Party's heritage, he confused in his mind the free market system with unconstitutional racial discrimination and he disdained the efforts of Presidents Eisenhower, Kennedy, and Johnson to extend to the South full implementation of the Constitution.

In the Republican National Convention hall, delegates at his command shouted down his opponents, astonishing millions of television viewers with the ugly implications of the new Republican standard-bearer's brand of "extremism in the defense of liberty." Eisenhower and Nixon expressed their dismay.

Goldwater supporters had earlier ousted most black Republicans from leadership positions in our Party. Said one of his southern supporters: "The black has been read out of the Republican Party of Georgia here today." In contrast to the multiracial Republican convention which had nominated Nixon, only 14 of the 1308 delegates in 1964 were black. The Goldwater forces so disgraced the Party of Thaddeus Stevens and Charles Sumner that tens of thousands of civil rights protesters gathered outside the convention hall. Martin Luther King, testifying to the Republican platform committee, appealed to the Party of Lincoln not to abandon its principles, but Goldwater supporters saw to it that the party platform dropped most of its traditional reverence for the constitutional rights of black Americans. The Fiasco of '64 made our Party nearly "lily-white" for the next three decades.

During the campaign, Goldwater threatened to launch nuclear

attacks on North Vietnam and political attacks on the Supreme Court with equal gusto, thereby undermining the creditability of his more sensible proposals, such as free trade, eliminating many federal government spending programs, making participation in Social Security voluntary, and privatizing TVA. Thinking that aping the segregationist Democrats was somehow the way to the White House, he infused into our Republican Party the Democrats' states rights argument as a means of combating President Johnson's socialist agenda. That September, Strom Thurmond, the Dixiecrat presidential candidate of 1948, joined the Republicans and endorsed Goldwater. In his speech, Thurmond actually denounced the Democrats – the Democrats! – for imposing "another Reconstruction," as if our Republican Party had never existed before he joined it.

President Johnson made the 1964 Civil Rights Act the centerpiece of his campaign, and to reinforce the point he selected its leading proponent in the Senate, Hubert Humphrey, as his running mate. Having given up on the Republicans after their convention, Martin Luther King shifted away from his previous bipartisan stance and campaigned for Johnson. In the presidential election, the percentage of blacks voting for the Democrat nominee rose from Kennedy's 70% to 94% for Johnson. Goldwater carried only his home state and five states of the Deep South. Johnson swept everywhere else, and he won the popular vote by 61% to 39%. In congressional races, our Party's share of seats fell to 32% in both the House of Representatives and the Senate.

The one bright spot in this dismal picture was the appearance of a new Republican star. By late October, Goldwater had so discredited himself that he dared not make one last televised appeal to the electorate. For that he turned to one of his foremost backers in California, the former movie actor and president of the Screen Actors Guild, Ronald Reagan. To a nationwide audience, Reagan delivered a masterful critique of the Democrats' socialist agenda while, just as importantly, not employing any of Goldwater's racist rhetoric. The country had to decide, said a thoughtful and temperate Reagan, "whether we believe in our capacity for self-government or whether we abandon the American Revolution and confess that a little intellectual elite in a far-distant capital can plan our lives better than we can plan them ourselves."

In January 1965, the month President Johnson was inaugurated for a full term, under the leadership of King and Abernathy the SCLC began a series of peaceful demonstrations in Selma, Alabama to protest the inability of blacks to vote in that Democrat-controlled state. In March, local police and state troopers commanded by Governor Wallace viciously attacked some 600 protesters who were attempting to march from Selma to Montgomery. No need to display bloody shirts as evidence of Democrat savagery – millions of shocked television viewers saw it for themselves.

Two days later, a second march turned back after Judge Frank Johnson ordered it halted to prevent more violence. Martin Luther King, the leader of this second march, complied with the order, knowing how important it was for the civil rights movement to preserve its law-abiding image. Six days after that, President Johnson gave a nationwide address comparing the protesters to the patriots at Lexington and Concord, repeating the movement's motto: "We shall overcome." The President ordered soldiers to protect marchers on a third and successful attempt to reach Montgomery from Selma.

After the President's ringing endorsement of the civil rights movement, there was no way another southern Democrat filibuster could halt his next goal, the Voting Rights Act of 1965, which authorized the federal government to abolish literacy tests and other means of preventing blacks from voting. Both houses of Congress passed the bill overwhelmingly in August, and it was signed into law that same month. In the House of Representatives, 85% of Republicans and 80% of Democrats voted for the Voting Rights Act. Seventeen Democrat Senators voted against it along with one Republican, Strom Thurmond.

The new law enabled millions of southern blacks to vote for the first time, while the Supreme Court's one-person, one-vote decision of June 1964 did away with the disproportionate power of rural voters in many states. The Civil Rights Act of 1968 gave the Attorney General greater powers to prevent use of interstate commerce to abridge someone's constitutional rights. The Fair Housing Act of 1968 prohibited most forms of racial discrimination in the private housing market.

As the Vietnam War intensified and disillusionment with the War on Poverty began to set in, our Party started to recover from its landslide loss in 1964. Rising prices and crime rates handed Republicans two more powerful campaign issues. Once the Civil Rights Act and the Voting Rights Act allowed southern blacks into the political process, southern whites who agreed with the Republicans on most other issues no longer felt compelled to vote for the Democratic Party. Another reason for the revival of our Party in the South was the millions of northern Republicans who had been moving there since World War II. The 1966 congressional midterm elections produced a Republican gain of 47 seats in the House of Representatives and 4 in the Senate. A big winner that year was Ronald Reagan, who achieved a stunning upset over Pat Brown, the Democrat who had defeated Richard Nixon for Governor of California in 1962.

In the mid-1960s, the Democrats began to pay a price for having oversold the War on Poverty as a cure-all for urban residents, particularly black men, who resented not sharing in the economic prosperity. The industrial jobs their fathers had held were moving overseas. In the new economy, education, not mechanical skill, was the key to success, but for the Johnson administration excellence in basic education was far outweighed as a priority by financial assistance to women and children. The war in Vietnam was another cause of unrest. Not only were thousands of inner city blacks being sent to kill and die overseas, but poor people everywhere resented the billions of dollars being spent to prop up a foreign government when so much needed to be done at home. Martin Luther King and most other veterans of the civil rights movement broke with President Johnson to oppose his war in Vietnam.

The first large-scale rioting by urban blacks took place in New York City in July 1964, and many incidents followed in other cities. In August 1965, just five days after the Voting Rights Act was signed, massive unrest seized the Watts section of Los Angeles. In July 1967, riots shook Detroit and Newark. When Martin Luther King was murdered in April 1968 a huge wave of rioting swept across the country. Impatient with the non-violent approach, militant black groups, such as the Black Panthers and the Black Muslims, emerged in the North. Unlike the black civil rights organizations, these made no common cause with white people. Also unlike the black civil rights organizations, the militant groups were counterproductive to their professed goals.

The rioting cost blacks the sympathy and commitment of most whites who had been dedicated to improving their condition. The black-white alliance exemplified by the NAACP and the Freedom Riders was shattered. A bewildered President Johnson backed away from further aggressive action for constitutional rights protection, and Congress turned its attention away from the inner cities. The rioting also engendered heightened emphasis on law-and-order policies, which replaced the civil rights movement as a major concern of both the Democrats and the Republicans. Tellingly, the political platforms of both parties in 1968 dropped most references to their commitment to black Americans.

Presidents Truman and Eisenhower were popular when they left office, but Lyndon Johnson was doing so as a defeated man. His vision for a Great Society had faded along with hopes for victory in Vietnam. The two principal contenders for the Democratic presidential nomination were Vice President Hubert Humphrey and Senator Robert Kennedy, who had resigned from the Cabinet four years earlier. Kennedy's murder in June made Humphrey the certain nominee. In the 1968 election campaign, the incumbent Democrats suffered relatively more from the nation's troubled mood than did our Party, as evidenced by their tumultuous convention in Chicago.

Unwilling to risk another fringe candidate, Republicans turned again to the tried and true Richard Nixon, who fended off another challenge by Governor Rockefeller and ones by Governor Reagan and Michigan Governor George Romney to win the nomination. Nixon offered the second spot on the ticket to the Governor of Maryland, Spiro Agnew, on the strength of his strong constitutional rights record, firm law enforcement stance, and appeal to southern voters.* The magnanimous Ronald Reagan moved that the convention make Nixon's nomination unanimous.

George Wallace did our Republican Party a tremendous favor by running for President as a third-party candidate. His American Independent Party absorbed much of the backward-leaning ideology of the American, or Know-Nothing, Party of the 1850s. Looking beyond his Dixiecrat base, Wallace also campaigned for the votes of northern whites. He attracted much of the Goldwater vote, thereby relieving the Republicans from having to tailor their campaign to accommodate opponents of the civil rights movement.

As election day neared, Nixon lost his large lead in the polls over Humphrey, but held on to win by a narrow margin. He received 43.4% of the popular vote, to 42.7% for Humphrey and 13.5% for Wallace. In the all-important Electoral College, Nixon won 301 votes, to 191 for Humphrey and 46 for Wallace. The American Independent Party did not field any candidates aside from Wallace and his running mate, General Curtis Le May. While Republicans picked up 5 seats in the House of Representatives and 6 in the Senate, Democrats retained control of both houses.

President Nixon's first major decision was appointing a successor to Chief Justice Earl Warren, who had retired in June 1968. Lyndon Johnson had nominated Associate Justice Abe Fortas for the position. There was a strong feeling among Senators that a new Chief Justice should be appointed by the next President and so Johnson's scandal-ridden pal was denied confirmation. The choice fell to Nixon.

Dwight Eisenhower recommended former Attorney General Brownell, on the strength of his labors on behalf of the Brown v. Board of Education decision and the 1957 Civil Rights Act, but Nixon feared picking a fight with southern Democrats so early in his presidency. This loss of nerve was, of course, a huge mistake that cost our Party a fabulous opportunity to refocus on the Radical Republican heritage. Nixon first offered the position to Thomas Dewey, to suc-

---

* The 12th amendment would have precluded California's Presidential Electors from voting for both Nixon and Reagan as presidential and vice presidential candidates.

ceed his 1948 running mate, but at 66 the former Republican standard-bearer thought he was too old. The President then named Warren Burger, Brownell's Assistant Attorney General for Civil Rights whom Eisenhower had appointed to the U.S. Court of Appeals in 1956. Warren Burger was fine, but Nixon's next two Supreme Court nominations were awful, two southern segregationists whom the Senate refused to confirm.

In October 1969, the Supreme Court ordered an immediate end to public school segregation, and by 1974 the percentage of black students in the South attending all-black public schools was down to 8% from the 68% when Johnson left office. In 1970, Nixon pushed for amendments to strengthen the 1965 Voting Rights Act. Under President Nixon, the Justice Department did more to implement the 1964 Civil Rights Act and the 1965 Voting Rights Act than it had during the Johnson administration.

Nixon was one of the most environmentally-minded Presidents since his hero, Theodore Roosevelt. Many of Nixon's economic policies, however, were less laudable. Just as Johnson had done, Nixon muddled lines of responsibility with various revenue-sharing schemes that matched federal government spending with state and local government outlays. Congress had the sense to reject Nixon's proposal to institutionalize this approach, which he called the New Federalism.

With Daniel Moynihan as his principal advisor on welfare policy, Nixon's policies on this issue were just as misguided as Johnson's had been. In 1969, Congress rejected Moynihan's Family Assistance Plan, a noble-sounding but terrible idea that would have given the federal government nearly complete control over the welfare system while avoiding any responsibility for the consequences. In 1971, Nixon imposed wage and price controls, a ridiculous power grab by the federal government that Lyndon Johnson would have admired. Nixon devalued the dollar, as Franklin Roosevelt had done.

In the 1970 congressional midterm elections, the Republicans did lose 12 seats in the House of Representatives but gained 2 in the

Senate, a result that boded well for our Party two years down the road. Nixon was renominated unopposed and ensured that the party platform contained a strong plank on guaranteeing constitutional rights, in contrast to the Democrats' feeble gesture in their platform. The economy was booming and U.S. military involvement in Southeast Asia was winding down, making a Republican victory likely.

Democrats nominated South Dakota Senator George McGovern for President and Johnson-era social engineer Sargent Shriver for Vice President. Nixon won in a landslide, by 61% to 38% in the popular vote and 520 to 17 in the Electoral College. Results in congressional races were mixed, with Republicans picking up 12 seats in the House of Representatives but losing 2 in the Senate.

One of the most significant events of Nixon's second term was the Supreme Court's 1973 Roe v. Wade decision, which struck down most state laws against abortion. While the majority opinion cited the due process clause of the 14th amendment to back up its discovery of a right to privacy, constitutional law was clearly not the true reasoning behind the decision. Rather, the seven Justices who voted in favor of it believed abortion should be permissible and Roe v. Wade was their opportunity to impose a final solution on the political controversy. However, once the Supreme Court declared a constitutional right to abortion it was no longer a political issue – one to be decided by the people's representatives and subject to change as public sentiment changed. As a result, both pro-choice and pro-life advocates hardened their positions and they could no longer afford to retreat an inch, turning an issue which would have been settled years ago into the most divisive of modern times.

Richard Nixon was forced to resign the presidency in August 1974 because of his involvement in the Watergate scandal. Bugging political opponents, though illegal, was nothing Lyndon Johnson had not done, even to fellow Democrats. President Nixon did try to obstruct the criminal and congressional investigations, very serious offenses, but he was not involved in the break-in itself.

Some other crimes Nixon did *not* commit include selling military secrets to Communist China, bombing foreign countries to distract attention from his legal troubles, and covering up the theft of thousands of top secret files by his CIA Director. To put Nixon's character in perspective, if Mephistopheles (the devil in Faust) had appeared to him and offered to make his political troubles go away if only he would sell military secrets to the Communist Chinese, can anyone doubt that Richard Nixon would have been appalled at the suggestion he betray his country to save himself?

Perhaps the best appointment President Nixon ever made was of Michigan's Gerald Ford to replace the disgraced Spiro Agnew as Vice President. Ford had been elected Minority Leader of the House of Representatives in 1965 after the Goldwater fiasco, and he chaired the Republican National Convention which nominated Nixon in 1968. Ford succeeded to the presidency and did an excellent job of restoring trust in government. To help heal a rift in our Party he named Nelson Rockefeller, Nixon's long-time rival, to be the new Vice President. Privately, not even top Democrats questioned President Ford's decision to pardon Nixon, in order to spare the nation protracted legal warfare, but his timing could have been much better. Doing so just a month after taking office, and without any preceding explanation, hurt our Party in the 1974 midterm elections two months later and proved to be the issue which more than anything else cost Ford the presidential election in 1976.

Former Governor Reagan challenged Ford for the Republican nomination that year, but lost to the incumbent President by a delegate count of 53% to 47%. Ever the class act, Reagan asked the convention to make Ford's nomination unanimous, just as he had for Nixon in 1968. After consulting with Reagan, Ford offered the vice presidential nomination to Kansas Senator Robert Dole. Given the tremendous acclaim his concession speech to the convention received, Ronald Reagan knew that the 1980 Republican presidential nomination would be his.

A two-year recession ended in the fall of 1976 but not soon enough to help Gerald Ford, whose late surge fell just short of the

Democrat nominee, former Georgia Governor Jimmy Carter. There were no big ideological differences between the two candidates, but Carter's greatest strength was his image as an honest outsider. Carter won 50% to 48% in the popular vote and 297 to 240 in the Electoral College. Jimmy Carter soon proved to be in over his head as President. Inflation and unemployment increased, and President Carter became an object of ridicule after a speech in which he blamed a national "malaise," not on himself, but on everybody else.

In 1980, former Governor Reagan turned back challenges from Bob Dole, George H. Bush, Howard Baker, and John Connally to win the Republican presidential nomination. Ronald Reagan's humble background and breadth of experience gave him a broad appeal which extended beyond Republicans to many Democrats and independents.

Born poor in tiny Tampico, Illinois, Reagan was a sports announcer before moving to Hollywood, where he worked his way up to considerable success as an actor during the 1930s and 1940s. Thirty years old when Pearl Harbor was attacked, army reserve Lt. Reagan was called up and assigned to stateside duty. After the war, Reagan served as president of the Screen Actors Guild for five terms. In 1954, he was hired by General Electric as a TV host and spokesman. This job afforded him an invaluable opportunity to travel around the country for eight years meeting with business executives and other employees. In 1964, the US Borax Company hired him to host its "Death Valley Days" program.

A firm supporter of Franklin Roosevelt initially, Reagan came to oppose the Democrats as their ideology became more socialist. He campaigned for Democrats as late as 1950, against Republican senatorial candidate Richard Nixon. Reagan campaigned for Eisenhower in 1952 and 1956 and for Nixon in 1960, but he did not join the GOP until 1962, when he supported Nixon for Governor of California.

Buoyed by his superb televised address in 1964, forever known as "The Speech," Reagan entered the Republican primary for Governor of California in 1966 and won it by more than 2 to 1. He then defeated the incumbent by 58% to 42%. Faced with the worst crime rate in the nation, high taxes, and bloated welfare rolls, he had campaigned to reduce all three. Impressed that he accomplished all three goals even though the legislature was largely controlled by Democrats, voters elected him to a second term.

Reagan clearly was a skillful politician, but he could have benefited from a more thorough grounding in the history of our Party, particularly the legacy of the Radical Republicans. Though no one could fairly accuse him of being a racist – one of his first acts as Governor was to promote the hiring of more blacks by the state government and for him racial prejudice was "a sickness" – Reagan opposed the 1964 Civil Rights Act and the 1965 Voting Rights Act as unconstitutional, even though these laws were the fulfillment of early Republican aspirations to uphold the Constitution.

Former President Ford declined to be his running mate, so Reagan offered the second place on the ticket to Nixon protégé George Bush, who had been his chief rival for the nomination. The Republican Party platform called for, among other things, rebuilding the neglected military to counter Soviet expansionism, tax cuts to spur economic growth, and less federal government regulation and less spending on domestic programs. President Carter fended off Massachusetts Senator Ted Kennedy to win nomination for another term. For the first time since the Wallace candidacy in 1968, a serious third-party challenger vied for the presidency, Illinois' Democrat-leaning Republican Representative John Anderson.

With the Carter administration mismanaging the economy and foreign policy, Reagan easily won the contest, by 51% to 41% and 7% for Anderson in the popular vote, and 489 to 49 in the Electoral College. On Reagan's coattails, Republicans gained a majority in the Senate for the first time since the 1950s and increased their share of the House of Representatives from 36% to 44%.

President Reagan wanted to get the federal government to stop interfering with foreign trade just as much he wanted it to stop impeding the domestic economy. Reagan was among the first to raise the possibility of a North American free trade zone. One of his first official acts was to abolish price controls on crude oil, gasoline, and heating oil. Shazam! Prices fell and lines at gas stations disappeared, as the free market brought forth greater supply to meet the demand.

Unlike Nixon, Reagan understood the dangers of matching-funds schemes that boosted the power of Washington bureaucrats over state governments and over the general public. Addressing the NAACP in July 1981, Reagan said: "Many in Washington over the years have been more dedicated to making needy people government dependent, rather than independent. Just as the Emancipation Proclamation freed black people 118 years ago, today we need to declare economic emancipation." That same year he named the first woman to the Supreme Court, Arizona's Sandra Day O'Connor. The current Chief Justice, Nixon-appointee William Rehnquist, Reagan promoted from Associate Justice in 1986.

The centerpiece of Reagan's economic policy was his proposal to cut taxes, as the Kennedy tax plan had done in the 1960s. Since then, marginal tax rates had crept up over the years, choking off entrepreneurial dynamism, and only lawyers and lobbyists could appreciate the added complexities of the tax code. As a description of Reagan's return to the Kennedy approach, the term "supply-side economics" came into vogue. Briefly, economic theory holds that at equilibrium, supply equals demand. For too long, economic policies focused almost exclusively on the demand-side of the equation, in order to elicit greater supply by increasing demand. Monetarism (strict limits on demand through proper monetary levels), fiscal policy (raising or lowering government spending and taxation), and monetary policy (adjusting interest rates, primarily) have their place, but so do policies intended to boost production of goods and services, which then generates higher demand for the greater supply.

Lowering taxes on producers, reducing regulatory impediments to production, and improving the economic infrastructure – these are all supply-side policies. Simple enough, but some supply-siders discredited themselves with fantastical claims that by lowering tax rates the federal government could boost economic growth so much that the increased tax revenues pouring into Washington would enable the federal government to spend even more, at no cost somehow to anyone. True Reaganites understand that government spending can be as much a cause of mischief as government taxation.

In his first State of the Union address, President Reagan asked for a 30% reduction in federal income taxes over three years. In July 1981, by margins of 238-195 and 89-11, Congress approved a 25% cut over three years. Convincing enough House Democrats to vote for his plan was a Reagan victory reminiscent of his earlier achievements dealing with the Democrat-controlled California legislature. The economic recession ended in early 1982, and the economic boom set off by Reagan's policy has not let up since.

The federal government deficit did grow fast, but not as a result of the tax cuts. For that, the Democrats holding the purse strings in the House of Representatives were the chief culprits. According to myth, the military buildup, which simply had to be done, was to blame, but in fact it was government spending on domestic programs that really got out of hand. While federal tax revenue was twice as high in 1989 as it had been in 1980, social programs expanded much faster than that.

⁓⧽⧽⧽⧽⧽⧽

Having restored our country's prestige abroad, revived economic growth, and lowered inflation from Carteresque heights, Ronald Reagan certainly deserved a second term. His opponent in 1984, Jimmy Carter's Vice President, Walter Mondale, offered little competition and actually campaigned for higher taxes. Reagan's campaign theme was "Morning in America." He won by 59% to 41% in the popular vote and 525 to 13 in the Electoral College. Republicans gained 16 seats in the House of Representatives but lost 1 in the Senate.

Progress in Reagan's second term was hampered by Iran-Contra, a term which covers two related but distinct scandals. In the first, the United States Government sold weapons to Iran to use in its war against Iraq, with President Reagan's permission. In the second, presidential underlings diverted money generated by the sale to support anti-Sandinista guerrillas in Nicaragua, this without the President's knowledge. Unlike the later Democrat scandals, personal or even

Party gain was not a motivation, and also in sharp contrast to the next Democrat to occupy the White House, the Reagan administration did not obstruct the congressional investigation. In fact, the President waived executive privilege and ordered everyone to provide Congress with any information requested.

By the end of Reagan's tenure in office, deficits were coming down and economic growth looked unstoppable, but then the President went along with the Tax Reform Act of 1986. While it did simplify the tax code, some taxes were raised. The basic idea of this law was that one dollar in higher taxes would be matched by two dollars in spending cuts. After the 1986 midterm elections, Democrats were in control of both houses of Congress, and they used their added clout to make sure that the tax hikes happened but that the spending cuts did not. The Republicans would only be able to accomplish their goal of balancing the federal government budget once they regained control of both houses of Congress in 1995.

Vice President Bush outlasted his chief rival, Senator Dole, to win the 1988 Republican presidential nomination, and he chose as his running mate Indiana Senator Dan Quayle. The youngest combat pilot in the U.S. Navy during World War II, Bush worked in the oil business in Texas before running unsuccessfully for the Senate in 1964. He did win a seat in the House of Representatives in 1966. Giving up his seat in the House of Representatives four years later to run for the Senate, he lost again but President Nixon named him Ambassador to the United Nations in 1971. Bush was then chairman of the Republican National Committee from 1973 to 1974. From 1974 to 1976 he was Ford's envoy to China, and his CIA Director from 1976 to 1977. The accomplished Bush owed his place on the 1980 Republican ticket to Ronald Reagan's effort to reach out to the Nixon wing of our Party.

Democrats nominated Massachusetts Governor Michael Dukakis for President and Texas Senator Lloyd Bentsen, the man who had defeated Bush's second Senate bid in 1970, for Vice President. Bush won 53% of the popular vote and 426 electoral votes to Dukakis' 46% and 111 electoral votes. In congressional races, Republicans lost 2 House seats, bring their share down to 40%, while their number of Senate seats held steady at 45.

Bush's nomination acceptance speech had called for a "kinder, gentler nation," a well-intentioned statement, which, however, was widely taken to be an implicit criticism of the way Ronald Reagan had been running things. Ominously, in his inaugural address President Bush appealed to Democrats in Congress to work with him in devising a new federal government budget. This was quite unlike the practice of President Reagan, who had delivered on his promises to the American people by appealing directly to them, not to the Democrats entrenched up on Capitol Hill.

During the campaign, Bush had vowed not to give in to Democrat demands that taxes be raised, but as President he was out-maneuvered by the wily Speaker of the House, Jim Wright, and the equally cunning Senate Majority Leader, George Mitchell. Thinking many moves ahead, both Democrats knew that the promises to cut spending they made to President Bush to convince him to sign their tax increase bill would be more than outweighed by being able to use his reversal against him in the 1992 campaign. In the 1990 midterm elections, Republicans lost 8 seats in the House and 1 in the Senate, not at all a bad showing for the party in the White House, but the Reagan wing of our Party was badly demoralized by the tax increases. Even worse, the tax hikes choked off economic growth and began a recession that badly hurt President Bush's reelection prospects.

The greatest achievement of the Bush presidency was the victory of the United States and our allies over Iraq in the Gulf War of January and February 1991. Most Democrats cowered before Saddam Hussein's threat to take over much of the world's oil supply, but the Commander-in-Chief rose to the challenge. Unfortunately, President Bush failed to finish off the Iraqi dictator. Going into Baghdad would have been a costly mistake, as would have been trying to install a new Iraqi regime, but the optimal move would have been to sweep across the country to destroy the Iraqi military before leaving.

Chagrin at having halted the troops short of complete victory left Bush unable to follow up at home on a war that never...quite...ended. So demoralized was the President by his blunder that he gave the electorate little reason to believe he actually wanted a second term. As late as the 1992 Republican National Convention, our Party could have averted a Democrat victory if President Bush and Vice President Quayle had been so bold as to decline the nomination. An open convention would have captivated the nation, energized our Party, and produced a ticket much more likely to have won the election. Badly weakened by a primary challenge, President Bush was forced to give the prime-time slot for the major convention speech, not to Ronald Reagan, but to Pat Buchanan, who gave millions of viewers a scary peek at a populist demagogue in action.

A somewhat less repugnant populist, Ross Perot, entered the presidential race with a campaign reminiscent of the wildly emotional and ill-considered Bull Moose movement of 1912. Democrats nominated Bill Clinton, an undistinguished Arkansas Governor. President Bush had one last chance to win the election, when during a debate the three candidates were asked to consider themselves our parents – that is to say, that We, the People should be considered children. Vigorously speaking up for the principles of American self-government at this point could have rallied Republicans to his standard, but President Bush let the opportunity slipped by. Clinton won the popular vote with 43%, to 38% for Bush and 19% for Perot. The Electoral College went to Clinton 370 to 168. Despite this defeat, Republicans increased their share of the House of Representatives from 38% to 41% and lost just one Senate seat, for a new total of 43.

Pushing for a national health care system was President Clinton's first major legislative initiative. Success here in enabling the federal government to grab control of one-seventh of the U.S. economy would have cemented Democratic Party dominance even more than did the New Deal and the War on Poverty. And why stop there?

Another few years and Democrats could have found it time for a national energy system, a national food system, or maybe a national entertainment system.

Clinton handed this ambitious if tricky assignment to his wife, who gathered a secret task force of academics and bureaucrats to draw up a blueprint for her massive social engineering project. HMOs and similar organizations, accused of being too powerful, were to be effectively replaced, in her scheme, by one gigantic federal government monopoly. Health care would have been impaired, innovation halted, and thousands of medical professionals prosecuted; but these failures would actually have amounted to a smashing success for Democrats. With the country carved up into hundreds of health care districts and federal bureaucrats empowered to arbitrate the firestorm of dissension they themselves created, the Democratic Party would have had no trouble implementing its "divide and conquer" strategy.

How easy and quick it would have been for a parliamentary democracy to have enacted this health care horror. Here we can appreciate the wisdom of our Founders. Under the American constitutional system, measures so drastic and vast can be rarely be enacted as quickly as socialists would prefer. Legislators in both houses of Congress, not beholden to some Prime Minister, insisted on analyzing and debating the plan first. Its opponents fought and won a battle in defense of freedom as great as the 1960s civil rights movement.

In 1994, the House Republicans' dynamic Minority Leader, Newt Gingrich, decided that the way for our Party to wrest control away from the Democrats was for congressional candidates to run on a common platform. Known as the "Contract with America," this was a series of measures Republicans committed themselves to passing in the House of Representatives if they gained a majority. In the 1994 midterm elections, Republicans won a majority of the House of Representatives for the first time in three decades, as well as a majority in the Senate. As promised, our Party then balanced the federal government budget, and has kept it in surplus ever since. Assuming that a majority in Congress made him a kind of Prime Minister, the proud Speaker Gingrich regrettably overplayed his hand, and within a year initiative reverted to the Democrats.

For the 1996 presidential election, our Party nominated Senate Majority Leader Robert Dole and former Housing Secretary Jack Kemp as his running mate. Dole's campaign lacked focus and a Perot candidacy again divided the Republican vote, assuring Clinton of reelection. In the popular vote, the tally was 50% for Clinton, 41% for Dole, and 9% for Perot. Clinton won 379 electoral votes to Dole's 159. Republicans fared better in congressional races, gaining 3 seats in the Senate while losing just 3 in the House of Representatives.

Obstruction of justice by the Clinton Justice Department and tenacious solidarity by congressional Democrats suppressed investigations into illegal campaign financing, espionage, and other scandals. The one investigation of Clinton that did proceed turned up strong evidence of crimes committed by the President involving a sexual affair, though these were trivial compared to some of his other offenses. Nonetheless, Republicans were unwilling to condone any criminal activity by the nation's chief law enforcement officer.

In December 1998, the House of Representatives impeached President Clinton, nearly every Republican voting yes and nearly every Democrat voting no. During his Senate trial, the Democrats closed ranks around their leader and voted to keep him in office. Even so, our Party could take pride in its courage because, as every Republican should know by now, doing the right thing is always the right thing to do.

Chapter Ten

OUR RENDEZVOUS
WITH DESTINY

And now, what is the right thing to do? Going forward, just which path should our Republican Party follow? Echoing Ronald Reagan's classic phrase, once again "we have come to a time for choosing." In the 1964 speech which launched his political career, he showed us the way: "They say the world has become too complex for simple answers. They are wrong. There are no easy answers, but there are simple answers."

Years from now, people will laugh and wonder what all the Social Security and Medicare fuss was about. They will find it particularly amusing how manipulative Democrats were and how gullible Republicans were, that amid soaring federal government surpluses worries about "saving Social Security" crossed anyone's mind.

As early as 1936, Republicans noted that *there is no Social Security trust fund. There never has been.* Rather, just as were the 19th century greenbacks, these obligations are backed by the promise of the federal government to pay them. Can these financial obligations of the federal government be considered any less imperative than the obligation to honor its other financial obligations, such as its 30-year Treasury bonds? Of course not. U.S. Treasury bonds are considered worldwide to be the most secure of financial investments. Their creditworthiness, reflecting the federal government's ability and willingness to honor them, is rated AAA.

Why is the ability of the federal government to repay its financial obligations beyond question? Because, surpluses aside, it could readily raise taxes on the American people to pay right back to the American people their Social Security and other transfer payments. Most foreign governments already tax their peoples to the limit, but onerous as the U.S. tax burden is, in an emergency it could go much higher.

Why is the willingness of the federal government to pay its financial obligations beyond question? Is it conceivable that the federal government – your federal government – would decide to dishonor its Social Security obligations any more than its 30-year Treasury bonds? Of course not. "The Social Security (or Medicare) fund might run out of money in ten years!" makes as little sense as a company worrying that if the cost of servicing a particular bond exceeds projections in ten years it will be forced to default on it, even if the company has sufficient funds elsewhere. In a family budget that has, say, $500 in monthly transportation costs (car payment, insurance, gas, etc.), if costs should rise to $600 would the family be forced to default on its car payment if it has sufficient funds elsewhere? Of course not. If that family or that company or that government has the ability and willingness to pay all its bills, then internal accounting devices are irrelevant to meeting its financial obligations.

Talk of shoring up Social Security, or earmarking funds for Medicare, or placing funds in a lockbox – it is all meaningless. Politicians going on about the dire consequences of this or that transfer payments fund running out are either exposing their ignorance or attempting to manipulate the electorate, knowing that confusion is a Democrat's best friend. Recipients of Social Security, Medicare, and other financial obligations of the federal government are fully guaranteed payment, and efforts to scare them into thinking otherwise are contemptible.

To be sure, the growth of transfer payments does indeed present serious problems for the country. Control over how other people's money is collected and spent is an excellent way to keep voters dependent. This control far outweighs any other motive, including the redistribution of wealth. Less than a fifth of federal transfer payments goes to people below the poverty line. Nearly half goes to people above the median income level, who are in effect employing federal bureaucrats to take money away from them and give it back again, minus a hefty handling fee. The most significant net transfer of wealth is from the young (those under 18 cannot vote) to the old (most of whom do).

Nearly a third of all federal government expenditures are transfer payments, that is, revenue taxed from some people and given to others – and this figure could rise to 60% in another two decades. Do We, the People of the United States want this to be the chief mission of the government established by the Constitution? Sloshing taxpayer funds from here to there has nothing to do with forming a more perfect Union or establishing Justice or ensuring domestic Tranquility or providing for the common defense. This revenue ritual does not secure the Blessings of Liberty, and the only general Welfare to be promoted is that of the institution which it benefits most, the Democratic Party.

Government-sanctioned discrimination on the basis of race is a Democratic Party policy for reasons that go back to well before the Civil War. In most countries of the western hemisphere with substantial black populations, there developed hierarchies of racial categories and terms to describe fine gradations of various ancestries of people with one or more black ancestors. But not in the United States, where there is a sharp line dividing white people from people with just one black grandparent. Why?

Though it is often regarded as an enlightened expression of ethnic pride, obsession with people's racial background is actually a legacy of the slave system. In early Brazil and the Caribbean, for example, whites were only a small minority, and so they needed to co-opt allies among people who were partially white, hence their strategy of racial gradation. In the pre-Civil War South, however, whites were a majority and so had no need for allies. For the slave master class then and many descendants of slaves now, any person with even one black ancestor is fully black.

How should the government classify a person with one black grandparent, one white, one Asian, and one Hispanic? What if that black grandparent had some white ancestry, or there were some Cherokee in the ancestry of that white grandparent? For some government preference program, how would an African-Polish-Irish-Armenian person rank against someone Mexican-Chinese-Swedish-Greek? Being in a position to arbitrate such disputes is a great source of power for the Democratic Party. No need for Democrats to devise a system of racial categorizations to assist them in sorting out racial admixtures; they could easily find one in the archives of the Confederacy, apartheid South Africa, or Nazi Germany.

Would it not be an action affirmative of, say, poor urban black children, to institute a policy which provides them with the same opportunity for a good education that wealthy suburban white children have? And what action could be more affirmative of black Americans and other racial minorities than to institute a policy – Martin Luther King's "Dream" – that we all "live in a nation where they will not be judged by the color of their skin, but by the content of their characters."?

"Poor people should be required to send their children to the designated government school, no matter how awful it may be, but wealthier parents should be allowed to choose their children's education." Who could advocate such a nasty policy? Democrats do, as this is the primary and secondary education system our country has now.

Advocates of forcing a poor child to attend the designated government school, no matter how awful it may be, fall back on the argument that vouchers would divert money from public schools. Here they reveal that their true concern is not the schoolchildren, but the schools, by which they mean the teachers and administrators, and ultimately, the Democratic Party, which protects their jobs in return for campaign contributions. In contrast, as the federal government dispenses housing vouchers to people fleeing public housing oppression, it arouses no great opposition to housing choice, because there is no disciplined, well-financed public housing employees union making payments to the Democratic Party.

It should be the responsibility of government to ensure that every child receives a good education. Must the government therefore operate the schools? The government should also ensure that people have adequate food and clothing. Must the government therefore operate the food and clothing stores? No, of course, to both questions. Consider a vast chain of government stores where most poor people bought their food and clothing. Can it be doubted that the service, selection, and quality would be terrible? If there were such a chain of stores, would the solution to these problems be higher salaries for clerks? More money for administration? Better facilities? No, of course, to all three questions. The solution would be to extend the free market society to the poor, so they could make their own choices. Fortunately, Americans receiving government assistance have the freedom to choose what they eat and what they wear, and so should they have the freedom to choose which schools their children attend.

We Republicans must avoid being distracted into expending our efforts in pointless sideshows. Prayer in public schools? This is an issue whose mere existence attests to the Democrats' success in leading our Party away from striving for the free market society. Think of the titanic struggles ahead for government schools as students of faiths other than Christianity and Judaism become more numerous and strident. Their rituals can be utterly distinct from any type of generic prayer the Supreme Court might permit in government schools. A decade or two from now, will separate prayer rooms be required? What if teachers of one faith refuse to lead or tolerate prayers of another? Inevitably, government schools will become arenas for religious and ethnic strife. Most Republicans have not thought this far ahead, but they should. As tensions escalate and education deteriorates, there will be the Democratic Party reveling in having one more problem to arbitrate. This issue is a can of worms – no, a barrel of snakes.

In accusing the media of harboring a pro-Democrat bias, Republicans allow themselves to be distracted into another pointless sideshow. More than just a source of aggravation, perception of media bias is one more issue whose mere existence attests to the Democrats' success in misleading our Party. Until the 1960s, most newspapers and radio and television stations were solidly Republican. The entertainment business, full of people who believe they are superior to others, is naturally a stronghold of socialism, so when the distinction between this industry and the news business blurred, most media outlets shifted away from our Party.

The Democrats taking control of them cleverly established a popular perception that the media was from then on to be impartial and that therefore the Democratic Party line should be regarded as the neutral, reasonable position. As a consequence, for the past thirty years, Republicans have been playing into their hands by agreeing that the media should somehow be neutral. Far better for Republicans to recognize that sources of Democrat propaganda are nothing more than sources of Democrat propaganda, and that the future is in non-traditional media such as the Internet.

The amount of money raised and spent on electoral campaigns and other political purposes in the United States is less than that spent to advertise soda or snacks. Try as Democrats might, there is just no getting around these fourteen little words: "Congress shall make no law...abridging the freedom of speech, or of the press." Rather than erect some oppressive and gargantuan mechanism by which the federal government, to the advantage of the Democratic Party, would infringe on our 1st amendment rights, the most simple, fair, and comprehensible campaign finance reform law could be written in just eight words: "Full disclosure. Individual donors only. No foreign money."* Gone would be political action committees, loopholes for unions, soft v. hard money, and all the rest of the mess brought to you by the Democrats. Restricting campaign contributions to individuals only would also eliminate the enormous loophole through which domestic subsidiaries of foreign companies make political contributions in this country.

Following the Radical Republicans' commitment to respect the Constitution can lead to many other simple, fair, and comprehensible policy solutions. For example, the Constitution would not have been ratified without the promise of a Bill of Rights, one of which is a guarantee that the federal government could not disarm the people. Neither duck hunting nor target shooting was the purpose of

---

* Kudos to George Will.

the 2nd Amendment right to "keep and bear Arms." Rather than seek to repeal it by the amendment procedure in Article V, most opponents of this constitutional right invoke some legal theory or panel of so-called experts to allege that this section of the Constitution does not in fact mean what it says. What protection does any section of the Constitution – from no quartering of troops during peacetime to a four-year presidential term – have if all that is required to get rid off the troublesome language is some very intense wishful-thinking by an assembly of academics?

Defenders of the 2nd amendment usually refuse to cede an inch to any gun control proposal because they understand that the ultimate goal of many backers of restrictions on guns is to confiscate them. Resolute defenders of the Constitution – every word of it – can in fact find plenty of room for reasonable restrictions on the use of guns. In the Old West, for instance, there were often controls to prevent their improper use. Few people complained and none did so on constitutional grounds, because government confiscation of guns was not even a remote possibility. Today, reasonable gun control measures would encounter far less resistance if confiscation were not even a remote possibility. Another point: the 2nd amendment does not apply to those so-called militia groups which are not "well regulated."

The strong popular sentiment for a government role in ensuring proper health care for every American can easily be accommodated within the Republican tradition, without the centralized bureaucratic control favored by Democrats. The starting point is to recognize that the current system in which people look to their employers to pay some or all of their medical costs is a historical accident, which began as a way for employers to get around World War II-era wage-and-price controls by offering medical care as a fringe benefit, instead of offering a salary increase. At present, policy-makers are trying to figure out ways to retain this employee dependency while enhancing the portability of health care coverage. Progress is slow and tortuous because the two goals are incompatible.

If instead of offering medical care benefits, employers in the 1940s had offered to finance part of employees' home mortgages, think of the endless wrangling we would be saddled with today. Should the employer pay the entire cost of a kitchen remodeling, or just a percentage? How can a person change jobs without having to change houses? What if the employer goes out of business during the course of a 30-year mortgage? With residents only paying part of the costs, housing prices might be double what they are today. Why should people look to their employers to pay for family health care any more than they do for home mortgages or college tuition?

<hr />

To keep us on the right path and reach journey's end, we Republicans must bear in mind the trail-blazing careers of Thaddeus Stevens and Charles Sumner. Stevens knew that for the emancipated slave, acquiring land of his own was a "sine qua non," meaning "without which, nothing." If Stevens had succeeded in implementing his proposal to provide each slave family with "40 acres and a mule," countless economic problems would never have arisen. If after the war Sumner's agenda for rigorous protection of constitutional rights had been enacted and enforced, the Democrats' political degradation of black Americans might have been prevented. Not taking these crucial first steps cost our nation a century of socialism and suffering.

The free market is voluntary cooperation, with self-interest the goal and societal advancement the result. Ronald Reagan was acutely aware that to preserve the free market society, the drift toward socialism has to be stopped. To seize and hold the policy initiative, we Republicans must charge right at the Democratic Party in a battle of ideas, our best weapon a clear vision of the free market society we are fighting for.

No distinction can be drawn between a free society and a free economy. Consider the numerous civilizations of the past which flowered when central government was unable to tighten its grip on the economy. For evidence of how socialism impedes progress, consider the cultural decline in Communist nations or the relative cultural stagnation of most West European countries today.

And now consider the United States – for Reagan a "shining city on a hill" – at its most vibrant in areas least controlled by government. No one planned one of our country's greatest contributions to the world, the Internet, or anticipated that it would be responsible for the most magnificent outpouring of prosperity in history. By no accident did the Internet arise here, where government is strong enough to safeguard constitutional rights and foster economic infrastructure yet still weak enough to permit a free people to freely create such an enterprise so spontaneously. As Bill Gates once testified to Congress: "The incredible success of [the high-tech industry] in the United States owes a lot to the light hand of government in the technology area, the fact that people can take incredible risks and if they're successful they can have incredible rewards… Overall, I'd say the light hand is working very well."

A century ago, economic transformation produced monopolies and other market failures for which the Progressive movement sought to compensate. Government action, particularly during the Theodore Roosevelt and Taft presidencies, was intended to promote the free market society, and so was progressive. But now, a century later, as the economy undergoes another transformation, decentralizing power and increasing the leverage of consumers at the expense of producers, regulation and other government intervention tend to impede the free market. Now, for government to get out of the way of this progress is truly progressive.

What is not progressive at all is the modern-day drive to extend the reach of government power over the individual. There is nothing democratic or progressive about socialism. Socialists chafe at restrictions imposed by the rule of law lest their planning be disrupted by predetermined rules which apply to everyone. Socialism is an attempt to fend off the future.

Innovation, by definition unforeseen, is a threat to the plans of the self-proclaimed enlightened, and so is to be suppressed. Based on what Friedrich Hayek called "a naïve and childlike…view of the world," central planning is "a fraud doomed to failure because no planner can possess all the knowledge needed to run a modern economy."

Centralization of power in a bureaucracy led by those who profess to know more and care more than anyone else is in fact the old, lamentably commonplace way nations have been governed since civilization began. It is government for the sake of the individual which is new.

We Republicans place ourselves at another disadvantage in the battle of ideas by ripping from socialists a label which describes them so well. Opponents of progress are those who want to conserve the age-old rule of the few over the many and the cultural stagnation this entails. Socialists are the true conservatives. Republicans try without success to affix this conservative label properly to our Party, using as adhesive such adjectives as "dynamic" or "compassionate" or "progressive." Trouble is, though our Republican Party definitely is dynamic and compassionate and progressive, conservative it is not.

Ironically, the socialists ripped from our Party a label which suits us so well and them not at all. As the term is understood everywhere in the world except where the Democrats appropriated it as their own, liberals have struggled for liberty by opposing government oppression and championing the free market. To quote Hayek once more: "The liberal position is based on courage and confidence, on a preparedness to let change run its course even if we cannot predict where it will lead... Conservatives are inclined to use the powers of government to prevent change or to limit its rate to whatever appeals to the more timid mind. In looking forward, they lack the faith in the spontaneous forces of adjustment which makes the liberal accept changes without apprehension, even though he does not know how the necessary adaptations will be brought about."

As political terms, "right" and "right wing," and "left" and "left wing," originated in 18th century France, where parliamentary allies of the king sat to the right of the speaker and his enemies to the left. The relevance of this arrangement to us today? None. Can there then be any real meaning to the terms "hard right" or perhaps "soft left?" No. In his essay "Politics and the English Language," George Orwell warned that "the slovenliness of our language makes it easier for us to have foolish thoughts...to think clearly is a necessary first step towards political regeneration."

In the speech accepting his second presidential nomination, Ronald Reagan explained the difference between Democrats and Republicans in a way that cannot be improved upon: "Two visions of the future, two fundamentally different ways of governing – their government of pessimism, fear and limits, or ours of hope, confidence, and growth. Their government sees people only as members of groups. Ours serves all the people of America as individuals. Theirs lives in the past, seeking to apply the old failed policies to an era that has passed them by. Ours learns from the past and strives to change by boldly charting a new course for the future."

They are socialists, we are liberals. They are conservatives, we are progressives. They are Democrats, we are Republicans. Ours is the Party of Thaddeus Stevens and Charles Sumner and Ronald Reagan. And yes, the Republican Party is *the Party of Lincoln.*

Index

Index

Index

Index

Index

Index

Index